Race, Real Estate,
and Education

In the series *Urban Life, Landscape, and Policy*,
edited by David Stradling, Larry Bennett, and Davarian Baldwin.
Founding editor, Zane L. Miller.

ALSO IN THIS SERIES:

A list of additional titles in this series appears at the back of this book.

Edward M. Epstein

Race, Real Estate, and Education

Inventing Gentrification in Philadelphia, 1960–2020

TEMPLE UNIVERSITY PRESS
Philadelphia • *Rome* • *Tokyo*

TEMPLE UNIVERSITY PRESS
Philadelphia, Pennsylvania 19122
tupress.temple.edu

Copyright © 2025 by Temple University—Of The Commonwealth System
of Higher Education
Published 2025

Library of Congress Cataloging-in-Publication Data

Names: Epstein, Edward M., 1966– author.
Title: Race, real estate, and education : inventing gentrification in
  Philadelphia, 1960–2020 / Edward M. Epstein.
Other titles: Urban life, landscape, and policy.
Description: Philadelphia : Temple University Press, 2025. | Series: Urban
  life, landscape, and policy | Includes bibliographical references and
  index. | Summary: "Explores the history of Philadelphia as a gentrifying
  city and the role of educational institutions in the city's
  transformation"— Provided by publisher.
Identifiers: LCCN 2025012693 (print) | LCCN 2025012694 (ebook) | ISBN
  9781439926314 (cloth) | ISBN 9781439926321 (paperback) | ISBN
  9781439926338 (pdf)
Subjects: LCSH: West Philadelphia Corporation (Philadelphia, Pa.) |
  Community and college—Pennsylvania—Philadelphia. |
  Gentrification—Pennsylvania—Philadelphia. | Public
  schools—Pennsylvania—Philadelphia. | Community
  development—Pennsylvania—Philadelphia. | Black Bottom (Philadelphia,
  Pa.)—History—20th century. | University City (Philadelphia,
  Pa.)—History—20th century. | Philadelphia (Pa.)—Race
  relations—History—20th century.
Classification: LCC LC238.3.P45 E67 2025 (print) | LCC LC238.3.P45
  (ebook) | DDC 307.1/416097481109045—dc23/eng/20250617
LC record available at https://lccn.loc.gov/2025012693
LC ebook record available at https://lccn.loc.gov/2025012694

The manufacturer's authorized representative in the EU for product safety is
Temple University Rome, Via di San Sebastianello, 16, 00187 Rome RM, Italy
(https://rome.temple.edu/).
tempress@temple.edu

9 8 7 6 5 4 3 2 1

CONTENTS

ACKNOWLEDGMENTS

I am greatly indebted to my mentor and dissertation chair, John L. Puckett, who inspired me to take on this topic. His comprehensive work on the subject furnished the backdrop for my own work, and his wide-ranging curiosity about history, politics, and social behavior goaded me to explore of new areas of literature, changing my thinking on so much of what I was studying. I am also grateful to committee members Matt Hartley and Jonathan Zimmerman, whose insightful comments led me to think more deeply about my topic.

Gathering data for this book was a community project. I am thankful to the scholars and leaders who worked with me to identify and interview neighbors who had experienced the events documented. Sociologist John Balzarini, scholar and activist Walter Palmer, community member Andre Black, and community organizer Gerald Bolling introduced me to many of the participants whose words are in this study. They helped acquaint me with the Black Bottom, a side of West Philadelphia I knew little about despite having lived in the neighborhood for more than a decade. I will continue to collaborate with them to spread the knowledge we have gathered and ensure the history recorded in this book is not forgotten.

As oral testimonies are a focal point of this book, I am especially grateful to my many research participants—interviewees who gave of their time and shared their life stories. Their memories, insights, and truths will inform future generations.

Primary source materials were also important to this study, and I am grateful to the archivists at Penn and Temple who led me to them. Particularly helpful was Penn public services archivist Tim Horning, who retrieved many boxes of papers and made scans for me. I would also like to acknowledge the staff at Temple University's Special Collections Research Center, especially librarian and coordinator of public services Josué Hurtado, who were equally helpful in providing materials for the book.

Along the way, numerous scholars gave me knowledge, advice, and inspiration. Laura Perna and Amy Hillier helped me discover the methodologies I wanted to use and discard the ones I did not. Joni Finney introduced me to an area of study I knew little about—finance—which now informs my thinking about the subject of this book and history at large. Davarian Baldwin, whose work is of critical importance in the field, helped me turn a wide-ranging paper into a succinct and straightforward discussion of education and redevelopment. Elaine Simon, Laura Wolf-Powers, Maia Cucchiara, and Linn Posey-Maddox, who have also made seminal contributions in this area, inspired and motivated me with their work.

I would like to thank Aaron Javsicas at Temple Press, who believed in my work and steered this project toward publication. The staff at Temple, especially Will Forrest and Gary Kramer, were most helpful and patient in getting me through the editing and production process.

Finally, I would like to thank the three people closest to me during this journey. First is my daughter, Chloë, who experienced West Philadelphia's evolution firsthand as a Penn Alexander School student and participant in her father's forays into community engagement, such as the 40th Street Artist-in-Residence Program and the University City Arts League. Second is my lifelong friend Tom McKean, who was my cheerleader during the many rewrites it took to produce this book. And third is my wife and life partner, Lindsay Metzker-Epstein who supported me with love and encouragement and whose knowledge of topics ranging from the sociology of education to the Horn and Hardart automat provided answers to so many vexing questions that arose during the writing process.

A Note on Racial Terminology

In this book, I capitalize terms for races: Black and White. I recognize that racial terms are artificial—there is no scientific validity behind these classifications, nor do they correspond to any agreed-on set of linguistic or cultural differences. Moreover, definitions of "Black" and "White" are subject to change; during the period covered by this research, who counted as White was in flux. Nevertheless, "Black" and "White" in this case refer to groups of people, and by capitalizing these terms, we distinguish them, as editor and copywriter Karen Yin points out, from colors—*black* hair versus *Black* hair, for example.[1] Moreover, it is important to be consistent: the previous example would apply equally to *White* hair. Throughout the book, I use "African American" interchangeably with "Black," as the people interviewed did.

Names of Organizations and Abbreviations

In this book, I refer to Philadelphia public schools as the School District of Philadelphia (SDP) and its governing body as the Board of Education. I refer to the University of Pennsylvania by its moniker "Penn" and Drexel University, formerly the Drexel Institute of Technology, as "Drexel." Other abbreviations appear throughout the book:

Lea for the H. C. Lea School
PAS for the Penn Alexander School
QPC for the Quadripartite Commission
RDA for the Redevelopment Authority
UCHS for University City High School
UCSC for the University City Science Center
URP for Universities-Related Program
WPC for West Philadelphia Corporation
WPHS for West Philadelphia High School

In my citations for archival material, I abbreviate the University of Pennsylvania's archives as UARC and Temple University's urban archives, located in the Special Collections Research Center, as SCRC.

Race, Real Estate,
and Education

Introduction

I arrived in Philadelphia as an artist looking for studio space, opportunities to exhibit my work, and employment in teaching. I found this postindustrial city to be fertile ground. In the area near the University of Pennsylvania where I lived, University City, there were plenty of under-maintained buildings that could be repurposed for the arts. Throughout the city were scrappy, artist-run galleries, and copious educational institutions—universities, K–12 schools, and community art centers.

In time, my career focus shifted toward education. I entered the Ed.D. program at the University of Pennsylvania's Graduate School of Education (GSE) expecting to study the role of the arts in schools. I planned to research arts-based interventions in K–12 education, especially those initiated by universities. My goal would be to learn how these interventions affect students and to identify best practices. I expected my degree to give me practical training for using the arts to improve academic outcomes in underperforming city schools. Luckily, there were plenty of local examples of university-based educational interventions, as the University of Pennsylvania—heretofore "Penn"—had been in that business for years. My dissertation advisor, John Puckett, suggested that I look at historical examples from the 1960s initiated by a Penn-controlled organization called the West Philadelphia Corporation (WPC).

What I found undermined many of my assumptions as an artist, educator, urban dweller, and person who appreciates the "diverse" character of the city. A trip to Penn's archives showed me that the WPC was a real estate entity set up by West Philadelphia's universities and hospitals for the purpose of redeveloping the area in a way that would spur faculty, staff, and students to relocate there. It revealed that the WPC's educational interventions were also intended to brand local public schools as safe for better-off, White families. It showed me that "University City" was a name devised to sell an area whose Black population had been increasing and make it appeal to a Whiter population. The WPC's most salient act in this regard, an act that continues to haunt the university community, was the use of urban renewal funding to drive a predominantly Black population from an area known as the Black Bottom.

My research showed me that the WPC was behind much of what I treasured in the neighborhood. Before entering the doctoral program at Penn, I had been director of the University City Arts League—a community arts center set up in 1967 with the support of the WPC. Later, I joined the University City Swim Club—a diverse neighborhood pool also set up with WPC backing. The turn-of-the-century house I lived in bore a historic plaque with a spiral pattern derived from a wrought iron fence, which the WPC had introduced in its 1963 promotional booklet *Elaborations on Living in University City*. And just after arriving in Philadelphia in 2003, I founded the 40th Street Artist-in-Residence Program, located in a building in Penn's portfolio of underperforming real estate assets. I learned that Penn had acquired properties like this during the urban renewal era and held them tax-free in anticipation of future expansion. Though this building was not part of the notorious Unit 3, the Black Bottom tract cleared at the WPC's behest, it was acquired for much the same reason.

Thus, much of what I thought was the result of conscientious urban dwellers trying to improve their city had been spurred by WPC actions. The WPC's purpose was to change the character of the neighborhood for the benefit of the area's major educational and medical institutions. And that change was racially tainted.

My dissertation covered the period 1960–1980, the era in which the WPC was active. I have since concluded that because the WPC's influence is still felt, it is necessary to extend the study to 2020. One of West Philadelphia's most attractive features, and the one that prompted my family to locate in the area, is the Sadie Tanner Mossell Alexander University of Pennsylvania Partnership School, commonly known as the Penn Alexander School (PAS). I enrolled my daughter in this K–8 school, a partnership created in 2001 between Penn and the School District of Philadelphia (SDP) to serve a racially and socioeconomically diverse swath of neighborhood residents. I learned from my research that the creation of a high-performing public school was also a WPC dream. In 1961, the organization proposed to build a science magnet school to appeal to university and hospital affiliates.

The school was to be located in the Black Bottom, its creation part of the justification for the city's demolition order for that area. Neighborhood opposition and citywide turmoil thwarted the original proposal, and a much different and ultimately unsuccessful school was built on the site.

PAS, by contrast, was largely successful. It boasted high-quality teachers, a light-filled, up-to-date building, and students who performed well on standardized tests. When it first opened, its enrollment bore some resemblance to the SDP's overall population makeup. The school's student body was 57 percent Black in 2002, and relations between students of different races seemed copacetic. By the 2017–2018 school year, however, that proportion had declined to 21 percent. Meanwhile, the neighborhood's affordability had evaporated. Housing prices had tripled in the PAS catchment, or attendance area, during the period 1998–2011.[1] What I thought had been a high-quality school for everyone had functioned as tool for gentrification.

The school's planners shrugged off responsibility for the area's increasing socioeconomic and racial divides. In her 2007 book on the subject, *The University and Urban Revival*, Penn president Judith Rodin, whose West Philadelphia Initiatives (WPI) created PAS, attributes the destruction of "racially, ethnically, and socioeconomically mixed communities" to "unintentional forces of upward mobility and the transmigration of populations from one neighborhood to another." However, my study led me to conclude that gentrification is anything but unintentional. In the case of West Philadelphia, the removal of Black residents north of the Penn and Drexel campuses enabled the stabilization of the White population to the west. From that point on, any neighborhood improvement, whether a park, a retail hub, or a school, was likely to benefit White people more than Black people. PAS consummated a plan the WPC had made years earlier to surround itself with prosperity—quietly shutting Black populations out.

The tendency to ignore the workings of racism in such situations is a hallmark of what theorist Charles Mills calls the "Racial Contract." He shows how the notion of political liberty that we identify with Western civilization is a two-tiered structure: on the one hand, a social contract defines the rights and responsibilities of free citizens, and on the other, a Racial Contract excludes certain people from the social contract. This dual system emerged as both a product of and justification for slavery and colonial hegemony during the European Enlightenment.[2] The Racial Contract is not merely an abstraction for theorists to ponder but, according to Mills, a description of how society operates. Most relevant to this book, it is an agreement to substitute for truth a racialized view of the world. It enables White people to treat non-White people unfairly while fully believing that they are living in a just society. As Mills puts it, under the Racial Contract, "one has an agreement to misinterpret the world."[3]

Such misinterpretation usually involves ignoring the effects of racial history in current circumstances. When the WPC disregarded the plight of Black residents in its neighborhood and wrote their homes off as blight, it was doing exactly what the Racial Contract required. When the Rodin administration ignored the fact that its redevelopment and educational initiatives were building on the WPC's displacements, it too was following the terms of the Racial Contract.

In the West Philadelphia where I had made my home, the public goods of neighborhood improvement, building rehabilitation and repurposing, and high-quality school creation concealed an agenda set by powerful institutions. Individual and community projects like green spaces, recreational facilities, art galleries, and restored historic homes were seeded by these institutions to support their agenda. As I delved further into history, I found that in Philadelphia, the business of urban revitalization began before the WPC was created in 1959. It can be traced back to the 1940s, when city planners, anticipating the decline of the city's industrial economy, set to work creating a "better Philadelphia"—a city that catered to cultural, educational, and scientific elites.[4] This was one of the origin points of urban pioneering and gentrification. The WPC's actions were an extension of the city's urban revitalization agenda, and the twenty-first-century development boom in West Philadelphia, including the creation of PAS, was its consummation.

The case of University City resembles other instances of university-initiated redevelopment around the United States, which, as documented in Davarian Baldwin's *In the Shadow of the Ivory Tower*, have created economic opportunity for technocratic elites at the expense of longtime neighborhood residents.[5] What makes University City different from these cases—and from the many nonuniversity sponsored redevelopment efforts around the United States and elsewhere—is the emphasis on school building. Penn and its collaborators recognized that to attract and keep the well-educated, affluent residents they desired, they would need to provide stable public schools that could compete with those in the suburbs. It was well known to twentieth-century WPC planners that school quality more than any other factor compelled well-educated residents to locate in the suburbs. It was equally well known to twenty-first-century WPI planners that what kept young, educated professionals from staying in the city was the realization that once they had school-aged children, there would be no public schools they regarded as suitable.

Much is known about Penn's campus expansion during the tenure of Gaylord Harnwell, from the early 1950s through 1970. Historians John Puckett and Mark Lloyd have written extensively on the university's efforts to create a verdant campus core and a surrounding compatible to educated elites who work and study at Penn. These authors, and more recently, Laura

Wolf-Powers, have shown how the WPC, whose governance and finances were controlled by Penn, branded the area "University City" as a marketing strategy in the 1960s.[6] Less is known about improved public K–12 education as a centerpiece of WPC's plan—and about the link between WPC educational initiatives and PAS. In the following chapters, I trace the factors that shaped the WPC agenda, the physical and educational modifications the organization proposed, and the consequences of its interventions during the 1960s, particularly for displaced residents of the Black Bottom. I show how, after laying fallow for many years, this agenda reemerged in a new guise in the 2000s—leading to an increase in the desirability of the neighborhood and contributing to a continued exodus of less well-off Black residents.

Chapter 1, "Salvaging a Run-Down City," provides citywide context for the plan to create University City in West Philadelphia. It discusses the deindustrialization of Philadelphia and the effort by planner Edmund Bacon and his collaborators to make the city a center for white-collar jobs. It describes the emergence of the Black Bottom, the neighborhood the WPC planned to eliminate, and the rise of Penn, the WPC's main backer, as a major presence in the area. The desire to demolish the Black Bottom predates the WPC's existence: in a 1947 memorandum, Bacon wrote of the need to eliminate an emerging "band of blight" in the university area. His memo also predicted the focus on education, calling for improved schools to attract "younger University faculty families."[7] Schools would be the at the center of all university-based neighborhood improvement efforts thereafter.

Chapter 2, "An Embattled School System," describes the history of segregation, overcrowding, and authoritarian management that plagued Philadelphia's public schools. It also covers attempts to fix these problems. When fears of crime and decay prompted university leadership to launch the WPC in 1959, the organization made school improvement one of its first projects. The corporation's Universities-Related Program (URP) designated certain schools as recipients of financial help and faculty support. Not long after, the appointment of reform-minded Superintendent Mark Shedd created an opening for experimentation in school curricula and diversification of staff and leadership. Reflecting Shedd's new direction and the 1960s zeitgeist, community groups founded experimental schools and programs of their own. These usually short-lived efforts raised key questions about how to reform a struggling urban school system. Could small, local school experiments become more than carve outs for a select group? Could a neighborhood school reflect the will of the community, both in its governance and its curriculum? These questions would reemerge in the twenty-first century with the creation of PAS.

Chapter 3, "Developing the Mind, Developing the Neighborhood," investigates the mixed ambitions of the WPC project, which ultimately led to its downfall. Citing accounts of former students and documents from the era, it shows how the corporation's interest in URP as a public relations tool overrode its interest in the quality of interventions. It also introduces the WPC's most ambitious project: the creation of University City High School (UCHS) as a science magnet school connected to a proposed science incubator, the University City Science Center (UCSC). This initiative was inextricably tied to the corporation's desire to eliminate the Black Bottom. By siting the school and science center in the heart of the neighborhood, the WPC hoped to obtain federal urban renewal funding to demolish it.

Chapter 4, "Conflict and Disillusionment," describes how community resistance and 1960s-era turmoil sidetracked the WPC agenda. As soon as the city announced its intention to implement the corporation's demolition plan in 1962, Black Bottom residents responded with protests, delaying the project's implementation. The SDP, mired in political upheavals, was unable to make UCHS the progressive, science-focused school the WPC wanted, instead creating a struggling neighborhood school. The chapter also shows how student opposition to the WPC agenda, which boiled over in the late 1960s, led to a community-supported sit-in on Penn's campus. The protest resulted in the creation of the Quadripartite Commission (QPC), expected to moderate community and university interests in future neighborhood redevelopment.

Chapter 5, "Dark Years in West Philadelphia," recounts how, in the wake of protest and financial strain, Penn put the WPC agenda on a back burner. The QPC bore little fruit, and in the absence of equitable planning and investment, forces of decline ruled West Philadelphia and the city at large. The 1985 MOVE bombing, in which police action incinerated an entire block of homes, represented a nadir for Philadelphia. Thereafter, Penn began to rethink community involvement. Ira Harkavy, a leader of the 1960s student protests at Penn, pioneered "academically based community service" (ABCS), a much different approach than the WPC's heavy-handed 1960s-era interventions. A spike in crime in the 1990s prompted the administration of Penn president Judith Rodin to revive the WPC agenda in a new guise, as the WPI. Informed by lessons learned in the 1960s and propelled by the prosperity of the 1990s, this new plan for revitalizing West Philadelphia showed promise.

Chapter 6, "A Jewel in Gentrification's Crown," describes how WPI's signature project, PAS, was initially successful as a university-assisted public school. Accounts from parents who enrolled their children there show that, while it did not always meet parent expectations, the school was good enough to overcome the perception that West Philadelphia offered no quality public educational opportunities. It attracted affluent, university- and hospital-affiliated parents to the neighborhood, affirming the WPC branding of the neighborhood as University City. With a diverse population and conventional curriculum, PAS initially withstood the criticism that had been leveled at WPC-era programs—that they were carve outs for a privileged group. Yet the school's presence, in combination with the amenities WPI provided, triggered rapid increases in housing prices, sapping neighborhood diversity and causing a sharp decline in PAS's Black population. Far from an unintended consequence, the neighborhood's gentrification was the realization of the WPC plan. From the beginning, this plan had called for the replacement of declining industrial, working-class, and Black districts with ones custom made for high-paid professionals.

Chapter 7, "Good Causes, Evil Effects," draws the book to a close by asking how such laudable projects as building a quality public school have resulted in increased segregation and gentrification. It finds that, given Philadelphia's—and the nation's—racial history, such results are predictable. The WPC embarked on school-building projects not just for education's sake but to brand the neighborhood as well off and White rather than poor and Black. Behind this racial labeling was an understanding, inherited from the nation's past as a slaveholding enterprise, that Black is a second-class status. To defeat the second-class citizenship prescribed for Black people by the Racial Contract, there must be a reckoning with history. The book proposes reparations as a spur to that reckoning.

Moreover, the book asks whether Philadelphia's overall approach to revitalizing an industrial city—an approach that has been lauded and copied—was misguided. Bacon and his colleagues, who preached that the built environment could be a force for social good, pushed the creation of a city with increased racial and socioeconomic stratification. The forces of money and influence won the day; instead of improving the lot of existing residents, the city sought more desirable replacements. The book views the redevelopment of West Philadelphia, and particularly the interventions into its public schools, as a cautionary tale. Absent the will to rectify historical wrongs and ensure that prosperity is shared, urban ideals such as historic preservation, walkable streets, dense and mixed-use development, cultural amenities, and especially quality public education are no more likely to create a better city than suburban sprawl.

1

Salvaging a Run-Down City

Travelers to central Philadelphia in 1950 would encounter a bleak landscape. The way east to city hall from 30th Street Station was shrouded by a twenty-foot-high concrete and stone viaduct known derogatorily as the Chinese Wall. This barrier terminated at the city's former Broad Street Station, which in a monumental act of corporate irresponsibility was left to crumble after a 1923 fire. Continuing east from city hall to the Delaware Waterfront, they would hardly notice Philadelphia's colonial-era buildings, hidden among nondescript architecture from other eras. Independence Hall was situated within a cluster of buildings on a city block rather than set off as a historic focal point. At Delaware Riverbank, they would find a grimy produce market crowded with trucks and trains. Everywhere, smoke from industries smudged the skies.[1]

To the west, the scene was much the same. The walk along Market Street toward the University of Pennsylvania and Drexel University (then called the Drexel Institute) was darkened by the Market-Frankford elevated line. Along that corridor was an array of small factories, shops, and decrepit row houses. Much of Philadelphia's blight persisted through the 1960s and is said to have inspired the nightmarish films of a young David Lynch, who lived in central Philadelphia as a student at the Pennsylvania Academy of the Fine Arts.[2] The photographs in figure 1.1, taken between 1912 and 1959, illustrate the industrial infrastructure and grimy condition of the city through the mid-twentieth century.

Figure 1.1 Industrial-age Philadelphia. *Clockwise from top left*: an unrestored 1797 Society Hill row house, 1959; view of Independence Hall, 1929, before adjacent buildings were demolished to create Independence National Historic Park in the 1950s; view toward West Philadelphia along the Market-Frankford elevated line, 1949; 1912 photo of the Chinese Wall and Broad Street Station, which burned in 1923 but was not demolished until 1953. (*PhillyHistory.org, a project of the Philadelphia Department of Records.*)

Yet in 1950, a new generation of leaders heralded the arrival of a metropolis that would cater to educated elites rather than factory workers. The new citizen would staff the office, lab, or operating room rather than the assembly line. The city's planners knew well that to appeal to this demographic, they had to fix Philadelphia's most decrepit corner: its public school system. How they approached this problem is a part of the story of creating a better Philadelphia that has yet to be told.

The Decline of Industry in Philadelphia

The grim factory landscape a 1950 visitor would have experienced had brought prosperity to the city for many years. From its founding by William Penn in 1682 to the end of World War II, Philadelphia was a center of trade and industry. Although railroads and shipbuilding were prominent, according to sociologist Carolyn Adams et al. in their study of the city's changing fortunes, *Philadelphia: Neighborhoods, Division, and Conflict in a Postindustrial City*, its biggest products were textiles and apparel. These sectors comprised 40 percent of the city's industrial output through the 1800s. They peaked in 1930 and, according to the authors, declined precipitously during the post–World War II era. The two industries lost 91,000 jobs (74 percent of their total) in the period 1947–1986, a figure that represented 79 percent of all job losses in the city.[3]

Suburbanization was one cause of job loss. Manufacturers preferred suburbs because their open spaces allowed the building of sprawling, single-story factories housing continuous-flow assembly lines. These plants could be serviced by newly constructed interstate highways. Ultimately, competition from other regions drained jobs from Philadelphia. At first, the Sunbelt cities, which had lower taxes and wages and offered subsidies to industry, attracted these jobs. By the end of the 1950s, many of them had gone overseas, where wages might be one-tenth those of U.S. workers.[4]

Black Philadelphians, who had trouble finding well-paid work due to racial discrimination, were hit hardest by industrial decline. Spurred by Jim Crow segregation and the collapse of the sharecropper system, the Great Migration had brought many Black people to Philadelphia from the South beginning in the early twentieth century. This movement of people persisted and even increased through the post–World War II era, as shown in table 1.1 and figure 1.2.[5] In 1910, before the influx of migrants from the South, Philadelphia's Black population was approximately 85,000, 5.5 percent of a total of 1.5 million people. By 1960, there were over 0.5 million Black residents in a city of 2 million, more than 25 percent of the population. They arrived expecting to find jobs in industry only to be blocked by discrimination in hiring and union membership. W. E. B. Du Bois's well-known 1899 study *The Philadelphia Negro* exposed the overcrowded living conditions and employment discrimination that existed for residents of the 7th Ward, then the center of African American settlement in Philadelphia.[6] According to Adams et al., this discrimination continued as new migrants arrived:

> In 1930, more than 80% of the black population lived in areas that were within one mile of five thousand or more industrial jobs, yet less than 13 percent of black workers were employed as manufactur-

TABLE 1.1. GROWTH OF PHILADELPHIA'S BLACK POPULATION, 1910–1970			
	Total Population	White	Black
1910	1,549,008	1,463,371	84,459
		94.5%	5.5%
1920	1,823,779	1,688,180	134,229
		92.6%	7.4%
1930	1,950,961	1,728,806	219,599
		88.6%	11.3%
1940	1,931,334	1,678,577	250,880
		86.9%	13.0%
1950	2,071,605	1,692,637	374,961
		81.7%	18.1%
1960	2,002,512	1,467,479	529,240
		73.3%	26.4%
1970	1,948,609	1,282,215	653,747
		65.8%	33.6%
Source: U.S. Census data, accessed through Social Explorer, https://www.socialexplorer.com.			

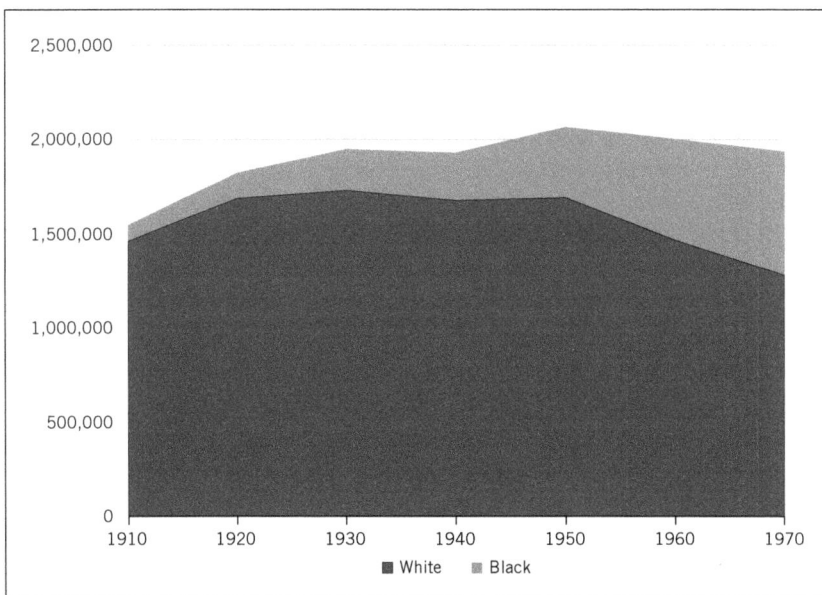

Figure 1.2 Makeup of Philadelphia's population by race. (*U.S. Census data, accessed through Social Explorer, www.socialexplorer.com.*)

ers. Blacks were more likely to be employed as laborers, servants and waiters.[7]

Discrimination persisted as the suburbs emerged. White Philadelphians moved to take factory jobs in these newly developed areas, but Black residents were blocked by racist housing practices.[8] With deindustrialization, service and information jobs became concentrated in the central city area, leading to a bifurcation of the workforce. By the end of the 1980s, employment in the lowest-paying and highest-paying categories had grown, while jobs had been lost in the middle category. According to Adams et al., between 1980 and 1987, the number of jobs earning more than twice the median income increased by 108 percent in Philadelphia; the number earning less than half the median income increased by 15 percent, and those earning one-half to twice the median decreased by 13 percent. In other words, the middle dropped out of the job market.[9]

Because of discrimination and disadvantages in education, Black Philadelphians' jobs tended to be clustered in lower-paid areas such as operative, labor, service, clerical, and—because of the prevalence of employment in nursing and teaching—in the nonprofit sector. Meanwhile, they were absent from areas like advanced technology services (i.e., research and development) because of the high educational barriers to entering these professions. Black workers also tended to be excluded from wholesale and retail sales jobs because of discrimination against them in people-oriented employment.[10] As we see in the next chapter, the disadvantages Black Philadelphians faced in schooling were baked into a public educational system with a long history of covert segregation and unequal funding.

Black residents who experienced life in Philadelphia during the mid to late twentieth century have spoken of the ongoing segregation and discrimination—sometimes subtle, sometimes overt—in various fields of employment. Those who lived in West Philadelphia neighborhoods adjacent to Penn, for example, rarely found anything other than low-paying jobs at the university. Jerry Davis, who grew up in Penn's shadow, recalled that "it was a bridge too far. It was just a different kind of universe."[11] Barriers to management-level employment persisted through the late twentieth century. Prentice Cole, a West Philadelphia resident who had been a student at the H. C. Lea School (a focus of Penn's educational improvement efforts, as noted in later chapters), experienced this racial discrimination firsthand. He described how, despite graduating from the prestigious Central High School and earning his BA from Penn, supervisors at one company rebuked him for "being loud, rude, abrupt, and . . . Black." He continued, "It ended up in a termination. I was the only Black employee to ever work out there."[12] Cole's experience is a case in point of discrimination against Black workers in people-oriented positions. The history recounted here of African American families migrating to seeking a better life and being consigned to declining urban neighborhoods and low-wage positions is hardly unique. Philadelphia followed the same trends as other Northern U.S. cities in this regard.[13] However, the city was also home to elite cultural, educational, and medical institutions, which would soon become a focal point of its rebound from economic distress.

The Emergence of the Black Bottom

The demographic and economic shifts that Philadelphia experienced in the early to mid-twentieth century were pronounced in Penn's environs, West Philadelphia. Originally a rural outpost of the city, this area developed, in the nineteenth century, in countervailing directions. We can visualize it as a triangle bisected by Market Street, Philadelphia's main east–west thoroughfare. The district to the north of Market Street was primarily industrial, developing first around wagon routes that brought trade from the west and later around the railroad. To the south was primarily residential. As early as 1850, investors began to create tract housing that appealed to middle-class Philadelphians seeking relief from the congestion of Center City.[14] Situated at the junction of these two areas was a neighborhood that was neither fully commercial nor fully residential and mixed in its racial composition. The area became home to diverse immigrant groups, including Irish, Germans, Italians, and Jews.[15] Among the settlers who populated the area was a small Black community that, according to 1850 census data, coalesced around Market Street and what is now 41st Street. A burial ground discovered during a 2018 construction project bore witness to the existence of this community.[16]

Longtime residents of the area remember that in the early years of the twentieth century, the area to the north remained a mixed-race neighborhood. For example, Cora Hill, who was born in 1919 at 3500 Warren Street, in the center of this district, recalled, "And when I was born, it was very well mixed. 1919. Most of our neighbors were White. Coming up, I had a very good childhood within the racial mixing."[17] The situation persisted into the mid-twentieth century. Andre Black (aka Tony Bond), born in 1949 in the same area, remembered playing with his White neighbors, Joseph and John Horne, when he was young:

> Everything seemed to disappear when you are playing hide-and-go-seek with your White friends who you didn't call White. We had a family called the Hornes; they were political people, they lived on . . . they might have been 24 North 36th. . . . Their grandfather was

a city council person, and their father was a lieutenant . . . a detective, so we played somewhat with Joseph and John because they were somewhere around the same age as we were.[18]

Hill's and Black's recollections of that era match those of Black Philadelphians from other parts of the city, who also experienced racial mixing. In his biography of public-school leader Marcus Foster, historian John Spencer notes that Foster's brother Alfred would play street games with Italian and Irish neighbors in South Philadelphia and that there was little tension between them.[19]

Because of its geographic location—near the Schuylkill River, at the "bottom" of West Philadelphia—residents called this area the Bottom. Yet as the demographics shifted in this roughly twenty-block area (bounded by 34th Street to the east, 38th Street to the west, Chestnut Street to the south, and Lancaster Avenue to the north), the neighborhood acquired a new moniker. According to Hill, "Well, each year . . . more and more Whites moved away, and that's how it became, they called it the Black Bottom."[20] Her nephew Butch Wilmore recalled using the term with his siblings during the 1930s:

> When we was there it was the Black Bottom. I was born in '33, so it must have been during that time. . . . I'm the oldest of them; that's why I said it had to be around 1933, because they're younger than me, and back then I can remember calling it the Black Bottom.[21]

Statistics corroborate residents' recollections of the changing demographics of this neighborhood. By 1960, the population of census tract 24, which contained the Black Bottom, was 78.8 percent Black.[22]

The testimony of Black Bottom residents gives a sense of the types of jobs available to African Americans in Philadelphia at the time. Their recollections align with the data given earlier in the chapter, showing an unequal economic playing field. Former resident and activist Walter Palmer noted in his interview with sociologist John Balzarini that Black people often worked odd jobs for White-owned businesses:

> Veterinary hospital, Crown Laundry—all White owned. Blacks worked in these places. That's how I got some part time work. I worked for a little grocery store. A blind home at 36th and Lancaster Avenue . . . many of us growing up were able to get work. We'd take blind people for walks, and you'd get tips get paid for it. We'd take groceries from the grocery store, and we'd get paid for it right. We'd take . . . I lived right next to 3647 [Market Street] was the junk shop, where

you could take rags and paper and iron and tin. And remember, this is the war time too.[23]

Ikey Davis, Jerry's brother, born in the Black Bottom in 1931, recalled that much of the work available to Black residents was informal. He remembered seeing Black women seek work in areas further west, which were more affluent:

And you would come to 52nd and Lancaster and the [White] women would be in cars and the other women, African American women . . . they [the White women] would say "You want a day's work?" . . . They'd say yes. And they'd get in the car and they [the White women] would bring them up here. Five dollars and car fare. And that was back in the '40s.[24]

Others found domestic work with White families in Wynnefield, close to the city limits. According to Butch Wilmore, however, police enforcement of unmarked racial boundaries made trips there perilous: "The cops would stop you. What are you doing there? Do you have a note? Who are you working for?"[25]

Much of the work available to Black residents at Penn, Drexel, or one of the hospitals was informal as well. Andre Black remembered shining shoes for students at fraternity and sorority houses; Butch Wilmore recalled parking cars for football game attendees. If they found employment at these institutions, it was usually in low-skilled positions. Andre Black, for example, quit school early to support his family: "I went on to University [of Pennsylvania] Hospital, where my grandmother had worked for over thirty years. . . . I did dietary [food service] work there, and I also did housekeeping work."[26]

Consistent with the data given earlier on types of occupations available to Black Philadelphians, skilled industrial labor seemed out of reach to Black Bottom residents. Passing on the street, Andre Black and his friends would marvel at the workings of the heavy equipment at the Stephen Green Printing Company at 34th and Market Streets (now part of the University City Science Center, or UCSC, and the location of Penn's archives): "And we used to go there and just look through the windows and see them rolling big paper and all that."[27] It never occurred to them, however, that they could become typesetters or press operators. The inaccessibility of higher paying jobs had consequences, and many families lacked funds to pay for necessities and relied on welfare for daily sustenance. Black remembered picking up staples at the armory on 33rd and Cuthbert Streets, where the government distributed surplus food: "powdered milk, butter, powdered eggs, canned spam, canned beef." He also remembered his family's inability to afford modern conveniences: "I lived with oil lamps because our electric was off. You didn't have a gas stove or what you have today. You had a wood stove that was cast iron." Similarly, Ikey Davis recalled the outdated system for providing hot water in his house: "You had a little thing in the basement that you would light—a gas thing—and that would make the water hot . . . and you know you don't keep it on long. Only long enough to make hot water so you could take baths."[28] The primitive conditions Black and Davis described are not surprising given the historical disparities between Black and White people in Philadelphia. For example, a 1921 survey found that only 10 percent of Black homes had adequate "sanitation, convenience and comfort," compared to 28 percent of White homes.[29] Reports from those who lived in the Black Bottom suggest that these conditions persisted through the mid-twentieth century.

Yet the neighborhood was not an economic desert. Although many were White owned, varied businesses in the neighborhood catered to the needs of residents. Among these were Henry Gross's clothing store; C. L. Presser's Hardware; Abbott's Dairy; the Modern Laundry; Marty's Junk Shop; the Horn and Hardart's automat; Jake Goldstein's grocery store; Barron's Drug Store; Club Zel-Mar; and as mentioned, the Stephen Green Printing Company. Many of these businesses are visible in a panoramic view of Market Street (fig. 1.3) taken in 1964, a few years before the demolition of the neighborhood. The view shows a bustling business strip with cars, trucks, and pedestrians rushing about.

City planner Edmund Bacon described this stretch of Market Street as "an extremely decadent" commercial area incompatible with the nearby universities. Yet as Black Bottom residents attest and the photograph suggests, it was the heart of a vibrant community.[30]

A certain number of the neighborhood's Black residents found their way to better opportunities. Walter Palmer had been a trailblazer at the Hospital of the University of Pennsylvania and the Children's Hospital of Philadelphia. Through his willingness to stand up to discrimination and with the support of a few well-placed allies, Palmer went from being a surgeon's assistant to a high-ranking member of a pulmonary care team led by C. Everett Koop, who later became U.S. surgeon general.[31] With Palmer's encouragement, Cora Hill also moved into the medical profession, quitting a job at the Modern Shoe Manufacturing Company and earning a nursing credential.[32] And Jerry Davis, who moved from public school to Catholic school in grade 8, told of how nuns and priests helped him regain ground he had lost in the School District of Philadelphia (SDP): "In 8th grade at seven o'clock, I'd go up to Saint Leonard's [the convent], and they would tutor me. They'd tutor me for a couple of hours. Every night I'd do my homework. And . . . over the course of the year, I finally . . . won a scholarship award for aca-

Figure 1.3 Panoramic view of Market Street, early 1960s. View east toward central Philadelphia. The photograph gives a sense of the Black Bottom's location to the west of Center City. (Architectural Forum, *vol. 121, August–September 1964, Acc. 350, box 11, "Unit 3-Clay Group Lawsuit." Special Collections Research Center, Temple University Libraries, Philadelphia, PA.*)

demic achievement." Davis would later earn a bachelor's degree from La Salle University and move into a management-level position in the public affairs department of the Atlantic Richfield oil company.[33] The situations of Cora Hill, Walter Palmer, and Jerry Davis, however, were exceptional. Statistics show that the experience of Andre Black, who did not complete a K–12 education and worked mostly in unskilled jobs, was more typical.

Another factor that influenced job prospects was political patronage. According to Cora Hill, there were jobs aplenty for friends of Republican committee member Frank Hahn. Hahn found work for African American men on a quid pro quo basis: he would deliver jobs with the expectation that they would vote Republican. In fact, Hahn was able to secure Butch Wilmore's father a job in the office of Bernard Samuel, mayor of Philadelphia from 1941 to 1952.[34] Such favors were short lived, however. As we see later in this chapter, the Republican machine for which Hahn worked would topple in 1951, diminishing the influence Hill, Wilmore, and others had in city hall.

With recent migrants from the South joining families that had lived in the area for generations, the Black Bottom became a nexus for Black culture. Walter Palmer vividly conveyed to sociologist John Balzarini the noisy vibrancy of the neighborhood during the 1940s, when he lived in a walk-up apartment on Market Street:

[The address] 3600 Market Street was really the heart of what was the highly populated area of the corner of the neighborhood that is referred to as the Black Bottom. . . . And I'm a kid from a small town, and I come here, and I see all these bright lights, and I'm lying on a bed listening to music at one, two o'clock in the morning coming out of the alley people playing horns and drums; I've never experienced anything like that before in my life. But it's exciting. My heart's pumping, just pumping, right . . . So the "El" [Market-Frankford elevated line] ran across down Market Street. . . . So I heard this clanging, clanging every night . . . how can a kid go to sleep, right? Well I didn't want to go to sleep because I was excited. The shadows, the noises, the music, the hollering, the screaming, the cursing . . . jazz music everywhere.[35]

According to Palmer, there were numerous venues in the neighborhood—including Club Zel-Mar on 37th and Market Streets, Powelton Bar at 40th and Filbert, and Fan's Theatre at 40th and Preston—that showcased jazz and Black entertainment. Among the performers who appeared in the 1940s, '50s, and '60s were jazz greats John Coltrane, Earl "Fatha" Hines, and Horace Silver; mambo pioneer José Curbelo; singer and actress Pearl Bailey; comedians Red Foxx and George Kirby; and dancers Bill Bailey, Chuck Green, and John Bubbles.[36]

Like many parts of Philadelphia, the neighborhood was not free of violence. Residents characterized some confrontations as protective—intended to fend off outside attackers at a time when racial and ethnic tensions were rampant throughout the city. Jerry Davis recalled this story about his brother Richard's reputation as a protector:

I didn't have to worry about somebody beating me up because Richard would take care of that . . . and these guys, six or seven of them. They grabbed me and stretched out my arms I'm like I'm being crucified. They're holding me like that. And this one guy was about to punch me, and this other guy grabbed me . . . and said, "What's your name?" I said, "J . . . J . . . Jerry Davis." He said, "You have a brother named Richard?" I said, "Yeah." He said, "Better leave him alone."[37]

For Andre Black, fighting was a skill needed to get through the school day. When he and his friends were bussed to a school outside of West Philadelphia, they endured frequent attacks: "We fought the Italians and Irish down in South Philly. We had to fight them to get to the bus."[38]

In other instances, the violence was senseless, fueled by alcohol and increasing hopelessness among residents. In the interview with Balzarini, Walter Palmer spoke of a man named Eagle Carter, who also looked out for his neighbors: "We all admired him because he was such a fighter, such a protector. You always knew you were safe." Unfortunately, fighting instincts

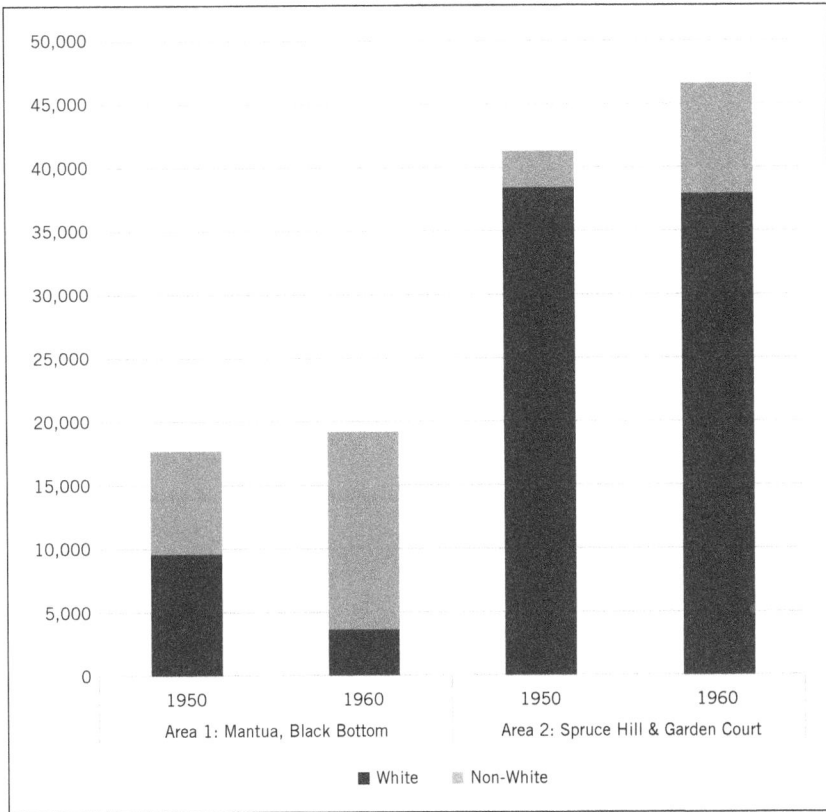

Figure 1.4 Population in West Philadelphia neighborhoods, 1950 and 1960. (*"A Profile of Basic Marketing Factors in West Philadelphia Corporation Market Area," UPA 4, box 74, folder "West Philadelphia Corporation 1955–1960, IV," UARC.*)

and alcohol got the best of Carter: "He got one of those drunk things, and . . . a guy cut his throat. He had to have a hundred stiches. Cut his body with a razor." Tragically, Palmer recalled, violence took the life of Carter's young brother Benny:

> Benny Carter was . . . he was a great guy, sweetheart, a little guy but a fighter. He had the same spirit as his brothers and sisters. And once the Bottom had gotten dismantled, he got into an argument. He got drunk . . . something he never did when we were kids growing up. And he always was sensible, right. Got into an argument with some guys in a bar on 40th and Market Street. And he went outside, and he was drunk. He sits on the pavement outside the bar; these two guys come out and see him. They take a beer bottle and beat him to death.[39]

Palmer's stories show that, while there was an element of neighborhood cohesion in the Black Bottom, there was also a dark edge, which grew more prominent in the minds of both residents and outsiders as segregation and poverty increased. A 1960 marketing report commissioned by the West Philadelphia Corporation (WPC), the entity formed by the area's universities and hospitals to redevelop the neighborhood, highlights how segregated West Philadelphia had become. As indicated in figure 1.4, the report found a dramatic increase in the non-White and a drain of the White population in Area 1, which contained the Black Bottom and the neighborhood to its north, Mantua. By contrast, the White population of Area 3, which included the more affluent Spruce Hill and Garden Court neighborhoods, remained relatively stable even as the Black population increased.[40]

An Ivy League Neighbor

The University of Pennsylvania was a relative latecomer to West Philadelphia. With roots in the colonial period, Penn was initially located on 4th Street, and later on 9th Street, in central Philadelphia. To escape the growing squalor of Center City, Penn relocated to West Philadelphia in 1872. The institution had a complicated history that intertwined a self-professed interest in the use of knowledge for the many with an elitism that reserved knowledge for the few.

Though more practical in their orientation and engaged with their locales than the English colleges of Oxford and Cambridge on which they were modeled, colonial American colleges like Penn were not necessarily more democratic. Historians John Thelin and James Axtell note that though they professed to cultivate a leadership class for the fledgling republic; in practice, they worked primarily to "complete and confirm" the qualifications of an already privileged group of young men.[41] These colleges also perpetuated the existing racial order of the colonies. According to Thelin, "nothing in their attitudes or actions with respect to race relations or slaveholding sets college officials and alumni apart from other colonists. There is no record of colonial commitment to the collegiate education of black students."[42] Penn, like many U.S. colleges and universities, had significant ties to the slave trade and the race-based pseudoscience emerging at the time. In his book *Ebony and Ivy: Race, Slavery and the Troubled History of America's Universities*, historian Craig Steven Wilder documents the many ways in which Penn benefited from slavery and contributed to an ideology of racial superiority.[43]

As it evolved, Penn came to exemplify the countervailing directions of U.S. higher education. In the nineteenth century, it was quick to embrace the model of the German university with its focus on professorial autonomy and laboratory research; to add professional schools in law, medicine, and business; and to adapt to the practical focus championed in the Morill Acts, which promoted research for industry and agriculture. Harley Etienne, author of *Pushing back the Gates: Neighborhood Perspectives on University-Driven Change in West Philadelphia*, notes that Penn's professional schools had an outward orientation like that of the land grant colleges funded by Morill—yet its focus on Ph.D.-level work was aligned with the German model.[44] Penn's Wharton School of Finance and Commerce encapsulated the wide-ranging directions of research and teaching at Penn. Known today for training corporate elites, Wharton was, from its founding in 1881 through World War I, a center for politically and socially progressive research. Notably, the school commissioned W. E. B. Du Bois's 1899 study of the conditions of Philadelphia's largely African American 7th Ward. Du Bois's survey of five thousand residents uncovered effects of race discrimination in housing and employment and anticipated the methods of the Chicago school of sociology during the early twentieth century.[45]

The post–World War II era saw enormous growth for Penn. The war had quickened the pace of scientific discovery, and Penn, which had hosted military-related projects such as the ENIAC computer, was well positioned to pursue federal research grants. The GI Bill encouraged returning soldiers to enroll in college, leading to an increase in the school's undergraduate population. Physicist Gaylord Harnwell, inaugurated as Penn's president in 1953, seemed well suited to lead the university during this era. Previously head of the navy's underwater research center in San Diego, Harnwell understood how to administer large-scale, government-sponsored research. By the end of Harnwell's administration in 1970, Penn's physical plant had increased to three times its size, university assets had grown by a factor of four, and the endowment had grown from $39 million to $200 million. Though the university had considered moving the campus to Valley Forge prior to Harnwell's presidency, Harnwell stood firmly on the side of growing within Philadelphia.[46] His choice to expand within the city had lasting implications for Philadelphia and the nation and aligned with the policies of an emerging city government that favored intellectual and cultural resources over industrial ones.

A Better Philadelphia

The decline in Philadelphia's industrial might spurred the rise of a liberal elite in city hall. According to historian Guian McKee, "liberals in Philadelphia recognized the problem of deindustrialization at a very early date and used the resources they had available to shape activist, public solutions to crucial economic problems." This new elite was broadly composed of groups wanting to clean up city government, but much of the cleaning up was aimed at the city's decrepit condition.[47] Reformers intended to not only correct the specific physical deficiencies of the city of Philadelphia but also restore public perceptions of city life overall.

How profound was the desire for change? It was strong enough to convince longtime Republicans in the business community to support New Deal Democrats in what amounted to a revolution in city government beginning in the late 1940s. At that time, leaders of commerce such as Harold Batten and C. Jared Ingersoll formed the Greater Philadelphia Movement to combat the corruption and physical decay they thought was driving away business.[48] Their first victory came in 1949, when state legislature gave approval for Philadelphia to draft a home rule charter reorganizing city government. The charter, approved by voters in 1951, established a strong mayor, diminished the role of patronage in key hiring decisions, and, most significantly, increased the power of Philadelphia's City Planning Commission. These changes paved the way for the election of Democrats Joseph S. Clark as mayor and Richardson Dilworth as district attorney in 1951—ending the reign of a Republican machine in place since the Civil War.[49] Clark served as mayor from 1952 to 1956 and was succeeded by Dilworth from 1956 to 1962. Though they both had patrician roots and Ivy League educations, the two supported New Deal policies and favored an active role for government in addressing social problems.[50] The reform era over which Clark and Dilworth presided saw an abatement of corruption and a transformation of Philadelphia's built environment.

A key figure in that transformation was planner Edmund N. Bacon. Like Clark and Dilworth, Bacon had the benefit of a privileged background and elite education. He had studied architecture at Cornell University and later at the Cranbrook Academy under the tutelage of Finnish architect Eliel Saarinen. German American modernist Oskar Stonorov was a mentor to Bacon, helping him find work as an architect and encouraging him to view city planning as a means for social as well as aesthetic transformation. Other mentors included public housing advocate Catherine Bauer and city planning historian and critic Lewis Mumford. Bacon is hailed as one of the most influential planners of the era and is often compared—favorably—to Robert Moses in New York. Unlike Moses, Bacon was a designer and visionary, not a boss. He influenced planning through salesmanship and the high regard in which he was held by his peers rather than through political and financial control.[51]

Following his mentors, Bacon developed an idea that planners could create an ideal "New Town," but he argued that the city, not the suburbs, would be the best location.[52] However, before Bacon came to Philadelphia, his attempts to effect social change in a city had ended in failure. Biographer

Gregory Heller describes how as a young planner in Flint, Michigan, Bacon had tried to utilize New Deal housing funds to improve living conditions for factory workers. Bacon had rallied the support of community groups, created elaborate visual models of his plans, and argued that with generous federal funding, the project made good economic sense for the city. However, Flint's conservative business leaders, wary of any Roosevelt-sponsored program, had quashed the plan and effectively ended Bacon's tenure as planner. Fortunately, Bacon had a fallback: he married a well-to-do New Yorker, Ruth Holmes, whose money helped him through the years between Flint and his next job in Philadelphia.[53] No mere socialite, Ruth Holmes Bacon was an educator who would help found an innovative preschool in Philadelphia, the Walnut Street Center. Her knowledge of the subject certainly affected Bacon's thinking about the role of education in redeveloping a city.[54]

In Philadelphia, Bacon applied the hard-earned lessons from his Flint years. His first challenge came in 1947, when his mentor, Oskar Stonorov, convinced him to take a position with Philadelphia's City Planning Commission. There, he was tasked with designing the monumental 1947 Better Philadelphia exhibition, which visualized a long-term plan for city redevelopment. In approaching the project, he used the same tools he had in Flint: community participation, elaborate visual displays, and economic as well as aesthetic arguments. This time, he was careful to also cultivate buy-in from top business leaders. Bacon garnered sponsorship for the show from Gimbels department store, which provided the space, and the Philadelphia Electric Company, whose president served as secretary of the exhibition committee.[55]

The Better Philadelphia exhibition was a spectacular success. The show, which occupied two floors of the Gimbels store, offered a rich array of multimedia displays. There were rotating models showing alternative plans for different sites; cartoons on such topics as "We All Plan," intended to convey the importance of city planning to a wide audience; a section entitled "Progress Must Be Bought and Paid For" justifying cost of redevelopment; and displays created by students from sixteen high schools who had been given instruction in model building by Bacon and Stonorov. During its thirty-eight-day run, the show attracted 385,000 visitors. Its $340,000 cost, equaling more than $4 million in 2024 dollars, was subsidized by $200,000 in contributions from the business community and a $125,000 grant from the mayor's office.[56] Better Philadelphia launched Bacon's career, paving the way for his appointment as director of city planning.[57] The show also envisioned the redevelopment of many of the blighted areas mentioned at the beginning of this chapter. It modeled a series of high-rise buildings in place of Broad Street Station and the Chinese Wall. And it showed the creation of a landscaped mall in front of Independence Hall, giving proper attention to the building and paving the way for the creation of a historic district in nearby Society Hill.[58]

Bacon was made director of city planning in 1949, and the election of Joseph Clark as mayor in 1951 boosted the power of his office. He first dealt with Broad Street Station. By 1959, the building and the Chinese Wall had been replaced by the first in a series of office towers in the Penn Center complex. With support from the Greater Philadelphia Movement, Bacon also began work on what would be Philadelphia's signature redevelopment effort, the Society Hill project. This project, begun in the mid-1950s, provided a model for what was to happen in West Philadelphia. Both involved the cooperation of private and public actors and what appeared to be an upswell of support from ordinary citizens. Both used what architectural critics called "penicillin, not surgery" to cure blight, restoring houses one at a time in favored areas and demolishing buildings in disfavored ones.[59] The creation of University City in West Philadelphia, however, would add one more element: transformation of the public schools serving the area.

From Society Hill to West Philadelphia

Like "University City," "Society Hill" was a name applied to an existing area to mold public perceptions. Bacon and his collaborators dubbed what was then referred to as the 5th Ward "Society Hill" to draw attention to its historical roots.[60] In the 1950s, the word "gentrification" had not yet been coined, but urban sociologist Neil Smith has cited Society Hill as one of the first examples of the phenomenon in an American city.[61] He analyzes its redevelopment in detail in his 1979 article, "Toward a Theory of Gentrification," and his 1996 book, *New Urban Frontier*.[62] In Smith's view, a key strategy in the Society Hill project—which would be repeated in West Philadelphia—was the promotion of a "back to the city" movement. Youthful residents would opt to locate there rather than the suburbs, investing sweat equity in the restoration of historic homes. They would contribute to the city as an educated workforce with money to spend. This was the beginning of the myth of the urban pioneer, which would reach its zenith in urban theorist Richard Florida's narratives about the creative class revitalizing cities.[63] The myth disguises the role of institutions—government, banks, developers, and, in the case of West Philadelphia, universities—in revitalization efforts. As we see, their investments turned these parts of the city in a way that favored Whiter and wealthier citizens.

The area now known as Society Hill had long been on the radar of powerful business leaders who wanted to stem decay. It was the seat of Philadelphia's original gentry but fell into decline beginning in the mid-nineteenth century, as industry made it increasingly grimy and congested. The neighborhood boasted a significant Black population dating to colonial times and was the site of some of America's first independent Black organizations. Among these was the African Methodist Episcopal Church, founded in 1794 when a White Methodist congregation refused to seat Black churchgoers. This led to the creation of the Mother Bethel AME Church on 6th Street in Society Hill, the current building of which is at the same location.[64] Through the nineteenth century, more affluent residents moved west to Rittenhouse Square—and some eventually to West Philadelphia—leaving behind a population that was a mix of working-class White immigrants and Black people.[65]

Both Society Hill and large parts of West Philadelphia were labeled "hazardous" in a 1937 federal lending map, resulting in a drain of capital.[66] By the 1950s, major banks were unwilling to underwrite loans in these areas. Those wishing to purchase properties had to borrow from marginal lenders that charged higher interest rates and required larger down payments.[67] Many owner-occupied houses were converted into rentals. Society Hill's population declined by one-half during the 1950s, and it lost 18 percent of its housing units; 3.2 percent of its properties were vacant at that time.[68] The condition of its housing is indicated in the photograph of the decrepit row house at the beginning of this chapter—an eighteenth-century building that would undergo a spectacular renovation.

But both areas had assets that presaged their importance in the twenty-first-century economy. Society Hill boasted one of the largest collections of colonial-era structures in the nation, and it was adjacent to historic buildings such as Independence Hall. West Philadelphia had universities and hospitals. Philadelphia's city leaders intuited that Society Hill's potential as a tourist destination and West Philadelphia's as center for what we now call "eds and meds" were part of the answer to the city's waning industrial economy.

A Philadelphia Electric Company advertisement placed in the *Saturday Evening Post* during the early 1960s (fig. 1.5) shows what city planners had in mind for these sections of the city and how they fit into a larger transformation the city hoped to enact. The top two illustrations picture Society Hill as a place where restored historic buildings coexist with office and residential towers. The lower right shows a "Proposed University City" in West Philadelphia, where picturesque campus buildings and a science research tower have replaced the industrial landscape of the Black Bottom. The ad's caption, "Freedom and progress go hand in hand in Greater Philadelphia," suggests elevating the city's history as a cradle of democracy while building a technocratic economy as the way forward. It is not surprising that the Philadelphia Electric Company placed such an ad, as it was a supporter of Bacon's 1947 Better Philadelphia exhibition.

Freedom and progress go hand in hand in Greater Philadelphia

FUTURE SKYLINE—WASHINGTON SQUARE EAST

INDEPENDENCE HALL MALL—ARTIST'S CONCEPT

As the birthplace of American liberty, the Philadelphia area attracts millions of visitors each year. It is also a steady drawing card for management and employees who value the private enterprise system that freedom founded here. For in this area are all the elements that create growth, prosperity, and pleasant living conditions. All this is evident in the new buildings, expressways, and expanding educational facilities which are already built, or being built or planned. Behind this surge of progress is plentiful electric power, ready to serve every need. It would pay you to locate in this Land of Opportunity.

PENN CENTER—VITAL NEW DEVELOPMENT

EXPRESSWAYS TO DOWNTOWN AREA

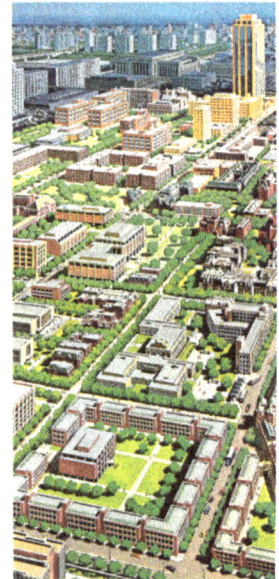

PROPOSED UNIVERSITY CITY

Philadelphia Electric Company

A tax-paying, investor-owned company with more than 100,000 stockholders   Serving the world's greatest industrial area, Delaware Valley

Figure 1.5 Philadelphia Electric Company advertisement. The advertisement's headline, "Freedom and Progress Go Hand in Hand in Greater Philadelphia," links the city's history as the birthplace of constitutional democracy to citywide urban renewal projects. Society Hill and Independence Mall are above. Below and to the left is Penn Center, which replaced Broad Street Station. Below and to the right is West Philadelphia, showing the science tower with the caption "Proposed University City." (Saturday Evening Post, *August 12, 1961. Used with permission.*)

A Planning Coalition

Philadelphia's business elites formed a nonprofit organization, the Old Philadelphia Development Corporation (OPDC), in 1956 to support redevelopment efforts in Society Hill. Though the city provided the overall vision and, through its Redevelopment Authority (RDA), power to demolish properties using urban renewal funds, businesses carried out restoration and building projects. Headed by the chairman of one of Philadelphia's major banks, the OPDC was able to find institutions to invest in the plan and developers to restore or rebuild targeted areas.[69] It also organized a publicity campaign that portrayed the transformation as the work of energetic families and individuals embracing city life. A September 1961 *Philadelphia Inquirer Magazine* article authored by Bacon heralds a "renewal of interest in center city living" and notes the "great amount of rehabilitation of older houses for family living" taking place, citing Society Hill and West Philadelphia as examples.[70] A page from a 1963 issue of the Bryn Mawr College alumni magazine (fig. 1.6) profiles the efforts of Agnes and Jared Ingersoll in restoring a historic Society Hill house. The wealthy couple became poster children for such efforts when, in 1959, the OPDC persuaded them to purchase a shell, 217 Spruce Street (depicted in fig. 1.1 in its unrestored condition), for $8,000. The Ingersolls subsequently invested $55,000 (more than half a million dollars in 2025) to return it to its historical grandeur.[71] Penned by Agnes Ingersoll, the article depicts home restoration as both fashionable and patriotic.

As this portrayal would have it, the couple walked accidentally into the renovation project: "Strolling about Society Hill one day in the fall of 1959 to look at the restoration in progress, we came upon a startlingly dilapidated, and yet, to our eyes, very charming old house."[72] In fact, the event was carefully orchestrated by the OPDC. Jared Ingersoll was a wealthy railroad executive and, as noted, a founder of the Greater Philadelphia Movement.

The WPC would play a similar role in West Philadelphia. It identified blighted areas and slated them either for restoration or demolition. Like the OPDC, it embarked on a public relations effort on behalf of urban living, producing the booklet *Elaborations on Living in University City* in 1963. As detailed in Chapter 3, this piece attempted to sell the neighborhood to university- and hospital-affiliated families through stories of adventurous families fixing up Victorian houses in much the same way the Ingersolls had their colonial-era home. For families that moved to University City, the piece also promised a quality public education at one of the neighborhood's emerging "Universities-Related" schools.

A
Society Hill
Restoration

Agnes Clement Ingersoll '23

Jared and I have been Philadelphia winter dwellers for many years in a house which after the marriage and departure of our five daughters was much too large for us. We began to think of finding something smaller, perhaps in Society Hill, the development of which we were very much interested in and anxious to help along. My husband had been a member of the Philadelphia Planning Commission when the idea of restoration of this area was being initiated.

Strolling about Society Hill one day in the fall of 1959 to look at the restoration in progress, we came upon a startlingly dilapidated, and yet, to our eyes, very charming old house. It was obviously of an earlier period than most of the houses on the street—also more bruised and battered and forlorn looking. We stood and looked at it a while, thinking aloud. "What a shambles. . . . Of course the rotted piece of cornice up there could be repaired and if the grimy red paint were scrubbed off the old bricks. . . . Yes, and if that gloomy brown paint that's peeling off the trim were a lighter color. . . . Oh look at that beautiful little pedimented frontispiece. . . . And the well-proportioned windows with nine-over-nine panes. . . . We'd have to replace the shutters, but, see, the turnbuckles and hinges are still there. . . . One, two, three, four stories, counting the one with the dormer. . . . What a quaint chunky chimney in the middle of the roof. . . . Probably lots of fireplaces inside." Just then the alley gate, hanging on one broken hinge, swung out, revealing through the arched brick tunnel a trash-littered muddy yard from which two ailanthus trees had risen above the grim surroundings. "And we'll lay a path of old brick in herringbone pattern back there with a bed on one side filled

"Situate on the North Side of Spruce St. between the Third and Second Streets from Delaware"

13

Figure 1.6 Page from article "A Society Hill Restoration." Agnes C. Ingersoll, *Bryn Mawr Alumnae Bulletin,* Winter 1963. (*Courtesy Bryn Mawr College Libraries Special Collections.*)

Government Foots the Bill

Urban renewal gave the infusion of cash necessary to restart investment in both Society Hill and West Philadelphia. As amended in 1954, the Federal Housing Act provided funds for the rehabilitation of existing homes as well as the construction of new buildings—exactly what was needed in Society

Hill and later in West Philadelphia. Title I of the legislation provided two-thirds of the funding for acquisition and demolition, a boost that made the Society Hill project worthwhile for developers by reducing costs and increasing profit margins. Since the maximum grant was $20 million, the RDA and OPDC split the project into three parts: units 1, 2, and 3.[73] In West Philadelphia, the WPC adopted a similar procedure, dividing target areas into five units. In Society Hill, the infusion of cash from the federal and local governments, which amounted to $38.6 million from 1959 to 1975, helped turn lending policies from redlining to greenlining. That era saw a return of large banks, which offered moderate interest rates and were willing to finance amounts higher than the purchase price of homes, providing a margin for renovation costs.[74]

As noted, Philadelphia's planners favored rehabilitation, especially for buildings with historic value. However, they also arranged for the demolition of buildings thought to be a nuisance or out of character with their aesthetic vision. One such structure in Society Hill was the grimy and congested food distribution center that dominated Dock Street. As shown in figure 1.7, this facility was replaced with the I. M. Pei–designed Society Hill Towers, a trio of high-rise residential buildings sited on a plinth overlooking the Delaware Riverfront. To finance such a large project required capital from the outside. The OPDC garnered funding first from New York real estate tycoon William Zeckendorf and later from aluminum producer ALCOA, which viewed real estate as a hedge against potential weaknesses in its extraction business. The redevelopment of West Philadelphia would comprise a similar mix of rehabilitation and replacement. The WPC promoted the renovation of historic houses in predominantly White areas such as Spruce Hill but planned the condemnation of the Black Bottom. Just as the OPDC had with the Dock Street Market, the WPC hoped to find corporate investors to replace the Black Bottom; this was the genesis of the University City Science Center (UCSC).[75]

OPDC public relations efforts, which promoted Society Hill as "the most historic square mile in the nation," were largely successful.[76] The media hailed its redevelopment as an "urban renaissance" and milestone in the effort to stem urban decay. To this day, many in architecture and urban planning view Society Hill in a positive light. Aside from the Pei-designed towers, the project preserved historic, human-scaled buildings, created walkable streets, and favored mixed commercial and residential development.[77] However, the process of awarding redevelopment contracts was hardly equitable. The OPDC favored developers who could contribute $40,000 per house in rehabilitation costs, and contracts were awarded strictly on a word-of-mouth basis. Neil Smith has shown that many of the renovations were done by affluent families that already lived in the city rather than

Figure 1.7 Transformation of Society Hill, 1950–1970. *Top:* Dock Street Market, 1953; *bottom:* Society Hill Towers, 1966. (*PhillyHistory.org, a project of the Philadelphia Department of Records.*)

suburbanites moving to the city.[78] The "most historic square mile" also became one of the most exclusive in the city. A time traveler from 1959 would recognize very little of today's Society Hill. The neighborhood has been sanitized, leaving only that which fits a specific range of the socioeconomic spectrum: restaurants, shops, and cinemas that appeal to an affluent customer; single-family homes; condominiums; and upscale rentals.[79]

Black Communities Ignored

The progress promised in publicity campaigns for both Society Hill and West Philadelphia never materialized for the African American residents of these neighborhoods. In Society Hill, approximately six thousand lower-income residents, many of them Black, were displaced. As most were renters, they were, according to Smith, evicted "on short notice, and with derisory relocation assistance and compensation."[80] Society Hill became primarily White and wealthy.[81]

In West Philadelphia's Black Bottom, 2,653 residents, 2,070 of them Black, were pushed out. Black Bottom residents were also unlikely to be homeowners. They faced the additional problem of living in a neighborhood that lacked officially demarcated boundaries. As theorist Katherine McKittrick shows, such situations are the legacy of racial bifurcation in the United States wherein Black people were consigned to marginal or expendable areas. Dispossessed since times of slavery, McKittrick says, Black people formed a sense of place "within, across, and outside commonsense cartographic and topographical texts."[82] Under urban renewal, communities formed around unconventional spaces were vulnerable to destruction. The Black Bottom— a borderland between industrial area and university campus that was never identified on a city map—amounted to little in the eyes of city planners. Challenged to recognize the Black Bottom as a community, WPC executive vice president Leo Molinaro quipped, "This area has never had any 'neighborhood' identification, or organization. It was from the beginning, marginal in use and occupancy."[83] Bacon referred to the area as simply "a wedge of Negro housing between Lancaster Avenue and Market Street."[84]

What Shall We Do about the Schools?

In Bacon's view, the area was a blight that, left unchecked, would thwart any effort to create a desirable university neighborhood. Before he was made head of the City Planning Commission, he had already identified Penn and Drexel's surroundings as pivotal to the city's future. Writing to planning director Raymond F. Leonard in 1947, he stated:

The University Area is a critical spot which will influence future trends in a large section of West Philadelphia. It is the apex of a triangle of good residential development extending westward to the city limits. If present deterioration in the University Area is allowed to spread, the good sections to the west will be cut off by a band of blight, and their rapid decline may be expected.[85]

The memo described areas to the north of Penn's campus as "a growing development of miscellaneous commercial uses mixed with residence" that had "no connection with the University" and the businesses around Market Street as "an extremely decadent commercial area." These areas were part of the Black Bottom.[86] Such descriptions would also be used by the WPC; became a euphemisms for "impoverished" and "Black."

Bacon's labeling of neighborhoods as "a band" of one kind or another was part of a tendency to view redevelopment as a chess game wherein pieces of residential settlement could be moved around to obtain a desired result. By eliminating one area and converting another, one might create continuous stretches of desirable development. Ignoring certain areas would result in decay. It is clear from Bacon's discussion that the Black Bottom was an area that needed to be eliminated. But it was not just physical structures that had to be changed. The planner devoted two pages of his memo to education. In Bacon's words, "The provision of acceptable educational opportunities is essential to the success of redevelopment in this area, and especially to attract the younger University faculty families." What followed was a detailed assessment of each neighborhood school and its potential to "meet the educational needs of University faculty."[87] Bacon made a series of suggestions on how to manipulate school catchment boundaries that modeled future conversations about West Philadelphia Schools—particularly in the covert way they refer to race.

His discussion of the H. C. Lea School is instructive in this regard and prognosticates the creation of the Penn Alexander School (PAS) fifty years hence. The planner gave the following assessment of Lea:

> The Lea School has a superior type of student, and by reputation, offers excellent instruction. However, the eastern boundary of its district is 42nd Street, and it is filled now almost to capacity.[88]

What did he mean by "a superior type of student"? Testimony by Barbara Pressman, who attended Lea during the 1940s, offers a clue. As discussed later in the book, Pressman went on to teach alongside Ruth Bacon at the Walnut Street Center, a pre-K–1 school. Pressman confirmed Bacon's assessment of the quality of instruction at Lea but also noted that the school's students were from south of Market Street—meaning largely White and middle class. Of the Black students at the school, Pressman observed, many were children of international students at Penn. It is clear, then, that "a superior type of student" had a certain race and class identification.[89]

With its eastern catchment boundary at 42nd Street and western boundary at 50th Street, Lea's center of gravity was too far to west to serve the university area. Meanwhile, the more centrally located Newton School had far too many students from the "low income triangle between Lancaster Avenue and Market Street"—the Black Bottom—in its feeder pattern, and therefore Bacon deemed it "unattractive to people of the type of University faculty."[90] Had Bacon thought it possible for Penn to create a university-assisted public school with excellent instruction and catchment boundaries coterminous with the Spruce Hill neighborhood, where university faculty tended to live, he might have suggested it.

Bacon's assessments acquiesced with the racism of the time. Any predominantly Black school was anathema to White residents, the thinking went, and nothing could change that. Speaking of two such schools located near Powelton, a mostly White area, the planner said:

> A marked anti-negro sentiment has been expressed in the Powelton area, and few children from this section attend either the McMichael or the Kendrick schools, both of which are almost entirely negro. . . . If the relocation and adjacent redevelopment of Kendrick School resulted in a substantial proportion of the students being white, this school might be well regarded and draw from the Powelton area also.[91]

Such acquiescence to entrenched racial arrangements echoes a similar capitulation to, and sometimes reinforcement of, racism by the SDP in the early twentieth century. The district would gerrymander school catchment boundaries to create single-race schools, then claim that parental preference had dictated that it be so.

Bacon's meandering speculations about school locations in the university area ended in a stalemate—he could think of no arrangement that created schools desirable to a more affluent, White resident. His successors, first at the Penn-sponsored WPC in the 1960s and later in Penn president Judith Rodin's brain trust, would propose more creative solutions. They would ultimately succeed in the endeavor.

Philadelphia in the 1950s was a city in decline, but a generation of new leaders saw reason for optimism. Its industrial economy was indeed on life support, but its cultural and intellectual assets were many, and a plan to favor those over factories stood the chance of creating a new type of city. By the late 1950s, city government and business were putting that theory to the test in Center City with the creation of an office tower hub, Penn Center, where Broad Street Station had stood, and the transformation of the city's oldest wards into Society Hill, the nation's most historic square mile. On the initiative of the University of Pennsylvania, they would soon attempt a more complete transformation in West Philadelphia. The creation of what planning historian Margaret Pugh O'Mara has termed a "city of knowledge"—a *University City*—would require more than an update to the area's physical infrastructure.[92] As in Center City, planners proposed to change what they viewed as an unsightly hodgepodge—an area mixed in appearance, socioeconomic makeup, and racial cast—to one that would appeal to a more affluent and educated group. But the biggest obstacle in this regard was the city's declining and embattled system of public education. As we see in the next chapter, this problem was long in the making. It encompassed a tangle of issues that divided Philadelphians along racial but also cultural and socioeconomic lines. In the 1950s, Clark, Dilworth, and their supporters among the city's business elites heralded a liberal government and focused on physical repair as the way toward a better Philadelphia. The question of how to repair the schools in the 1960s ignited a culture war that brought down the liberal city government.

2

An Embattled School System

Planner Edmund Bacon envisioned a city inviting to well-educated people but inherited one with an inferior school system. The School District of Philadelphia (SDP) was plagued by segregation, overcrowding, and an authoritarian mindset in its curriculum and governance. These conditions, which could be traced to the origins of the system in the nineteenth century, coalesced in the early twentieth, when the system was unified and its enrollment began to shift from majority White to majority Black. It would interfere with Bacon's vision and especially with that of the West Philadelphia Corporation (WPC), which during the 1960s sought to create a "brainsville" in the area surrounding Penn. Understanding the history of public schooling in Philadelphia enables us to see why, when Penn and its collaborators created a good, integrated school in the twenty-first century, it quickly resegregated.

A History of Segregation and Discrimination

From their beginning in 1818, Philadelphia's public schools treated Black students differently from White students. In his book *The Education of Black Philadelphia*, historian V. P. Franklin documents the origins of this discriminatory treatment and shows how it persisted through the 1950s. When the first public schools opened, slavery had not been abolished for long in Pennsylvania, and even White people who believed in education for Black citizens did not think it should happen in an integrated setting. Thus, the first public school in Philadelphia was for White children only, and a school for Black children did not open until 1822.[1] As more schools were created, a hand-me-down pattern was established wherein new buildings were designated Whites only and old ones were given to Black children. The system also discriminated against Black educators. When the Institute for Colored Youth (now Cheyney University) was established as a school for Black teachers, Philadelphia's public schools refused to hire its graduates.[2] Unequal schooling persisted even after the U.S. Civil War, when Pennsylvania enacted legislation to forbid segregation.[3]

An important milestone was the 1904 unification of Philadelphia's schools, which had hitherto operated as a collection of quasi-independent districts.[4] Under central governance, the system enacted new policies and practices intended to respond to the social pressures of the era, such as industrialization and immigration. Many of these policies were implemented under the second superintendent of the newly formed SDP, Martin Brumbaugh (1906–1914). Having studied at Harvard and the University of Jena in Germany and earned a Ph.D. from the University of Pennsylvania, Brumbaugh was well prepared for the task. He promoted innovations we might regard as progressive, such as an arts curriculum and a "teachers' institute" to advance the professional development of teaching staff.[5] In alignment with Progressive-era thinking, Brumbaugh also promoted the idea that schools could solve social problems, diverting the uneducated masses from indigence and criminality to productive existence. This transformation, he thought, could be accomplished by bringing scientific management to the system. Brumbaugh's approach borrowed from the social efficiency model, which utilized management techniques pioneered on the industrial assembly line: breaking educational tasks into step-by-step procedures and using standardized testing to assess results and steer students on the path best suited to their abilities.[6]

Historian V. P. Franklin has shown that Brumbaugh's approach had a detrimental effect on the city's growing Black population. Black migrants from the South, who had received inferior education under the Jim Crow system, were held back or shunted into vocational tracks in Philadelphia. Using the excuse that parents preferred separate schools, or that they better met student needs, the district quietly adopted practices that reinforced segregation. One was the "tipping point" phenomenon: when a school's Black population reached a certain threshold, White students were encouraged to enroll elsewhere and Black teachers were hired. Segregated employment eligibility lists, which steered Black teachers to Black schools, facilitated this process. Middle and high schools, which aggregated enrollment from different neighborhoods and were therefore racially mixed, did not employ Black teachers or principals. And the system continued the hand-me-down approach to school facilities, wherein White populations were provided new buildings and Black ones left with the old.[7]

The experiences of noted Black educator Ruth Wright Hayre reveal the district's discriminatory practices and the negative attitudes they fostered. Hayre attended the city's public schools in the first half of the twentieth century and later became a teacher, principal, and, ultimately, school board president. Though she was top of her class, Hayre recalled a middle-grades counselor steering her toward a vocational rather than college preparatory track in high school. Only after her mother confronted central administration was Hayre allowed to enroll in a course of study that matched her abilities.[8] While studying for her education degree at Penn, Hayre was required to complete her practicum at a Black school in Chester, Pennsylvania, rather than the nearby West Philadelphia High School (WPHS) because of the SDP's refusal to employ Black teachers in the upper grades.[9] When community resistance forced the district to discontinue this policy, Hayre was one of two Black teachers hired at Sulzberger Junior High School. There she encountered firsthand the low expectations and opinion many of her White colleagues held of their Black students. According to Hayre, one such teacher said, "You can't teach them anything," and another, "I'm going to transfer where I can teach children, instead of animals."[10] Moreover, years of preferential treatment by the district—and the preceding history of slavery and segregation—had instilled in her White colleagues that no Black person should rise to a position of authority over White people. Hayre reported that when a Black man, Tanner Duckrey, was finally elevated to the position of principal at Sulzberger, one teacher asked to be transferred, saying, "I just can't let my friends know that I'm working under a colored principal."[11]

From the early through mid-twentieth century, the Philadelphia Board of Education's fiscally conservative governance structure reinforced racist policies and prevented the district from making necessary improvements to its physical plant. According to historian Jon S. Birger, the fifteen-member board was under the thumb of Philadelphia's business elites, whose main concern was keeping taxes low and avoiding controversy. Under this system of governance, business manager Add Anderson became the most important person in the district, constraining important educational decisions by holding the system's purse strings. From his appointment in 1936 to his death in 1962, Anderson was, according to Birger, more powerful than the superintendent. Though officially, he controlled operational decisions such as the provision of janitorial services and building repairs, he would use his authority to dissuade principals from altering the educational program in ways he did not approve. Moreover, he was at the center of a patronage system: he awarded jobs to friends of city ward leaders or city council members, cementing his influence in political circles. Anderson's fiscal conservatism prevented the district from moving forward on multiple fronts. He not only thwarted expenditures on new schools but also made such short-sighted decisions as declining federal funds for meal programs for malnourished students, citing additional cost to the district. Such decisions pleased the business interests that dominated board of education politics.[12]

The segregation, discrimination, and overall toxic environment in the Philadelphia public schools continued to be felt through the mid-twentieth century. To parents and children who were part of the district during the 1950s, 1960s, and 1970s, it manifested itself as a pervasive indifference to the needs of Blacks in the system. It meant low expectations of Black students' abilities; condescension toward parents requesting information about their children's education; and a tendency, despite laws forbidding the practice, to acquiesce in segregated enrollment patterns. Rochelle Nichols-Solomon, who grew up in South Philadelphia and sent her children to the H. C. Lea School in West Philadelphia during the 1970s, remembered the struggles her mother, Mamie Nichols, had with district administration over the placement of her own children. She recalled that although her mother had not yet completed her high school education at the time, she could recognize a high-quality school and fought hard to ensure her children attended one:

> And [she] was always reading and finding out information about transfers. . . . And so each of us were transferred out of our neighborhood to go to junior high someplace else. . . . Not without trepidation. I mean, the first one, the District said fine. The second one, my brother, they said no. My mother said all right, he won't go to school. So she kept him home until they said yes, and he went. Then it was me, and I had a twin brother. It was our time, they said no. My mother said fine, they won't go to school. . . . And I think by the fifth child or the sixth, the District was just like, it's Mamie Nichols, just let her do it.[13]

These fights were critical, Nichols-Solomon remembered, because the consequence of going to the wrong school could be devastating. She recalled, for example, that at the time she and her brothers and sisters were attending high school, during the 1960s, low-performing students were tracked into a "modified," major, meaning they received a certificate instead of a high school diploma. The district had planned to apply this designation to her brother, who struggled academically:

> So my oldest brother, Russell, was a kid who never did well in school. He did not need to sit down at a desk, he just was not that kind of kid. He needed to be active, and needed to be doing things. So he

never did well in school. So when he gets to high school, they were going to put him in "modified." And my mother, who was again the activist, was like, "like hell you're putting him in modified!"[14]

Tracking her brother as "general" rather than "modified" meant he earned a full high school diploma. This enabled him to serve as a dental assistant when he enlisted in the armed forces during the Vietnam era. According to Nichols-Solomon, her brother took the necessary college-preparatory courses after returning from military service, went to college, and earned a DDM degree. One can imagine that his path would have been vastly different had his mother allowed him to be shunted into the "modified" track.[15]

Agitating for Better Schools

Concerted efforts by community groups led to modest improvements in the SDP's treatment of Black Philadelphians. Beginning in the 1930s, E. Washington Rhodes, publisher of the *Philadelphia Tribune*, the city's Black newspaper, joined forces with Floyd L. Logan, a Black U.S. Customs agent who had been a frequent contributor to the *Tribune*, to form the Educational Equality League (EEL). This organization scored an important victory in 1937 when it persuaded the SDP to eliminate segregated eligibility lists for employment in its schools. The change enabled a trickle of Black teachers and principals—among them Ruth Wright Hayre—to be hired at high schools or promoted to higher positions in administration.[16] Yet the SDP found other ways of segregating employment—first marking African Americans' employment records with a "C" for "colored" and, after that practice was forbidden by Pennsylvania's Fair Employment Practices Commission, assigning teachers to schools near their homes with the understanding that residential segregation would perpetuate employment segregation.[17]

In their push to end discrimination, the EEL and other Black citizens groups used the same methods as the nationwide civil rights movement emerging at the time. These included public pressure through boycotts and marches as well as legal action to challenge racist laws and practices. Yet such challenges had limited effect because segregation and discrimination in Philadelphia were largely de facto, relying on segregated housing and ingrained cultural tendencies. An example was the effort to desegregate the Anna B. Day School in the Germantown section of Philadelphia. This mostly White and well-equipped school was located not far from the overcrowded and entirely Black Emlen Elementary School. Citizens' groups petitioned the SDP to integrate Day Elementary School in 1956 but were rebuffed. By 1961, overcrowding at Emlen had reached a critical point, with students attending classes in trailers. Drawing inspiration from national civil rights protests and local campaigns against employment discrimination, the citizens' groups asked the NAACP to back their desegregation bid. Philadelphia's NAACP chapter filed *Chisholm v. Board of Public Education* in federal district court in June 1961.[18]

The settlement of this case in 1963 required the SDP to desegregate its schools but relied on citizen oversight to detect and report violations. The district's implementation of the plan was haphazard, leading to threats of protest and boycotting by the NAACP and other activist groups. Ultimately, no further actions were taken. Beginning in 1964, White reaction against SDP plans to bus students further sapped the momentum behind desegregation.[19]

Other school reform groups that emerged during the post–World War II era were White-led or mixed in composition. These organizations pushed for greater transparency and integrity in SDP governance, as well as better conditions in schools—and in some cases also opposed segregation. Among these were the Citizens Committee on Public Education in Philadelphia (CCPEP), formed in 1953 by Annette Temin, a Penn-educated White woman who had been president of her local home and school association. Temin rallied a cohort of influential players to the cause—many with ties to the reformist circles that had ejected the Republican machine from city hall. Members of the committee included Ruth Bacon, wife of city planning director Edmund Bacon. The body gained support from various organizations, including the NAACP, the Chamber of Commerce, and various churches. It resisted the stingy decisions of district business manager Add Anderson and had some success in reforming the city's school tax system. The group would be instrumental in overthrowing the conservative board of education in the 1960s, a move resulting in a brief and tumultuous period of reform in the SDP.[20]

Another mixed-race school reform group was the West Philadelphia Schools Committee (WPSC), founded in 1960 to promote equal opportunity and integration in West Philadelphia schools. Among its members were George Hutt, who would become the first Black member of the Philadelphia Board of Education.[21] The organization opposed the SDP's 1962 building plan, which it said discriminated against Black neighborhoods. It dismissed the district's claim that Black families that had migrated from the South were responsible for poor school performance, instead placing the blame on the SDP's overcrowded, segregated schools and poor quality teachers.[22] Under the leadership of Helen Oakes, a White, middle-class parent who, like Temin, had begun as a home and school association member, the WPSC proposed an alternative plan for school building called "educational parks." Large campuses would educate students at all grade levels and draw from various neighborhoods—overcoming neighborhood schools' tendency to reinforce residential segregation patterns. Despite Oakes's vigorous advocacy for educational parks, none were built. The WPSC disbanded in 1971, its members frustrated by their inability to combat entrenched power structures within the SDP.[23]

Enter the West Philadelphia Corporation

Beginning in 1960, the newly formed West Philadelphia Corporation (WPC) joined the school improvement fray. Its efforts also reflected parents' widespread discontent with schools, but motivated primarily by Penn's desire to make its surroundings more appealing to well-educated, affluent families. Launched and funded by Penn, the WPC had more than persuasion at its disposal. Its parent organization boasted one of the top graduate schools of education and of architecture in the country. It also had the ear of Philadelphia's city planning apparatus, which was willing to demolish neighborhoods at its behest.

Planner Edmund Bacon's 1947 insight that the university area was a "critical spot that would influence future trends in a large section of West Philadelphia" suddenly gained traction in 1958, when mayhem hit the neighborhood. The murder of a Korean graduate student, In Ho-Oh, by local youth propelled Penn to join forces with other educational institutions and hospitals in the neighborhood to create the WPC.[24] The form and purpose of the organization were seeded in 1956 by Martin Meyerson, a city planning professor who would later become Penn's president. Writing to G. Holmes Perkins, dean of Penn's Graduate School of Fine Arts and chair of Philadelphia's City Planning Commission, Meyerson repeated Bacon's 1947 warnings:

> The University of Pennsylvania is located in an area which is on the brink of blight. . . . only a vigorous program of planning redevelopment and rehabilitation of a large area will prevent West Philadelphia from becoming a sea of residential slums with commercial and institutional islands.[25]

In his previous role at the University of Chicago, Meyerson had gained extensive experience in redevelopment and rehabilitation. He had helped create the South East Chicago Commission (SECC) in 1952, attempting to stem what historian Arnold Hirsch calls "racial succession" in the neighborhoods surrounding the University of Chicago as Black populations increased and White flight took hold.[26] Together with Morningside Heights Incorporated (MHI), formed by Columbia University in 1947 to thwart a similar succession in its neighborhood, SECC provided a model for the WPC. Both organizations had prominent board members and ties to city government, ensuring any plans put before it would be rubber stamped.[27]

The SECC and MHI used urban renewal legislation to displace neighborhood residents, putting them at odds with their communities. Stefan Bradley, author of *Harlem vs. Columbia University: Black Student Power in the Late 1960s*, describes how Columbia's interventions in Morningside Heights during the 1960s led to accusations of segregation and contributed to the campus uprisings in 1968.[28] Similarly, in *In the Shadow of the Ivory Tower*, Davarian Baldwin recounts the anger of neighborhood residents toward the University of Chicago because of the displacement of Black residents beginning in the 1950s, largely through plans developed by the SECC.[29]

The WPC had a local antecedent in the Old Philadelphia Development Corporation (OPDC). Recall that the OPDC grew out of Philadelphia's political reform movement in the 1950s and launched the Society Hill redevelopment project in 1956. Though it also used urban renewal funding to clear "problem" areas, it differed from SECC and MHI in the broad nature of its goals. In alignment with Edmund Bacon's approach, it emphasized rehabilitation over demolition and sought to promote the city as offering a superior quality of life. The WPC adopted the same approach but added the element of education. It recognized that to appeal to an affluent, well-educated family, a city had to offer strong schools as well as cultural amenities and a good physical appearance.

The WPC's leader, Leo Molinaro, was at the center of redevelopment circles at the time. In his previous role as director of the American Council to Improve Our Neighborhoods (ACTION), Molinaro had educated the public about urban renewal policies. Martin Meyerson had also worked for ACTION and likely played a role in Molinaro's selection.[30] Beginning in 1958, ACTION was headed by developer James Rouse, a promoter of new urban communities. Such communities attempted to combine elements of city and suburb, balancing density and walkability with open space. Molinaro would work for Rouse after he left the WPC.[31] In addition to knowledge of city planning, Molinaro also had a university background and an interest in education, having worked as an assistant professor at the Institute of Citizenship at Kansas State College (1951–1952) and been associated with the Akron Adult Education Foundation in Ohio.[32] Like Bacon, Molinaro was a planning visionary who believed that improvements in the built environment could strengthen society's social fabric. He also believed that education was a critical factor in realizing these improvements.

From its inception, the WPC had the blessing of the reformist politicians who had dominated city hall since the early 1950s. In a 1959 letter to university vice president John Moore, Mayor Richardson Dilworth proclaimed that "the setting up of the West Philadelphia Corporation is a splendid step toward improving and rehabilitating a key area of our City. It deserves the commendation of all or our citizens because unless blight is checked all the rest of us will have to pay the price."[33]

Following Bacon's model, the WPC sought the input of community groups in its decision-making. In addition to representatives from partner institutions Penn, Drexel, Philadelphia College of Pharmacy, and area hospitals, its board included leaders of homeowners' associations in the areas surrounding Penn and Drexel: Benjamin L. Barkan, Joseph Moloznik, and John M. Marshall.[34] The WPC also formed a community relations advisory consisting of various neighborhood organizations[35] and arranged for grant funding for social work doctoral student Bettie Livermore to conduct a "social audit" of faculty and staff living in West Philadelphia.[36]

Livermore's study showed that better schools, as much as safety and neighborhood amenities, were of critical importance to university faculty and staff.[37] As noted, however, public education was in bad shape. A 1960 Graduate School of Education (GSE) survey commissioned by the WPC exposed deplorable conditions and overcrowding in West Philadelphia schools, many of which had been built in the nineteenth century.[38] Feedback from the school committees of three neighborhood groups led the WPC to conclude that there were no good options for parents who wanted their children to attend high school in West Philadelphia, causing many to leave the area. These groups suggested that "particular attention be given to experimental situations in the local schools which could be reenforced to strengthen the educational resources available in West Philadelphia."[39] From the beginning, the WPC knew that its constituents not only wanted higher quality schools but also embraced progressive thinking about education.

Universities-Related Program

Armed with this knowledge, the WPC concocted a series of school interventions called the Universities-Related Program (URP). Interventions included aid for elementary and middle schools in the form of curriculum development and investment in facilities. They also encompassed a college readiness initiative, the Motivation Program, at area high schools. The WPC first implemented these programs at the K–9 H. C. Lea School and WPHS, the schools closest to Spruce Hill and Garden Court, neighborhoods where Penn faculty and staff tended to live.[40] It later expanded the elementary-middle programs to six other schools in surrounding neighborhoods. At the same time, the Motivation Program's director, Rebecca Segal, introduced the program into other high schools around the city.[41]

Spruce Hill, the quiet, shady neighborhood to the west of Penn, was one of the "good sections to the west" that planner Edmund Bacon feared would

be "cut off by a band of blight." One of America's first instances of suburbanization, the neighborhood was an outgrowth of Hamilton Village,
formed by the subdivision of William Hamilton's estate in the pre–Civil
War era.[42] It remained middle class and predominantly White through the
1960s (see fig. 1.4). Former Spruce Hill resident Carol Williamson, who at
that time lived on St. Mark's Square, a block adjacent to the now-defunct
Philadelphia Divinity School, described her street thus:

> I think that being on St. Mark's Square was kind of its own little
> bubble. The Seminary [divinity school] owned five houses on the
> block, so our family and four other Seminary families lived there . . .
> most of the other people who were not connected to seminary, there
> were a lot of, you know, Penn professors and people. There were lots
> of kids. And of course, before they had done all that building on the
> seminary property [42nd to 43rd between Spruce and Locust Streets,
> where PAS now stands], there was all this woods from the middle of
> the block and on down.[43]

Children could safely play, she noted, on the street or in the wooded area
adjacent to the divinity school. Williamson attended the H. C. Lea School
from 1962 through 1969 and then University City High School (UCHS),
both of which received assistance from the WPC. Notably, the divinity
school site would be chosen, during Penn's second wave of neighborhood
interventions in the early 2000s, as the location for its highly successful Penn
Alexander School (PAS).

The WPC understood that its liberal-leaning, university-affiliated constituents were against segregation. Livermore's study, for example, found
that the typical Penn faculty or staff member living in the area desired diversity: they "spoke in favor of neighborhoods with a mixture of people from
different races, socio-economic classes and religions" and "expressed concern or caution about a 'community of scholars' that would be composed
almost exclusively of university people."[44] For this reason, the WPC joined
activist and community groups in opposing segregated schools. For example, it stood with the WPSC, CCPEP, NAACP, and Urban League in speaking out against the SDP's plan to build a junior high school at 46th and
Market Streets, which groups believed would increase segregation.[45] And the
WPC was careful to emphasize in its publicity for the URP that school interventions were intended for everyone, not just the children of university-
and hospital-affiliated parents.

Having heard from advisory groups that secondary education in West
Philadelphia was weak, the WPC added another plank to its educational
platform: a science-themed high school. The proposed UCHS took inspira-

tion from Bronx High School of Science in New York and the Baltimore Polytechnic Institute, the latter of which had ties to Drexel. In alignment with its professed commitment to serving the entire neighborhood, however, the WPC planned to omit the rigorous admission process these other schools used. Instead, it would enroll students from a feeder pattern of elementary and middle schools in the neighborhood.[46]

The educational proposals the WPC made early in its history seemed reasonable enough. Responding to long-standing discontent with Philadelphia's public school system, it planned to intervene at every level, to both improve existing schools and create a new school. Though the WPC's plans did not eliminate segregation in education, they did not appear to increase it, as would have been the case if the WPC had proposed a separate system for university- and hospital-affiliated students. Instead, the group's approach was to start with mixed-race schools like Lea and make improvements it claimed would reverse White flight. The proposed UCHS was similarly expected to serve both Black students from surrounding neighborhoods and White students from university- and hospital-affiliated families.

While the WPC's educational arm was proposing to make better schools for all, its real estate arm was launching efforts to drain the neighborhood of less well-off Black residents. As we see in succeeding chapters, the organization's plan unraveled when the tumult of the 1960s exposed its dual nature.

Counterculture Invades the Board of Education

A critical moment in the history of Philadelphia's schools came in 1965, when reformers prompted an overthrow of the board of education. Democratic Mayor Tate appointed a new board, elevating liberal former mayor Richardson Dilworth to its presidency. Dilworth's choice for superintendent was Harvard-trained Mark Shedd, who began his term of service in 1967.[47] The new leader would bring progressive ideas to Philadelphia's schools, elevate Black employees to positions of prominence, and promote greater community input into the running of schools. While the reformist tenor of Shedd's administration appeared favorable to the WPC's plans, it provoked a conservative backlash that threw the system into turmoil and ultimately undermined the URP agenda.

Shedd studied at Harvard at a time when the institution was a hotbed for new ideas about education. Figures of importance at Harvard included Theodore Sizer, a noted critic of traditional high schools who became dean of Harvard's GSE. Sizer recommended Shedd as a candidate for superintendent to board president Richardson Dilworth. Harvard's faculty also included Jerome Bruner, an educational psychologist who pioneered the idea of scaffolding. Rather than feeding ideas to the learner, scaffolding provides a framework for the learner to discover on their own. The approach was part of a larger ecosystem of progressive educational ideas that had been evolving since the early twentieth century.[48] To encourage students' discovery process, schools built around progressive education shed boundaries between classrooms, grade levels, disciplines, and school and community. They also shunned grades, standardized tests, and tracking. In all respects, they opposed the social efficiency model that, as mentioned earlier in the chapter, had dominated the SDP since reorganization in 1904.

From his appointment as superintendent in 1967, Shedd began to introduce progressive ideas into the curriculum. His administration initiated the Parkway Schools, a kind of school-without-walls program in which students learned at various cultural and scientific sites. Breaking with SDP tradition, he railed against authoritarian control and placed a high value on student expression. According to Shedd, "Nothing frightens me more than the possible impact on a barely articulate child—whose crying need is for self-expression—if he enters a classroom with a harsh emphasis on absolute order and, above all, absolute silence."[49] He therefore made "affective education," the development of students' internal awareness and ability to communicate their feelings, a key part of the curriculum.[50]

Shedd's progressive approach extended to governance as well as curriculum. Where in the past, the tight-fisted policies of business manager Add Anderson had dictated school budgets, the new superintendent gave broad leeway to principals. And to counter past discrimination, he encouraged the hiring of Black administrators—promoting such people as Constance Clayton, who would later become the SDP's first Black superintendent, to positions of authority. He also took chances by hiring leaders who were exceptionally young or from nontraditional backgrounds. For example, he hired Terry Borton, age twenty-eight and a fellow Harvard graduate, to promote his affective curriculum.[51] Borton in turn brought on Norman Newberg, who was trained in theater, not education, to assist him. Newberg introduced acting to a kindergarten class at the SDP's Henry Elementary School as a tool for overcoming disabilities. He recalled that his background was no impediment to being hired by the Shedd administration:

> He [Shedd] wasn't especially interested in people who had a degree in education. He was interested in people who knew how to relate to children and who had a connection to the community, which he was a big advocate of.[52]

According to Newberg, in developing their affective curriculum, he and Borton emphasized the importance of putting students in touch with their feelings: "We talked a lot about how you could create literacy, a language that people would use and feel. And we got to thinking about the limitations that kids had, and their parents, to use what we called the language of feelings. And we taught that. We published a book."[53]

In his effort to improve race relations in the SDP, Shedd instituted a series of off-site sensitivity retreats. Among the people tasked with organizing them was Newberg, who used his theater background in the effort. Newberg organized gatherings of teachers, students, parents, and administrators, Black and White—sometimes overnight and at locations outside of the city—in which participants would use theater exercises to work through their differences. WPHS graduate Norman Brown, a Black student who was president of his school class, attended one of these events in the wake of a 1967 student march on the school district offices. Brown came to admire Shedd's commitment to improving the schools:

> Right after the protest, Mark Shedd pulled an all-city conference in Atlantic City. The cool thing about Mark Shedd is that his daughter went to Germantown High School. I mean, unlike superintendents now—I don't know where their students go to school—Mark's people, his kids went to his high school. So we had a conference, which was headed up by Marcus Foster in Atlantic City. Never been to Atlantic City in the wintertime, and I didn't want to go either. But he rented a hotel. It was like seventy of us. They said, let's get out of the city; let's take all these kids down here to Atlantic City, pay for transportation, pay the room, and we had a conference.[54]

The event, Brown noted, generated several new ideas, including the Parkway Schools program, and resulted in the introduction of an African American curriculum. Brown described a conference with quite a bit of drama—perhaps owing to Norm Newberg's theater background and Shedd's focus on "gut issues": "We had reps from every high school, and we were in Atlantic City, working it out ourselves, busting and fighting, arguing about what, you know. We came back with a plan, and, you know, it was good."[55]

Jettie Newkirk, a counselor at WPHS from 1965 through 1971, also saw Shedd as an effective leader: "I thought Mark Shedd was brilliant. He listened, he was young, he was energetic. He had charisma. He had an inclusive rather than exclusive attitude."[56] From Newkirk's perspective, conditions regarding race improved during that era, though it was not clear that Shedd was responsible. Newkirk saw an increase in number of Black counselors, which she believed made a difference in educational outcomes for Black students:

There were counselors there who had a reputation of telling Black students they weren't college material and therefore couldn't go to college—very discouraging in terms of future goals for the students. So with the increase in number of Black counselors, we were able to control that and cut it down.[57]

As an activist educator who would go on to cofound an experimental school, Newkirk was herself committed to combatting the racism that plagued Philadelphia's school system.[58]

Many of those viewing the situation from the outside also had the perception that Shedd was a true innovator and that Philadelphia was leading the nation in urban school reform. For example, James "Torch" Lytle, who had just earned his doctorate from Stanford University and had an interest in urban education, was drawn to Philadelphia because of Shedd: "In 1967–68 through 1970, Philadelphia was perceived as the most interesting urban school reform district in the country."[59] Through a connection in the Philadelphia district's central office, Lytle was able to secure a position as assistant to deputy superintendent David Horwitz. Characteristic of the Shedd era, Lytle was hired with little experience for a vaguely defined position that enabled him to shadow his supervisor, listen in at meetings, and generally gain experience on the job. Lytle would later teach at Penn GSE and hold the position of principal at UCHS, the SDP school planned by the WPC.[60]

Not everyone viewed Shedd's approach favorably. Historian John Birger notes that teachers found the retreats confrontational. They claimed to be "subjected to verbal abuse and intimidation by black community activists" at the events.[61] The teachers' union opposed certain of Shedd's personnel decisions, particularly the removal of WPHS history teacher George Fishman at the request of student protesters. Students accused Fishman of racism because he refused to include Black history in a course he was teaching. However, Fishman had the respect of his fellow teachers and regarded himself as nonracist, having published scholarly articles on civil rights. Moreover, the student who initiated the complaint had failed Fishman's class the previous semester because he had attended only four sessions in a five-month period. Shedd backed down when the union threatened to strike if Fishman was removed.[62]

Ruth Wright Hayre, who, as noted, was one of the first African Americans to serve in the highest levels of SDP administration, had mixed views of Shedd. Though she valued his efforts, she thought students would benefit from a more disciplined approach:

Many people saw the student demonstration as characteristic of the Shedd administration—uncontrolled, without focus or positive result. Dr. Shedd was sincere on issues of diversity and innovative programming. He was a risk-taker committed to making a positive difference. However, I believe his tenure would have been quite different had he focused more on instruction and carefully considered educational objectives, especially student achievement.[63]

Shedd's most famous detractor was outside the SDP: police commissioner and rising political star Frank Rizzo. The feud between the two would bring an abrupt end to school reform and result in a rift in Philadelphia's two-decades-old Democratic party leadership.[64] The fact that Shedd had only lukewarm support from prominent African American administrators like Hayre further weakened his position.

Do-It-Yourself School Reform

While Shedd and his colleagues were trying to make change from within, community members were launching their own school experiments. These initiatives exemplified the ideals of school reform but also exposed the difficulty of fixing a broken system: the problem of creating a boutique program within an otherwise failing system and the tension between community control and expertise.

A School within a School: The Lea Learning Lab

In some instances, parents came together to create progressive educational programs in existing schools. One such program was the Lea Learning Lab, initiated by a group of Penn-affiliated parents during the late 1960s. While children of all backgrounds benefited from the lab, it created a parallel environment in the school sheltered from the problems of the mainstream.

The group that founded the program included Susan Bank, who held a master's degree in education from Villanova University and whose husband, William Bank, was a neurologist at the Hospital of the University of Pennsylvania, and Nina Segrè, married to Penn physics professor Gino Segrè. They modeled the program on the British Infant School, which had become popular in the United States during the 1960s. Not actually a school for infants, this type of school served children ages five through seven in an open classroom. Rather than separating children by grade, it put students of different ages together in "family" groups according to interest and abilities, encouraging older students to mentor younger ones.[65] Segrè, Bank, and their collaborators launched a version of this program as the Lea Learning Lab in 1968 with the help of Charlotte Levens, the WPC's URP coordinator at Lea. According to a proposal document coauthored by Levens, "the school we have in mind would devote itself to helping children feel good about themselves. That is to say, everything that happens at school would aim at moving children toward feeling that they are worthwhile, trusted, important, capable and responsible individuals."[66] As it included students from older grades, the lab—often referred to as the "open classroom"—did not follow the British model exactly. Moreover, by using overflow space on and off the Lea campus, the program served the secondary purpose of relieving the overcrowding Lea was experiencing at the time.[67]

Carol Williamson, who was part of the program's first cohort of students in 1968, recalled that she was one of three in the lab, all of them White.[68] By the 1970s, however, the program had grown, both in size and diversity. A Black student named Pat Spann remembered being picked for the program in grade 5 (1969–1970) because of her strong grades. She enjoyed having fewer students in the class, more freedom, and an assortment of animals in the classroom (e.g., a spider monkey).[69] Dorothea Camp, a friend of Michelle Segrè—whose mother, Nina, was a founder of the program—remembered her open classroom teacher Judy Buchanan as one of the best she had. According to Camp, Buchanan, her teacher from 1977 through 1979, made effective use of the progressive approach: "She would teach, obviously, but there were times of the day where you could kind of pick what you wanted to do. It was very laid back, and she was just so nice."[70]

Rochelle Nichols-Solomon, a Black parent who had her children transferred to Lea in 1978, had an outsider perspective on Lea's progressive experiment. She too remembered Judy Buchanan as a standout teacher. However, she enrolled her children at Lea not because of the lab but because the school offered an all-day kindergarten program, essential for her as a working parent. Nichols-Solomon saw the lab as a fad: "open classroom was 'what's hot, what's not' in education at that time." She sensed but was not fully informed of the connections between Penn, the lab, and the Little Red Schoolhouse, another progressive project at Lea:

> So there were a lot of West Philly hippies who sent their kids to Lea. I would not be surprised if there was affiliation with Penn; I just don't know about it. But they probably . . . when you think about the Little Red Schoolhouse, and the open classroom and that kind of thing, there probably was something there.[71]

What linked Penn and progressive education at Lea was the WPC. As noted, the corporation had made Lea the focus of its efforts to draw White parents to the neighborhood. Faculty members around campus were keen to see WPC efforts succeed. Respondents to a 1968 survey of the educational needs of university families gave "overcrowding, large classes, severe discipline problems, and excessive regimentation" as reasons not to enroll their children in public schools. The survey cited the "educational deficiency" of area schools as the most frequent reason for moving to the suburbs. Parents envisioned a community school, separate from but supported by Penn and the SDP, as the ideal way to meet their needs.[72] Charlotte Levens's 1968 plan reflected that interest:

> We would like what has just been described to be put into practice in a school building which is physically and organizationally separated from, but institutionally supported by, the School District of Philadelphia and the University of Pennsylvania. That separation and support may be achieved by sub-contracting the planning and execution of the school program to a group of individuals with the combined talents necessary to the success of the enterprise.[73]

Segrè, Bank, and other parents in their circle were just the "group of individuals with combined talents" needed to create such a program.

In the context of an overcrowded and segregated school, creating such a "physically and organizationally separated" program was problematic. Parents with a great deal of social and intellectual capital carved out a unique educational space. And while it benefited some families that were not part of their circle—like the Spanns and the Nichols-Solomons—those families were shut out of its formation and management. Nichols-Solomon, whose later career was in educational philanthropy, lamented that typical parents in the SDP had little control over their schools:

> One of the reasons that people couldn't connect with their schools was they wouldn't know how to connect with their schools. . . . Lea had home and school . . . but it was a pretty traditional parent teacher association. . . . But it wasn't about transforming or changing schools.[74]

As detailed in Chapter 4, students at Lea who were not selected for the Lea Learning Lab continued to receive inferior education.

Local Preschool, Celebrity Cred

As noted, in the late 1960s, working parents had few options for all-day preschool or kindergarten. One that emerged in West Philadelphia was the Walnut Street Center, originally located in a house on 40th and Walnut Streets near the Penn campus. Funded by a Department of Education grant, this school offered progressive education in a racially and socioeconomically integrated environment. It boasted a diverse, capable, and caring staff. The Walnut Street Center's full-day program meant that supporting career women was part of its progressive agenda.[75] Ruth Bacon, wife of city planner Edmund Bacon, was both a teacher at the school and an author of its founding documents. As noted, Ruth Bacon was a trained early-childhood educator and an educational activist. She was a member of the Delaware Valley Association for the Education of Young Children (DVAEYC) and the CCPEP.[76]

A statement of the school's philosophy drafted by Bacon describes a child-centered school that foregrounds emotional learning: "Walnut Street Center must be a place where the child can grow fully in an atmosphere of warmth and complete acceptance." Important too in the school's racially integrated environment was the acceptance of difference: "As a staff we feel a strong obligation to become more deeply aware and respectful of the varied experience that is part of each child."[77] Other aspects of progressive education the school embraced were parental involvement in the school and questioning and self-expression by the children. Above all, it sought to eliminate walls between school and city, making real-world experience a central part of children's learning process:

> The experience of the wider community will interweave as the child and his group of friends moves out and back into the port, the fountains, the Museums, the market, the pet-shop, the public transportation, the pipe being layed [sic], the building going up, the parkland.[78]

In this regard, Ruth Bacon's educational approach meshed with her husband's métier: the built environment was the classroom.

The experiences of those who attended the school speak to its child-centered approach. Lois Gelfand, who grew up in West Philadelphia and went to the school in 1970–1973, remembered the diversity of the students (shown in fig. 2.1) and the sensitivity of the staff. In the school's rich environment, children interacted with a variety of play materials and even animals. Gelfand had fond memories of Bacon, whom she recalled had a soft touch with children. On one occasion, Gelfand recalled, she was distraught over missing her turn to bring home the class guinea pig, and Bacon arrived at her home with the animal in hand. According to Gelfand, the center "felt like a little utopia to me."[79]

Bacon portrayed the school's kind environment and experiential model of education in the 1969 short film "Let's Go out Together," produced by the CCPEP. In the fragment of the film that still exists, one sees teacher Barbara Pressman and other teachers taking children on field trips to the city's open-air Italian market, the Philadelphia Museum of Art, an agricultural

Figure 2.1 Walnut Street Center pre-K class, 1970–1971. Ruth Bacon is in the back row, far left; Lois Gelfand, middle row, second from right. (*Image courtesy of Rob Stevens.*)

school and farm, a firehouse, the fountain at Logan Square, the Delaware Riverfront, and a construction site. In each location, we see children manipulating materials and asking questions. The film's background music and theme, "Let's Go out Together," were composed and performed by Bacon sons Kevin and Michael, who would go on to careers in film and music.[80]

As an experiment, the school showed promise. Its student body and staff were diverse, and its progressive approach was appreciated by parents whose children were enrolled there. It was doubtful, however, that such a specialized environment could be replicated given the SDP's rigid system and pervasive shortages of space and equipment. One reason for the school's success was that it selected students whose families were favorably disposed toward its approach and had the means to clear its admissions hurdles. Bacon's planning documents called for parents to undergo an admissions interview to facilitate "understanding and planning for the individual child."[81] Gelfand and her mother reported going through such a screening process.[82]

There was concern that the center's claim of serving neighborhood children was misstated. A 1969 report on the school by the Penn Faculty Senate's Ad Hoc Committee on Education in University City found that it catered to the children of university affiliates. The report stated that much of the school's economic diversity came from graduate students who enrolled their children there—families that were "classified" as low income but may have come from affluent circumstances.[83] According to Barbara Pressman, the center enrolled children of prominent Black Philadelphians—including Wilson Goode, who would serve as mayor in 1984–1992—as well as Black teachers, lawyers, and other professionals. Pressman said that there was always a waiting list for admission to the school.[84]

The SDP's inability to provide a suitable location for the center hastened the program's demise. Originally housed in a Penn-owned brownstone, it was forced to move when the building was demolished in 1970. The district planned to rehouse the center at either the Drew School or the Powel School, both located north of Market Street. These plans faced opposition because the Walnut Street Center's grant funding provided its teachers a higher pay scale than rank-and-file SDP teachers. White parents were reluctant to enroll their children in a program that met in a heavily Black neighborhood, while Black parents resisted having a Title I–funded program that appeared to cater to affluent White people in their schools. The SDP eventually found space for the program, but it folded in 1978 because of budget cuts.[85]

A Penn Professor Visits Your High School

In 1968, recently appointed Penn English professor Peter Conn began a teaching exchange with Penn Ph.D. graduate Barry Slepian, who had been lecturing in the Penn English Department and started teaching English at WPHS that year. With adjacent offices in Penn's English Department, they bonded over a shared concern for the problems of public education and disdain for the academic elitism that separated Ivy League professors from K–12 teachers. When Slepian took a job teaching English at WPHS, the two arranged a program of informal two-week swaps in which Slepian would teach at Penn and Conn at WPHS. According to Slepian, other Penn professors, including Michael Zuckerman, joined the program. Although the swaps were never officially part of the WPHS curriculum, students like Glenn Bryan and Norman Brown remembered Conn, Slepian, and Slepian's wife, Ruth—who also taught at WPHS and held a Ph.D. in English from Penn— as being among the most influential teachers they had at WPHS. Brown, for example, was thrilled by the level of instruction he received: "They were supportive of us. They were cool; I mean, they were really cool, and the manner that they taught was different—it was just, I mean, totally different way of instructing."

The success of this exchange speaks to the value of university professors sharing their knowledge in a K–12 setting. It also points to the importance of faculty initiative in university-community engagement. Informal though it was, the partnership grew out of an understanding between a professor and a teacher about community needs, and both participated in its planning and implementation. This conception was much different from the WPC's URP, which was driven by the interests of university administration. Faculty participants in URP would grow wary of contributing to programs in which they had little input and which seemed intended to serve public relations more than community need.

A Community-Controlled School in Mantua-Powelton

Residents of Mantua, a predominantly Black area north of the Black Bottom, joined neighbors in the heavily White Powelton neighborhood to form the Mantua-Powelton Minischool in 1967. Though its student population was primarily Black, the school also sought to address the drain of White students, whose parents tended to pull them out of public school in the upper grades. According to author Henry Resnik, "while the need for a sense of black identity was vitally important, the minischool was never separatist."[86] Part of the glue that held the two groups together was the building effort of John Ciccone, a Penn architecture student who dropped out to form the Mantua Workshop, which was devoted to rehabilitating homes in the neighborhood on behalf of Black residents. The workshop operated under the umbrella of the Black-led Mantua Community Planners, whose motto was "Plan or Be Planned For!" A core idea of the minischool was that it would meet in multiple buildings that Ciccone and his team of volunteers would rehabilitate.[87] Connecting physical rebuilding and education, the minischool echoed the WPC agenda under community aegis.

The minischool's scattered site idea found a supporter in SDP official Rick de Lone, a Shedd lieutenant who had applied the same idea to the district's Parkway Schools. When minischool planners presented their proposal to de Leon, he helped garner a $100,000 Rockefeller grant for the project and arranged for $27,000 additional funding from the SDP budget. The school drew teaching ideas from the Philadelphia Cooperative Schools program, a haven for Shedd's affective curriculum. It brought together several elements of progressive education, including parental involvement in teaching and governance, open classrooms, and experiential learning.[88] As its first principal, the minischool appointed Forrest Adams, a charismatic young Black man who lived in Powelton but related well to the Mantua community. Adams's intellectual outlook included elements of progressive education and Black radicalism.[89]

The minischool's do-it-yourself spirit was both its strength and its Achilles' heel. Despite the best efforts of Ciccone and his team, the scattered site idea was dropped in favor of a single building that the Redevelopment Authority (RDA) would lease to the school for a dollar per year.[90] The new site, a converted factory, was not ready in time for classes to start, leading to chaos for teachers and students. Teachers and community members disagreed over how loose the curriculum should be, with some arguing that basic skills such as reading and math should be taught using a more teacher-centered approach. There were breakdowns in discipline, and according to Resnik, Adams's "antipathy to structure" prevented him from building a cohesive staff. At one point, a math teacher who preferred structure purchased plywood and walled off an open area to create separate classrooms. Adams summarily dismissed this teacher, who complained to the Mantua Community Planners. That organization was not the school's governing body, however. The minischool lacked a board of directors, and there was no process for handling dismissals. The question of *who* in the community controlled this community school was never resolved, and the school closed when a fire broke out in the building during its second year of operation.[91]

Yet there was no question that the minischool garnered community buy-in. Neighborhood children attended the school, and neighbors were involved at all levels—from building construction to teaching to governance. And according to Resnik's reports, the progressive features of its curriculum worked. Students were engaged and answered teachers' questions eagerly. The school encouraged creativity and engaged students in self-directed projects. In his view, the students seemed happier because of the freedom they enjoyed.[92]

Many Problems, Few Easy Answers

When it introduced the URP in 1961, the WPC entered a fray underway since the 1800s. West Philadelphia's schools were not merely in need of better libraries, math curriculums, or college access programs, as URP proposed. Schools like Lea and WPHS belonged to a system that had been set up on a segregated basis, placing Black students in substandard buildings and discounting their educational abilities. When the district was organized in its current form in 1904, it continued these practices through covert means. By drawing school catchment boundaries that tracked neighborhood segregation and using segregated employment eligibility lists, it created all-Black schools. As Philadelphia's Black population increased, these schools became increasingly overcrowded, but the district's stingy and authoritarian board declined to expand or improve facilities.

Black-led citizens' groups such as the EEL and NAACP pressured the district to change its policies. While their efforts led to the repeal of segregated employment lists and eventually to a federal desegregation settlement, the educational divide between Black and White Philadelphians continued to grow through the 1960s. White-led groups such as the CCPEP also pushed for change, ushering in a reform era under Richardson Dilworth and Mark Shedd. However, the reforms they instituted, including the hiring and promotion of Black administrators, precipitated fierce backlash.

Parents, individuals, and neighborhood groups propounded their own ideas for better schooling. Some created models of progressive schooling within the district. Programs like the Lea Learning Lab and Walnut Street Center were little utopias of diversity and child-centered learning. Yet within a school system whose funding was inadequate and whose leadership was constantly in flux, the prospect of sustaining and spreading these models was dim; they showed promise but ultimately served a select group of families rather than the broader population.

A few educational experiments envisioned a more democratic system of schooling. The Conn-Slepian teaching exchange at WPHS sidestepped traditional hierarchies, showing how professors could inspire K–12 students and modeling faculty control of university-community engagement projects. The Mantua-Powelton Minischool showed what could happen if a district turned over power and funding to groups that have traditionally been disenfranchised. Though it would have benefited from more structure, the minischool was, in its short existence, a true community school. It represented the culture of the community in which it was located, and community members literally made the school.

What would the WPC contribute to schools? Would URP fix schools by fixing inequality, or would it merely carve out a special niche for the children of university- and hospital-affiliated families? The next chapter describes the progress of URP and the unfolding of the most ambitious part of the WPC plan: the creation of the entirely new UCHS. The land use plan for this school would throw the WPC project into turmoil, change West Philadelphia irreversibly, and inflict long-term damage on the universities' relationship with their neighbors.

3

Developing the Mind, Developing the Neighborhood

In his epigraph for the second (1961) annual West Philadelphia Corporation (WPC) report, Executive Vice President Leo Molinaro struck a lofty chord with these excerpts from Walt Whitman's "The Great City":

> *Where thrift is in its place, and prudence is in its place . . .*
> *Where outside authority enters always after the precedence of inside*
>   *authority . . .*
> *There the greatest city stands.*[1]

On whose authority the corporation would carve University City out of West Philadelphia was a question that would occupy the minds of residents in for the next decade.

Having determined that education was key to building the kind of city where university and hospital families would like to live, the WPC set to work on its Universities-Related Program (URP). By 1962, it had begun providing aid to the Lea School and launched the Motivation Program at West Philadelphia High School (WPHS). Soon, URP would spread to several other schools in West Philadelphia, including the Alexander Wilson School (grades K–6), the Thomas Dunlap School (K–6), the Drew School (K–6), the Octavius Catto School (10–12), and the Samuel Powel School (K–6).

A Public School for You

Situated on the edge of Penn's neighborhood at 47th and Locust Streets, the
H. C. Lea School served the Spruce Hill neighborhood, and would have been
the most likely place for a university-affiliated family to enroll their children—if they used the public schools. The population of its catchment was
approximately 84 percent White but decreasing numbers of White families
were choosing to enroll their children there.[2] It was a logical place, therefore,
for the WPC to begin its campaign of interventions, accompanied by publicity, to convince such families that West Philadelphia's public schools were a
viable option for them.

In addition to Spruce Hill, the Lea served a patchwork of neighborhoods
with varying demographics. To its south was Garden Court, which former
Lea student Brenda Bonhomme described as a "middle class, family, friendly neighborhood," and an integrated area. Bonhomme was Black, and the
sister of Prentice Cole, mentioned in Chapter 1 in connection with the racial
climate in Philadelphia industries. She recalled that her parents had moved
to Garden Court in 1963 so that their children could attend Lea, which she
said had a "very decent" reputation.[3] Lea's catchment also included areas to
the north and west that were more heavily Black. At that time the school was
designated as "open," meaning it drew enrollment from around the city, a
factor that added to the school's diversity.[4] Former Lea students I interviewed noted that the Penn-affiliated families added another element to the
school's population, as many had immigrated from other countries for research and teaching opportunities at the University.[5]

A 1961 report by the West Philadelphia Realty Board confirmed Lea's
reputation, describing it as "one of the outstanding public elementary schools
in the City of Philadelphia with a very alert, progressive program." However, people who attended Lea or enrolled their children there reported overcrowding, serious deficiencies in the facilities, a weak academic program,
and growing racial tensions in the school. Bonhomme recalled a friend of
her brother Prentice walking to Lea every day from 42nd and Haverford
Streets, an area north of Market Street with very different demographics
from Spruce Hill and Garden Court. On his walk to Lea, this friend said he
worried about his safety.[6] As shown later, students coming to Lea from less
affluent circumstances did not fare as well in the school.[7]

Among the White, Penn-affiliated students who attended the school was
Amy T. Orr, daughter of Penn campus planner Harold Taubin. Orr attended Lea from 1960 to 1969, her entire elementary and middle school career.
She described her family as liberal. In his work as Penn's planner, her father
was an early promoter of accommodations for people with disabilities. Her
mother, a psychologist, was an advocate of sex education. Orr recalled that

the school's diversity extended beyond Black and White to groups from many countries and that the school touted its identity as a diverse place. Of the immigrant population at Lea, Orr said, "I grew up in this neighborhood thinking everyone was first-generation American. There were already people from all over the world, and their parents were from India, their parents were from Italy, because of Penn."[8] She recalled that among the programs designed to highlight the school's diversity was an international dance class, which afforded her and her classmates the opportunity to perform at civic functions, as shown in figure 3.1.

A URP planning committee report stated that between 1962 and 1964, the program garnered significant personnel, material, and curriculum resources for the school. The report mentioned improvements in the following areas at Lea:

Personnel. According to the report, URP hired teacher Therese Senesky as a full-time, salaried program coordinator. It documented the placement of additional "practice teachers" (i.e., student teachers) from Penn and Cheyney University.[9]

Books. In consultation with Drexel's library science program, URP created a new library, increasing the number of volumes Lea held from nine hundred to thirty-six hundred and providing shelving. The cost of the physical improvements and acquisitions was $5,500 ($56,800 in 2025 dollars), and the report anticipated spending $5,500 each of the next three years for the acquisition of books and hiring of an additional librarian, a student intern, and a full-time secretary.[10] The library was one part of the Lea school that former students recalled as being unique. Brenda Bonhomme, who returned to Lea as a tutor years after attending the school, described it as "a big bright room that had lots of low shelves," and remembered "liking it when I was a kid and still liking it very much as an adult."[11]

Science programs. The report stated that Penn professor Robert Crimmins assisted Lea's science coordinator in the development of a new curriculum, and URP contributed $1,500 in lab equipment ($15,500 in 2025 dollars) to the school.[12]

Curriculum resources. In reading, Penn professor Mary E. Coleman initiated experimental programs and brought in a full-time reading coordinator. The report claimed that these additions resulted in Lea students showing improvement in reading scores on standardized tests. In math, the program introduced the "Greater Cleveland Plan," a well-regarded math curriculum at the time, for grades K–1 and gave students access to what was

Figure 3.1 Lea School dancers, 1964. Amy T. Orr is on the left. (*Amy T. Orr, personal collection.*)

then cutting-edge computing equipment. The report noted that foreign language instruction was nonexistent at the school in 1962 and claimed that by 1963, URP had introduced French, Spanish, and Russian. It anticipated the hiring of another language teacher for grades 6–8, the creation of a language lab, and the purchasing of additional textbooks.[13]

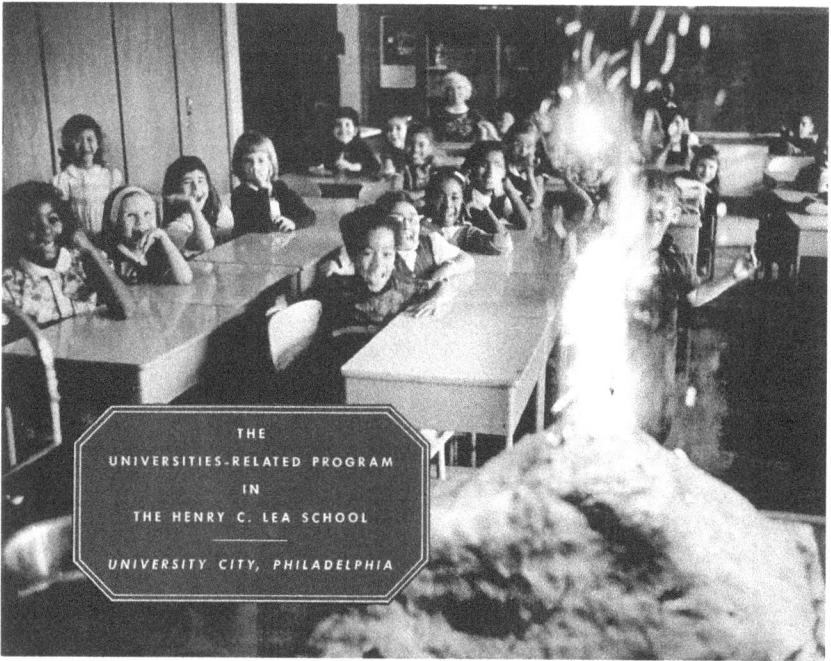

Figure 3.2 Cover of WPC booklet *The Universities-Related Program in the Henry C. Lea School*, January 1964. (*Amy T. Orr, personal collection.*)

As these improvements were being implemented, the WPC was busy promoting them to the public. The attractive cover of the booklet *The Universities-Related Program in the Henry C. Lea School*, seen in figure 3.2, shows a mixed-race group of elementary school students watching what appears to be a baking-soda volcano eruption. Inside, the publication trumpets the accomplishments mentioned in the planning committee report: the new library, science lab, and enhanced programs in reading, math, and foreign languages. It also boasts of the cooperation of Penn and Drexel faculty in the implementation of URP, mentioning Penn Graduate School of Education (GSE) professor Mary Coleman and a host of others from the fields of education, science, psychology, and business.[14]

Though URP contributed significantly to Lea, its contributions were not enough to reverse the growing divide between the more privileged university- and hospital- affiliated students and the rest of the school's population, which was increasingly Black and disadvantaged. That the WPC recognized the existence of this divide—and that parents were aware of it—is evident in another publication used to promote the Lea School. The front panel of a 1963 trifold (fig. 3.3) shows a diverse array of faces from Lea, its headline proclaiming, "A Place for Every Child—Kindergarten through Eighth

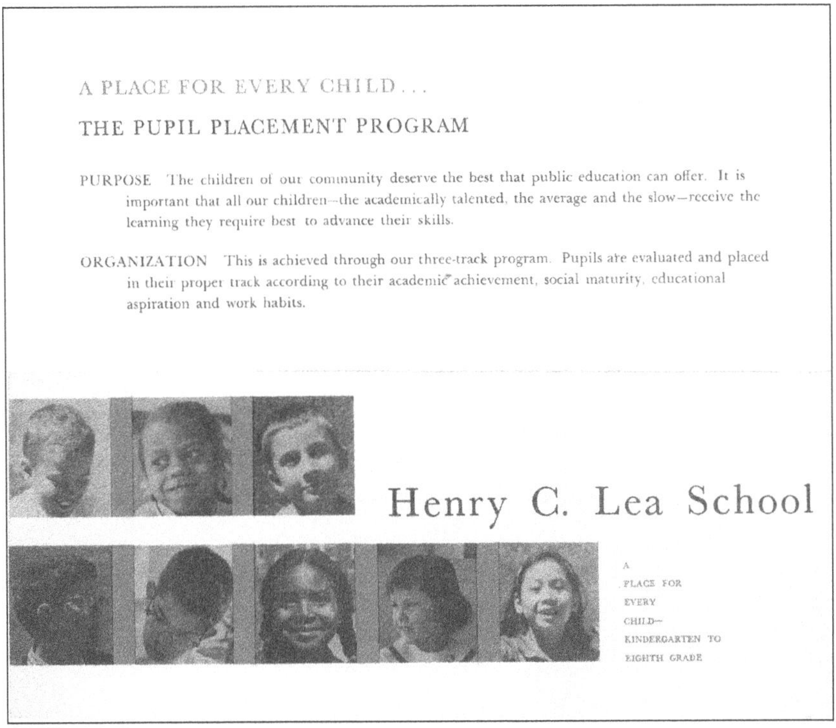

A PLACE FOR EVERY CHILD . . .

THE PUPIL PLACEMENT PROGRAM

PURPOSE The children of our community deserve the best that public education can offer. It is
important that all our children—the academically talented, the average and the slow—receive the
learning they require best to advance their skills.

ORGANIZATION This is achieved through our three-track program. Pupils are evaluated and placed
in their proper track according to their academic achievement, social maturity, educational
aspiration and work habits.

Henry C. Lea School

A
PLACE FOR
EVERY
CHILD—
KINDERGARTEN TO
EIGHTH GRADE

Figure 3.3 Henry C. Lea School brochure. Lea Home and School Association, 1963.
(*Amy T. Orr, personal collection.*)

Grade." The publication was primarily devoted to the "Pupil Placement Program," the school's tracking system, conveying two messages to parents:
every student is welcome at Lea, but your child need not be *placed* with every
other student.[15] The consequences of such division within the school would
be uncovered in a 1968 appraisal of Lea by Penn GSE, discussed in Chapter 4.

That tracking might have been used to signal to White families that their
children were safe in an urban school is not an implausible conclusion, con-
sidering the reports given by Lea School graduates. Brenda Bonhomme, for
example, recalled that the tracks were not as evenly mixed as the school
overall. "I would have been in first track [i.e., more advanced] classes along
with my brother, and those were the more integrated classes. You could see
that as the kids that were in the slightly slower tracks were less integrated
than the kids in the first track."[16] Former Lea student Malcolm Bonner, who
was also Black, had a similar impression:

All the White kids were on first track, and I was like, "How can this
be?" You know, because some of the White kids were smart, John

Molinaro, Jay Mitchell, you know what I mean? They were smart kids—Tony Nixon, smart kids, good students, whatever. But some of them, I don't want to mention names . . . some of them, man, were not sharp, were not the sharpest knives in the drawer, and I say that 'cause, you know, we were all friends; I would help them with their homework. . . . So that was really my first personal experience with racism.[17]

The John Molinaro whom Bonner mentions was the son of WPC executive vice president Leo Molinaro, who enrolled both of his children in West Philadelphia public schools. The WPC head believed in integration and felt that his decisions about where to live and educate his children showed he was on the right side of arguments about race in the neighborhood.

College Readiness: The Motivation Program

WPHS was the closest public high school to Penn and Drexel and the one that served surrounding neighborhoods such as Spruce Hill and Garden Court. During the 1960s, however, the school acquired a reputation for being overcrowded, segregated, and low achieving.[18] By boosting college attendance by WPHS graduates, the WPC hoped to counter that reputation. It launched the Motivation, Program, sometimes called just "Motivation," or "M," in 1961, with funds from a $25,000 gift (worth more than $258,000 in 2025 dollars). The WPC intended the program to run for five years, by which time it was hoped that the school climate would have shifted.[19] In the words of community relations advisory coordinator Barry Freeman, the hope was "to spur high school students to achievements more closely related to their capacities."[20]

After a lackluster pilot program led by a part-time teacher liaison and with Penn students as tutors, the WPC launched a robust version of the Motivation Program in 1962.[21] Under the capable leadership of WPHS English teacher Rebecca Segal, the program produced many graduates who attended college and pursued successful careers.[22] Prior to her teaching career, Segal had served as national president of the Women's American Organization for Rehabilitation through Training (ORT), a Jewish educational philanthropy formed in the nineteenth century to provide career training to impoverished Jews in czarist Russia. She had assisted with ORT efforts to resettle Holocaust survivors in the fledgling state of Israel and training programs for both Jews and Arabs in North Africa. Her 1972 memoir, *Got No Time to Fool Around*, describes an internationalist perspective and optimism about uplift through education: "I came to believe that all human beings, no matter what their origin, their religion, their politics, are intrinsically alike:

they react to love, hunger, pain. They respond with almost predictable reactions to various stimuli in the achievement of certain goals."[23]

Segal touted the features of her Motivation Program in a 1964 *Wall Street Journal* editorial. Students enrolled in grades 10 through 12, which at the time was their entire high school career, as junior high school covered grades 7 through 9. The program featured special college-preparatory courses and extensive tutoring designed to enable students to persist beyond the first year of college. It also offered need-based scholarships ranging from $100 to $2,600 ($1,000 to $26,800 in 2025 dollars) for students who qualified for admission to Penn.[24] The Motivation Program took students who, according to the criteria of the day, showed promise of success. They had to have a minimum IQ score of 100, an grade 8 reading score, and be in the SDP's "College Prep" or "Commercial A" tracks.[25] Through diligent recruiting, Segal boosted enrollment from an initial 60 to 276.[26]

Many Black students did benefit from the program. Among those were Norman Brown, Glenn Bryan, and Craig Taylor, who were enrolled in the program at WPHS from 1967 to 1970, and K. Rose Samuel-Evans, enrolled from 1970 to 1973. All credited the Motivation Program with giving them tools to succeed in college and beyond by steering them into a more rigorous course of study; enabling them to acclimate to Penn and other college campuses; providing them with cultural enrichment; and putting them in a social milieu with other college-bound students. By the time these students enrolled, the Motivation Program had gained such a reputation that some students were transferring to WPHS to enroll in it. Norman Brown, who would walk three miles per day to attend WPHS, was one.[27]

Graduates of the program recounted being enrolled in special college-preparatory courses in English and math. They recalled that teachers of Motivation-level classes were of high caliber, had high expectations for their students, and, like program staff, were committed to student success. Brown, who later worked as a teacher, said of his instructors,

> The staff at the time—and having been a teacher for sixteen, seventeen years, I can't say that my commitment to my students was any less than theirs—but they, they . . . were there for us. I mean, we didn't have a tutorial program, but when we had trouble, they stayed after school. Whatever we needed, they'd make it happen.[28]

Brown, Bryan, Samuel-Evans, and Taylor all recalled the rigor of Motivation Program courses as preparing them well for college. Samuel-Evans remembered a Motivation-level course introducing her to the works of Shakespeare, which she did not encounter in regular classes. Brown said of the education he received, "I didn't feel like I couldn't function at Dartmouth or at Penn and

Harvard, wherever . . . and I didn't have to go and take supplementary courses to catch up."[29]

For Motivation Program graduates, preparation for college went beyond coursework to include field trips to museums, historical sites, and performances. According to Samuel-Evans,

> They were exposing us to culture . . . things we normally wouldn't do—plays, the Franklin Institute, the Art Museum, the Betsy Ross House, the typical places in Philadelphia that you weren't going to on the weekends with your family. . . . And then we went to see a play in New York, *Don't Bother Me I Can't Cope*. . . . It was my first [professionally produced] play.[30]

She also noted that the Motivation Program offered a study-abroad experience in Spain in which her brother, also a WPHS Motivation graduate, participated.[31] Norman Brown had a similar recollection of the program's field trips, which also included university tours: "We had block tickets; we had shows at the Academy of Music; we had ballet; we had a spectrum; we'd take trips to universities—I mean, we toured Penn, that was a memorable experience."[32] Such college tours were a key part of the program, which helped students with all aspects of the admissions process. It ensured they made standardized test dates and application deadlines; it also assisted with essay writing for college applications.[33] For Brown, Bryan, and Samuel-Evans, campus visits were pathways to admissions—Brown to Dartmouth, Bryan to Penn, and Samuel-Evans to Boston College.

The three were not alone in attending college. They each estimated that fifty to sixty students from their class were enrolled in the program, and approximately 85 percent the Motivation cohort went to college.[34] Their reports matched with those of the program's leadership. According to Rebecca Segal, during the 1960s, "approximately 75 percent of each 'M' group were matriculating and staying in college. The evaluation of 1971 showed approximately 81 percent going through the second year in the face of appalling national attrition figures in the first year of college."[35]

Former Motivation Program students averred that the strong support given them by teachers and staff contributed to their success in college and beyond. Samuel-Evans, who is currently assistant director of community engagement at Drexel University, and Bryan, who is assistant vice president of community relations at Penn, believe that it gave them the confidence and academic preparation to compete with college students from more privileged backgrounds. Samuel-Evans said that her success at the predominantly White and Catholic Boston College, where she graduated cum laude in 1977, was due in large part to the Motivation Program: "I was the first African

American and the first female at Boston College to win their persuasive argumentation contest. . . . I was the chairman's pick. He recognized that I was a gifted orator and he wanted to work with me." When she had doubts about her ability to succeed in that predominantly White environment, she could call on the reservoir of confidence the Motivation Program gave her: "I think that it helped me confront the fact that, 'OK, colored girl, you can do this.'"[36] Bryan, whose position at Penn has familiarized him with current educational interventions, believes that the Motivation Program's comprehensive nature and dedicated staff made it unique and that it has yet to be matched by contemporary college access programs.[37]

As with URP at the Lea School, the WPC began publicizing the work of the Motivation Program almost as soon as it was launched. A 1963 WPC annual report, reproduced in figure 3.4, dedicates a full page to the program. The photograph seems carefully selected to show WPHS as having a significant White population when, in fact, the White population was dwindling by that time. Notable also is the apparent size of the Motivation Program's enrollment—large enough to fill an auditorium. The program's accomplishments in the 1962–1963 school year provided Leo Molinaro with a talking point he could deploy in support of the WPC plan. In a 1963 report to the board, the WPC leader cited the program as part of the overall picture of neighborhood improvement, one result of which was that the number of Penn families living in West Philadelphia had grown from 329 to 753.[38]

In its initial years, the Motivation Program was clearly tied to the WPC and its agenda for neighborhood improvement. In her memoir, Segal gives this description of her work redeveloping the program the summer before its relaunch in fall 1962: "All summer I hammered out my own ideas and what I believed to be those of my associates at West Philadelphia High School and also of Leo Molinaro, Executive Vice President of the West Philadelphia Corporation, a subsidiary of the University of Pennsylvania (and my friend), and officials of the three universities of University City."[39] Molinaro and Segal were neighbors, in fact, at the University Mews apartment building in West Philadelphia.[40]

While the program had the potential to help students from African American families, the WPC was most clearly focused on convincing affluent White families that WPHS was an appropriate destination for their children. This focus was evident in a report cowritten by the SDP regional superintendent for West Philadelphia and WPHS principal Jack H. Neulight, which touted the Motivation Program as an initiative to "improve the school and its image within the community, and to attract to the school college bound students [who] were leaving the neighborhood in search of better educational opportunities."[41] The WPC's goals were even more evident in conversations between the Motivation Program's second coordinator, Eileen

THE MOTIVATION PROGRAM

At the high school level, the Motivation Program which enrolled 135 students in September, 1962, now enrolls 276 students at the West Philadelphia High School. The Motivation Program includes an enriched curriculum and on-campus study-visits at the University of Pennsylvania, Drexel Institute of Technology, and the Philadelphia College of Pharmacy and Science. After-school cultural events attended by the "M" students range from a Shakespeare offering at Drexel Institute of Technology to a lecture at the University of Pennsylvania, or a play at a Center City theatre. A full time teacher-coordinator supervises the program.

Drexel Institute of Technology provides extensive testing services and professional advisory services in library science. The University of Pennsylvania participates through its Graduate School of Education which has provided professional guidance in launching new reading and mathematics programs and in-service teacher training in science education. University students participate in a vigorous tutorial program. The University of Pennsylvania has allocated a number of scholarships for qualified West Philadelphia High School graduates as has the Philadelphia College of Pharmacy and Science.

Whatever success the program enjoys is due to the hard work of the faculties and students of the two participating schools, the unflagging support of the Board of Public Education, the institutions of higher learning, the Home and School Associations and the several community associations in the area.

Students in "M" Program, West Philadelphia High School, March, 1963

Figure 3.4 WPC Annual Report, 1963, p. 13. Page highlights the accomplishments of the Motivation Program. (*Acc. 350, box 1, folder "Annual Report-4th, 1962–63," Special Collections Research Center, Temple University Libraries, Philadelphia, PA.*)

Brown, and WPC officials. Though WPHS was a neighborhood high school, students from outside the school's catchment could choose to attend specifically to enroll in the program. Brown recalled that sometime after she took the helm in 1967, a WPC official questioned her about her success in recruiting students from outside the catchment area to attend the school. "How many of them are White?" he asked. When Brown replied that applications did not ask about students' race, he responded testily, "What do you think all of this is about?" The official's remark confirmed Brown's view of what the Motivation Program meant to the WPC: "The moral of the story for him was that they truly wanted more White kids to go to West Philly so that the University's professors and staff-people's kids would be more likely to go . . . he was not happy that I had somehow missed one of the key goals."[42]

Brainsville in West Philadelphia

The WPC's URP was in large part intended to sell the neighborhood as a place with excellent schools. This tactic was situated within a larger strategy that included improving housing, enhancing the quality of life, and creating jobs. As well as marketing University City to potential residents—"responsible citizens" it hoped would relocate there—the WPC was also promoting the area to Philadelphia's planning apparatus, which could authorize the use of federal funding for redevelopment. The ideas it touted, therefore, were in line with city planner Edmund Bacon's vision for a Better Philadelphia. Just as the OPDC had done in Society Hill, the WPC would restore its neighborhood's historic housing stock. It would also replace the declining factory economy with one that employed well-educated professionals. Given the strengths of WPC member institutions in science and medicine, a natural way to approach this goal was by creating a science incubator. Said one 1959 report, "a research center of laboratory and office complexes seems to be a compatible use for an area containing the University, Drexel, and so many hospitals."[43]

A New Athens

What would a university city look like, and who would live there? The corporation's smartly designed 1963 publication, *Elaborations on Living in University City*, gives us a picture of its intentions. The cover image, a leafy spiral design from a Victorian fence shown in figure 3.5, has become ubiquitous as the marker of West Philadelphia's historically designated houses.

Like the WPC's annual reports, the booklet used high-minded rhetoric, favorably comparing the new University City to the ancient Greek capital:

> Like ancient Athens, University City is an urban place where human culture may flourish and grow from the individual talents of its citizens. But unlike Athens, people of every race, from every corner of the globe, have come to dwell in University City.[44]

Thus, the *Elaborations* booklet presented diversity as a value of the WPC redevelopment program. It profiled West Philadelphia residents of varying races and ages who appreciated not only the practical advantages of city life but also its charms, erudite pursuits, and richness.

One featured couple, the Jannettas (shown in fig. 3.6), spoke of the convenience of residing within walking distance of work. Peter Jannetta, chief of surgery at the Hospital of the University of Pennsylvania at the time, said in the booklet, "If I'm called, it takes me eight minutes to walk to the hospital. . . . I have colleagues who live out in the suburbs. If they've got trouble brewing, they're stuck here. Sometimes they don't see much of their families."[45] The booklet also highlighted the Jannetta couple's adventures restoring a Victorian house:

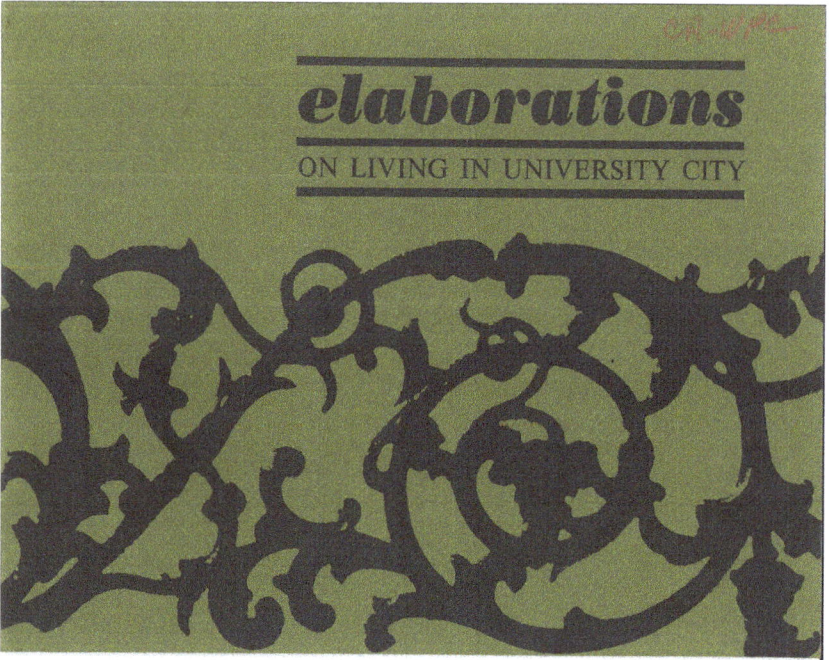

Figure 3.5 *Elaborations on Living in University City*, September 1963, cover. (*UPA 4, box 152, folder "Community Relations—West Phila. Corp. V 1960–65," UARC.*)

Peter and Ann Jannetta have an imposing hobby—a three story, ninety-year old hobby of a house. For them the house is neither an obsession nor a burden, it's pure fun and they've devoted almost three years to the enjoyable task of fixing it up.[46]

This jaunty description of the delight the Jannettas took in their renovation project resembled that of the Ingersolls, the Society Hill urban pioneers profiled in the Bryn Mawr alumni bulletin piece from Chapter 1.

Like generations of urban hipsters to come, the Gopniks, another family profiled in the piece, had eclectic tastes and delighted in repurposing urban flotsam and jetsam. In their living room, the publication said, "a clean-cut couch by Charles Eames lives comfortably with a handsome ice-box-turned-liquor cabinet which the Gopniks bought for two dollars and stripped down to the bare wood."[47] As a migrant to West Philadelphia who fixed up a house in the early 2000s, I was under the impression that my generation had invented the DIY aesthetic. The profiles of 1960s do-it-your-selfers in *Elaborations* corrected that assumption. Authored by the WPC, the booklet also belied the notion that urban pioneering was a countercultural endeavor.

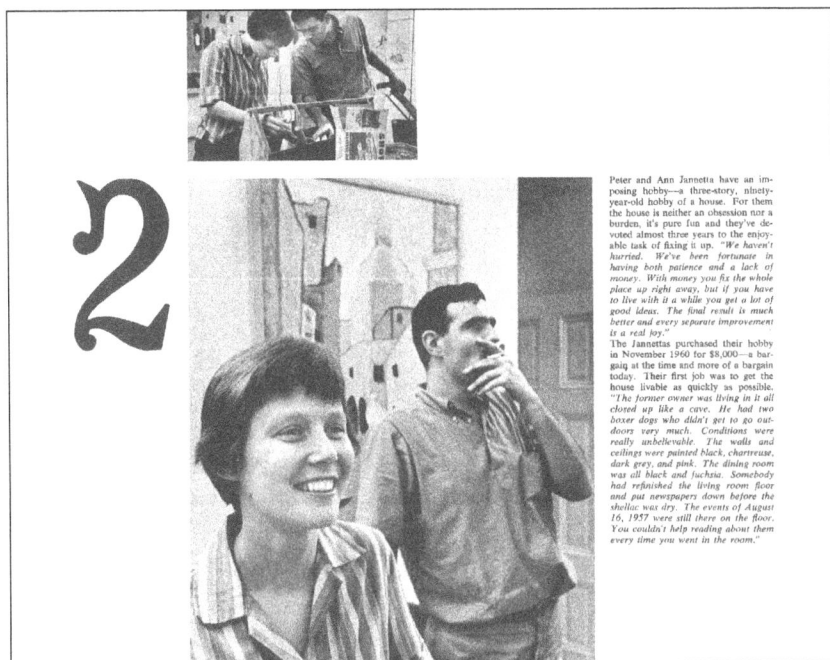

Peter and Ann Jannetta have an imposing hobby—a three-story, ninety-year-old hobby of a house. For them the house is neither an obsession nor a burden, it's pure fun and they've devoted almost three years to the enjoyable task of fixing it up. "We haven't hurried. We've been fortunate in having both patience and a lack of money. With money you fix the whole place up right away, but if you have to live with it a while you get a lot of good ideas. The final result is much better and every separate improvement is a real joy."

The Jannettas purchased their hobby in November 1960 for $8,000—a bargain at the time and more of a bargain today. Their first job was to get the house livable as quickly as possible. "The former owner was living in it all closed up like a cave. He had two boxer dogs who didn't get to go outdoors very much. Conditions were really unbelievable. The walls and ceilings were painted black, chartreuse, dark grey, and pink. The dining room was all black and fuchsia. Somebody had refinished the living room floor and put newspapers down before the shellac was dry. The events of August 16, 1957 were still there on the floor. You couldn't help reading about them every time you went in the room."

Figure 3.6 *Elaborations on Living in University City*, September 1963, p. 7. (*UPA 4, box 152, folder "Community Relations—West Phila. Corp. V 1960–65," UARC.*)

For Irving Gopnik, an English professor at Rutgers University in Camden, and Myrna Gopnik, a linguistics student at Penn, one of West Philadelphia's chief attractions was its proximity to the university's cultural offerings. The booklet showed a family field trip to the Wistar Institute (fig. 3.7) and named some of the Gopnik children's erudite pursuits: "at seven, Alison [their daughter] has already read all of Shakespeare's comedies."

Elaborations noted that the Gopniks chose the 71 School for their children's education. The publication devoted five of its twenty-two pages to Lea, echoing themes from the booklet *The Universities-Related Program in the Henry C. Lea School*. It touted the school's diversity above all: "Role call reads like a United Nations roster in this second-year class at the Lea Elementary School. Sonia is from India, Xuan Mai and Tung from South Vietnam, Vivian from Germany." Yet, the booklet noted, these diverse children's families shared an academic or professional affiliation: "Their fathers have come to University City on a variety of special assignments: advanced study or teaching at the University of Pennsylvania, research for a private firm, professional work, specialized training at one of the many hospitals."[48]

Though Annabelle McDaniels, shown in figure 3.8, was the sole Black resident profiled in the publication, *Elaborations* went to great lengths to

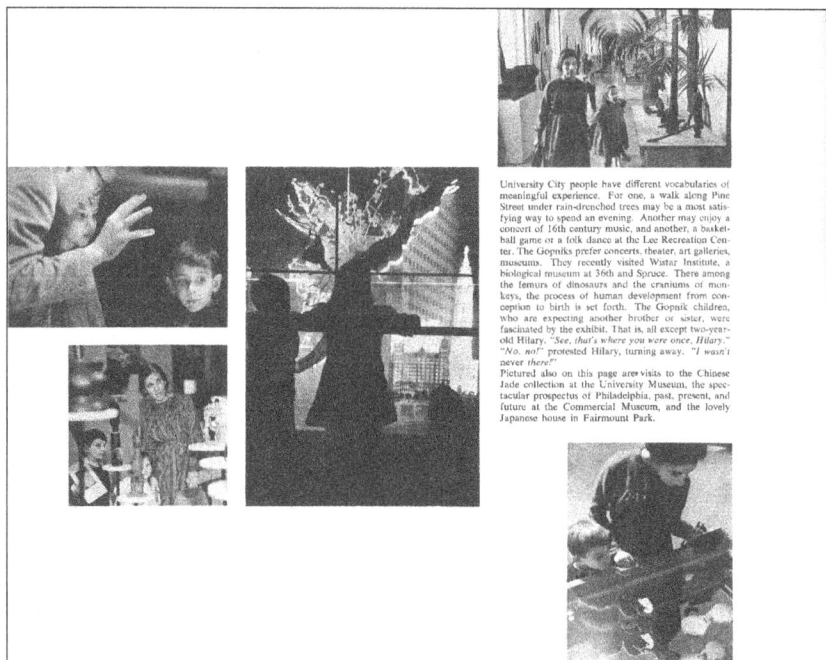

University City people have different vocabularies of meaningful experience. For one, a walk along Pine Street under rain-drenched trees may be a most satisfying way to spend an evening. Another may enjoy a concert of 16th century music, and another, a basketball game or a folk dance at the Lee Recreation Center. The Gopniks prefer concerts, theater, art galleries, museums. They recently visited Wistar Institute, a biological museum at 36th and Spruce. There among the femurs of dinosaurs and the craniums of monkeys, the process of human development from conception to birth is set forth. The Gopnik children, who are expecting another brother or sister, were fascinated by the exhibit. That is, all except two-year-old Hilary. "See, that's where you were once, Hilary." "No, no!" protested Hilary, turning away. "I wasn't never there!"

Pictured also on this page are visits to the Chinese Jade collection at the University Museum, the spectacular prospectus of Philadelphia, past, present, and future at the Commercial Museum, and the lovely Japanese house in Fairmount Park.

Figure 3.7 *Elaborations on Living in University City*, September 1963, p. 12. (*UPA 4, box 152, folder "Community Relations—West Phila. Corp. V 1960–65," UARC.*)

explain that her presence in the neighborhood was unremarkable. Describing the attitudes of other residents, it said, "it suits them to live in a community so diverse that a Negro is simply a neighbor, not a 'cause' to launch a crusade—or form a blockade."[49] Yet McDaniels was anything but unremarkable. At age forty-two, the text stated, she went back to Penn to earn her nursing degree while continuing her roles "as a mother, housekeeper, community worker, and wife."[50] With her deft handling of this list of burdens, it is hard to imagine a more "responsible type of citizen" than McDaniels. The message was clear: respectable Black people are welcome in University City.

Through upbeat prose, candid photos, and quirky anecdotes, this publication outlined bedrock themes of the urbanist project. City life, it declared, was not only more convenient than suburban; for the well-educated, liberal resident, it was also more nourishing to the soul. One could live in a charming Victorian home, enjoy the city's cultural attractions, and have a respectable Black neighbor. In the metropolitan paradise that was University City, one also had a suitable public school around the corner. Given how nicely this booklet aligned with the urban revival project in Society Hill, it is not surprising that it caught the attention of Edmund Bacon. Said Phila-

Mary Jo Larsen protests, "*I don't have a career. I work. We need the money to help with Ben's business.*" (Her husband—the only supplier of potable water to ships anchored in the Port of Philadelphia, is currently expanding his operations.) True enough. Mary Jo's three jobs buttress the family's finances, but, if her commitment to teaching art and the amount of responsibility she carries are any measure of a career, Mary Jo qualifies in spite of herself. Trained as an art teacher at the Philadelphia Museum College of Art, she gave up teaching to marry and raise four children. Then, a few years ago, with three of the children settled in school and the financial uncertainty of Ben's new enterprise looming large, she accepted a job teaching children's art classes at the Lea Community Art Center. Soon she was also conducting Saturday classes at Fleisher Art Memorial, and last year she became Supervisor of Student Teachers at the Museum College. Despite her busy schedule, Mary Jo sees a lot of her children, both at home and as students in her classes. "*I'm grateful to my kids. They help me keep a balance between home and work, and I find being a mother makes me a better teacher.*"

Annabelle McDaniels is fully engaged. At 42 she's engaged in the most demanding job of her life, a job that requires all her resourcefulness, all her energy, intelligence, and enthusiasm. After fifteen years of keeping house and raising two children, she has enrolled as a full-time undergraduate at the University of Pennsylvania. In addition to this, of course, her former duties as mother, housekeeper, community worker, and wife continue unabated. How does Annabelle react to this formidable challenge? She loves it. She feels alive and stimulated as never before. She finds that relationships with her family are, if anything, closer than ever. And, best of all, she's discovered a new sense of purpose—a new appreciation of her abilities as she prepares to take up a career in elementary school teaching.

Figure 3.8 *Elaborations on Living in University City,* September 1963, p. 14. Profile of Annabelle McDaniels (left). (*UPA 4, box 152, folder "Community Relations—West Phila. Corp. V 1960–65," UARC.*)

delphia's city planner in a letter to Penn President Harnwell, "I was so impressed with the publication *Elaborations on Living In University City,* that I felt it quite appropriate to write you, in addition to Leo, expressing my admiration for his splendid work."[51]

University City Science Center

With the successes of the Stanford Research Park, the North Carolina Research Triangle, and the Harvard-MIT research corridor in mind—and the knowledge that Penn faculty had great potential to garner federal science grants—WPC planners contemplated building an urban science incubator in West Philadelphia. In this regard, a 1962 WPC publicity piece stated exuberantly, "Witness the clustering of research firms around Harvard University and MIT. Such laboratories can be physically attractive and economically salutary, and they bring to a community a responsible type of citizen."[52]

To make the case for a science incubator to its friends in city hall, the WPC touted the research center's potential economic benefits. In a 1963 summary of its redevelopment proposals, the WPC boasted that such a center would "capture a greater share of research and development expenditures and jobs for Philadelphia" and increase the "economic base of Philadelphia by providing more municipal income in wage taxes and real estate taxes." The science incubator's economic effect, the WPC claimed, would be statewide, "providing a strong research emphasis attractive to industry."[53]

The WPC first proposed locating the science incubator in a research tower to be constructed on disused industrial land to the east of the Penn and Drexel campuses and adjacent to the Schuylkill River. A May 1960 letter to Gaylord Harnwell from Philadelphia Industrial Development Corporation (PIDC) executive director Richard Graves described a twenty-story, 250,000 square-foot building to be erected on an empty site adjacent to the Pennsylvania Railroad's former freight depot, which was being used as a parking lot. Graves noted that the WPC board had already requested preliminary drawings of the tower and mentioned the importance of arranging for the railroad to give or sell the land for it. Conveniently, Pennsylvania Railroad vice president J. Benton Jones was on the WPC board.[54] A survey the WPC conducted of potential tenants for the science incubator suggested that many would be happy with a high-rise building.[55] An artist's rendering of the tower appeared in the bottom right of the *Saturday Evening Post* ad reproduced in Chapter 1.

Yet by 1961, the corporation had rejected the tower idea in favor of a much more expansive vision. This new plan would move the tower to a site at 34th and Market Streets and add several low-rise buildings, giving the proposed science incubator 1.5 million square feet in total. Rather than using unoccupied land, the new plan would require the city to displace both residents and commercial enterprises.[56] What provoked the change?

Design aesthetics provides one explanation. In her book *Cities of Knowledge: Cold War Science and the Search for the Next Silicon Valley*, planning historian Margaret Pugh O'Mara discusses the rise of research parks in the 1950s and 1960s. These developments, initiated by universities, mimicked the pastoral feel of campus architecture. With low-rise buildings in carefully landscaped settings, "the prevailing design and architectural choices of American colleges and universities reflected the deep-seated cultural presumption that the urban environment was no place for intellectual discovery."[57] WPC planners might have preferred a campus-like design for their science incubator to a tower situated on a city street. But as O'Mara points out—and WPC papers reveal—prospective clients were happy with the original design. An *Evening Bulletin* article from the period reported that 25 percent of the tower could have been rented "immediately."[58]

The reason for the change becomes clear when we consider the WPC's background and mandate. Recall that as early as 1947, Edmund Bacon warned of a deteriorating "wedge of negro housing between Lancaster Avenue and Market Street"; and in 1956, Martin Meyerson described Penn and Drexel as an island amid "a sea of residential slums." Such thinking permeated the WPC's early planning documents, which called for the elimination of the Black Bottom. A 1959 report described it as containing "predominantly deteriorated buildings with only a scattering of poor to fair buildings," making redevelopment "necessary in this area." Redevelopment would create a "residential link with Powelton for Drexel and Penn, the Powelton Area already containing many professional people as well as persons connected with the institutions of the 'University City.'" To realize this goal, the document bluntly called for the elimination of 4,208 occupied dwelling units and the displacement of 13,634 residents over twenty years. In their place would be housed 11,850 university affiliates. The residential development, it said, "would not be public housing."[59] The creation of a science incubator on a sprawling campus, then, provided a pretext to eliminate this problem area.[60]

It was not only institutional insiders who called for the Black Bottom's destruction. In a 1961 letter to the City Planning Commission, Leo Molinaro gave as one of the priorities of Powelton Neighbors president John Marshall and Spruce Hill Community Association president Joseph Moloznik "wiping out the worst slums in University City which lie just north of Market Street between 34th and 38th Streets." This desire is not surprising given the proximity of their neighborhoods to the Black Bottom and the fact that their home values might increase or decrease depending on its fate.[61]

Visual materials included in WPC files give a clear picture of how it viewed West Philadelphia. A map from a 1959 fact sheet, shown in figure 3.9, defines the corporation's "area of interest" and within it, the footprint of member institutions and boundaries of neighborhood homeowners' associations. These were the constituencies represented on the WPC board. The black outline, labeled "Enlarged University City Area," is the area targeted by the corporation for redevelopment. The red and blue shaded areas to the right represent the Penn and Drexel campuses, respectively. The areas bounded by the blue, green, and gold outlines are the Garden Court, Spruce Hill, and Powelton neighborhoods, respectively. Not included is the Black Bottom, which lacked an official boundary and had no board representation.[62]

The maps in figure 3.10, produced by the author, offer an interpretation of the WPC perspective. The first map shows Bacon's worst-case scenario, where decay spreads from the Black Bottom and Mantua to the Powelton neighborhood—and eventually to neighborhoods to the west like Spruce Hill—creating a "band of blight" around the universities. The second posits the repurposing of the Black Bottom, creating a "band of affluence" and preserving the predominantly White makeup of Powelton, Spruce Hill, and Garden Court.

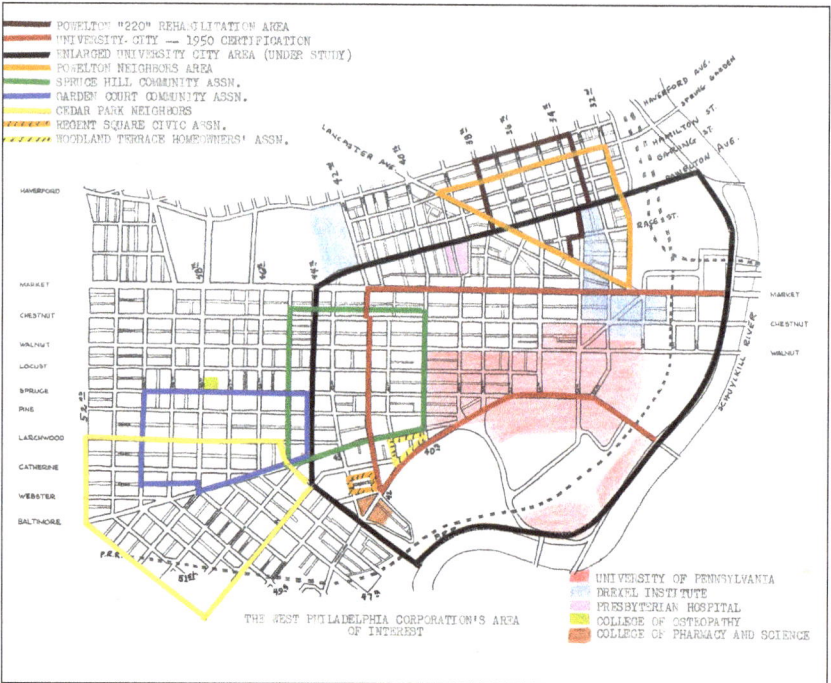

Figure 3.9 Map of WPC "Area of Interest." Orange, green, blue, and yellow lines indicate key civic association boundaries. (*Fact sheet "The West Philadelphia Corporation," undated, fall 1959, UPA 4, box 73, folder "Community Relations, the West Philadelphia Corporation 1955–60 I," UARC.*)

Clearing the roughly eighty-three acres north of Chestnut Street, south of Powelton and Lancaster Avenues, and sandwiched between 34th and 40th Streets would require design expertise, political influence, and money. The WPC was not lacking for these. As mentioned in Chapter 2, Penn had initiated the formation of the corporation. Its president, Gaylord Harnwell, was also president of the WPC board, and the university provided the bulk of its funding.[63] Penn boasted one of the premiere schools of architecture in the nation, with faculty including Louis Kahn, Robert Venturi, Denise Scott Brown, Robert Geddes, and Ian McHarg. Architectural critic Lewis Mumford, whose views influenced Edmund Bacon, taught at Penn during the 1950s.[64] Moreover, there was no wall between Penn elites and Philadelphia's city planning apparatus. Penn alumnus Edward Hopkinson chaired Philadelphia's City Planning Commission from 1943 to 1956. He was followed by G. Holmes Perkins, who was dean of Penn's School of Fine Arts, which housed the architecture and city planning programs. Edmund Bacon also taught at Penn.

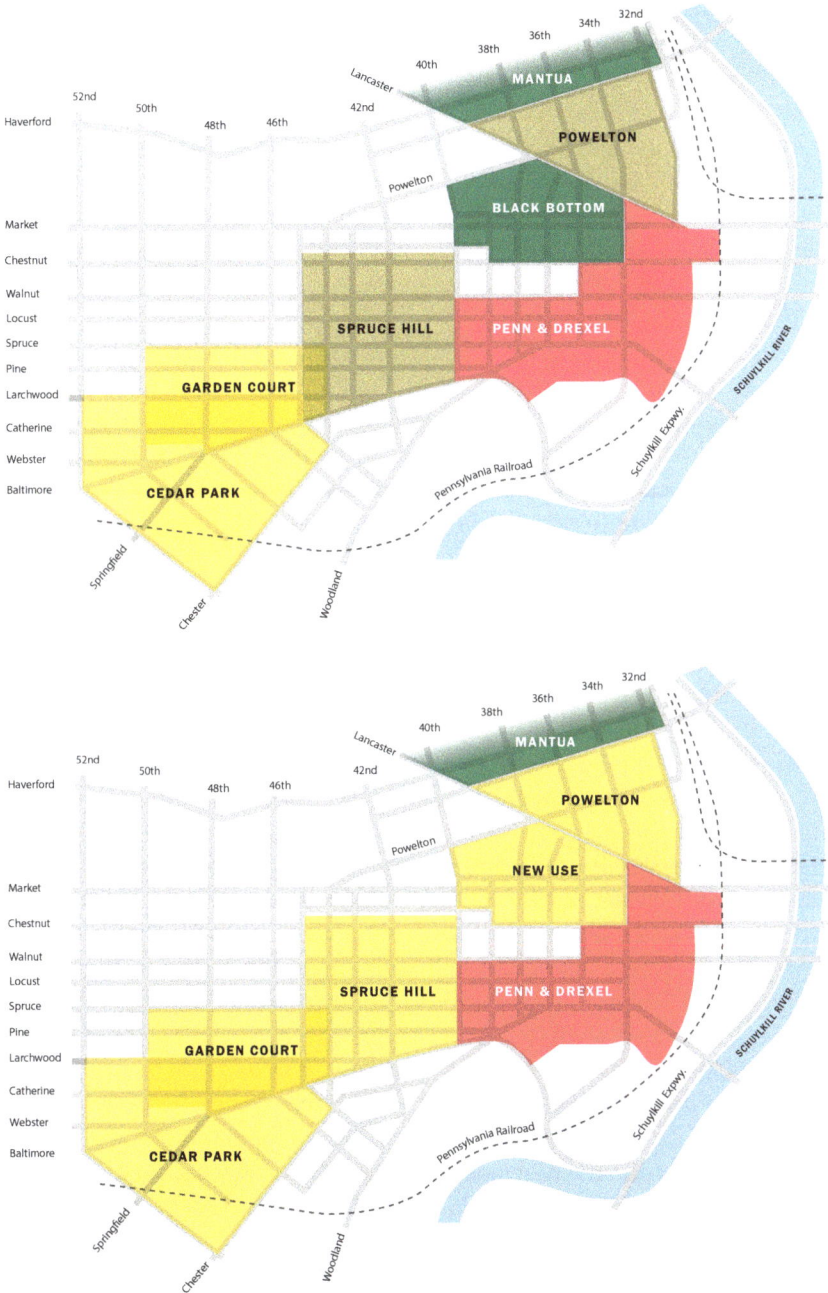

Figure 3.10 University City in 1960, showing alternate scenarios envisioned by the WPC. Predominantly Black areas are represented in green, predominantly White and middle-class areas in yellow. In the first scenario, formerly White, middle-class Powelton and Spruce Hill deteriorate, creating the "band of blight" of which planner Edmund Bacon warned. In the second, the Black Bottom is redeveloped, surrounding the universities with a band of affluence. (*Maps by the author.*)

Penn's influence was not limited to design but extended to the political sphere. During the 1960s, Penn trustee Gustave Amsterdam served as executive director of the Redevelopment Authority (RDA), the agency empowered to exercise eminent domain and clear blighted buildings.[65] Richardson Dilworth, who, along with Joseph S. Clark, had ushered in Philadelphia's reform era by overturning the Republican machine in 1951, was friendly with Penn president Gaylord Harnwell. Dilworth served as mayor when the WPC was formed in 1959, was briefly on the WPC board, and was president of the Philadelphia Board of Education beginning in 1965, during the height of the WPC's school interventions.[66]

The WPC's most important connection with regard to its redevelopment plans was to Joseph Clark. A Penn Law School alumnus, Clark became a U.S. senator after his term as mayor of Philadelphia ended in 1956. He served on the committee that oversaw urban renewal legislation and, in that role, helped write section 112 of the 1959 amendment to the Housing Act, which allowed federal urban renewal funds to be used for university projects.[67] With this legislation in place and friends in city government, the WPC could arrange for the clearing and redevelopment of vast tracts of land with minimal outlays of cash by institutional sponsors.

As with Society Hill, planners divided the West Philadelphia project into multiple tracts—Units 1 through 5—enabling the city to receive the maximum amount of funding for each. In August 1961, Philadelphia's city council approved an application for urban renewal for Unit 3, slating for clearance eighty-three acres directly north of Penn's campus and west of Drexel's. This was the area interviewees mentioned in Chapter 1—the Hills, Wilmores, Davises, Bonds, and Palmers—called home: the Black Bottom. It was to be cleared to make way for the WPC's science incubator, the University City Science Center (UCSC). Architectural models reproduced in the WPC's 1963 annual report showed research labs, university classroom buildings, and housing for university and science center affiliates. Yet even in this expanded guise, the research park was not enough to consume Unit 3's land. The WPC added one more element to complete the plan: the science-focused University City High School (UCHS).

Images from the 1963 report describe how this roughly pentagonal-shaped tract would be apportioned. The first, figure 3.11, is a page from the WPC 1963 annual report showing a model of the proposed development and explaining its purpose. The second, figure 3.12, identifies the breakup of the land. Around Market Street to the south are labs and housing for the science center. To the north, below the tract's apex at the intersection of Powelton and Lancaster Avenues, is the high school, surrounded by expansive athletic fields. Areas not covered by UCSC and UCHS would be used by Presbyterian Hospital, Penn, or Drexel for institutional purposes.

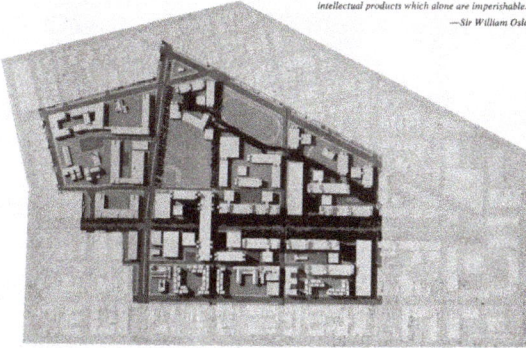

"We forget that the measure of the value of a nation to the world is neither the bushel nor the barrel, but mind; and that wheat and pork, though useful and necessary, are but dross in comparison with those intellectual products which alone are imperishable."

—Sir William Osler

According to current data developed by the National Science Foundation, there are now two and a half million Americans working as scientists, engineers, and technicians. This is three times the number just twenty years ago. By 1970, the number is estimated at almost four million. The University of Pennsylvania, last year, accounted for $26 million in research contracts. Drexel Institute of Technology numbers almost a third of all practicing engineers in Philadelphia among its graduates. The Presbyterian Hospital has recently activated a new million-dollar laboratory building. The Philadelphia College of Pharmacy and Science reflects a growing emphasis upon pharmaceutical sciences and related research. These factors and Philadelphia's diversified industrial base make the development of a University City Science Center a sound investment for the welfare of the entire city. Over the past three years the Corporation has pursued a course of action to realize this concept.

The Redevelopment Authority and the City Planning Commission have cooperated in the preparation of a plan which locates the Center in the heart of University City, between 34th and 38th Streets along both sides of Market Street. In this site, the Center effectively relates to the scientific and educational resources of University City. Equally important, the plan for the Center relates to Center City developments west

Photograph of a model showing illustrative site plan for University City Science Center

Figure 3.11 WPC annual report, 1963, p. 5. Shows model of proposed University City Science Center and scienced-focused school. (*WPC Annual Report, 1963, Acc. 350, box 1, folder "Annual Report-4th, 1962–63," Special Collections Research Center, Temple University Libraries, Philadelphia, PA.*)

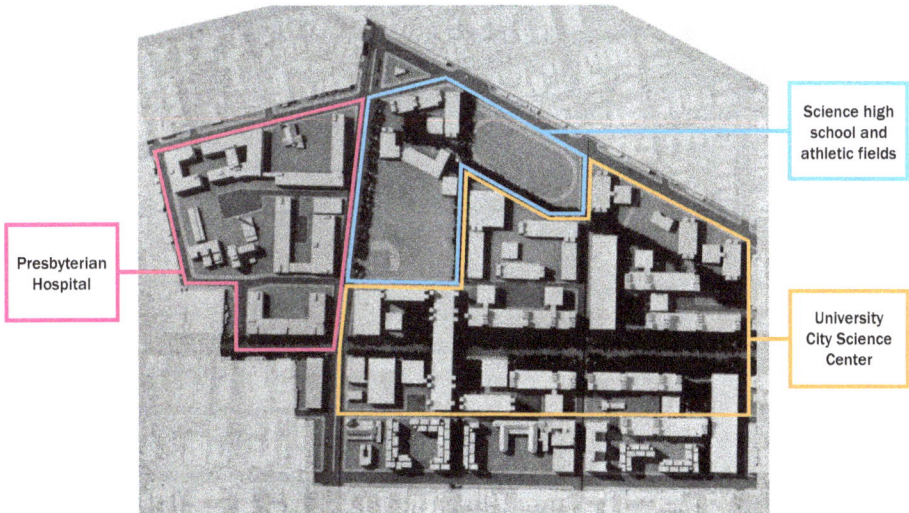

Figure 3.12 Enlargement of figure 3.11 showing planned uses of Unit 3. (*WPC Annual Report, 1963, Acc. 350, box 1, folder "Annual Report-4th, 1962–63," Special Collections Research Center, Temple University Libraries, Philadelphia, PA. Author's annotations.*)

A Science High School in West Philadelphia

As noted in the previous chapter, the WPC conceived of UCHS as an innovative project that would serve the surrounding neighborhood. Unlike the elite science schools on which it was modeled, it would accept students from nearby feeder schools rather than through a competitive screening process. This system presumably made the school palatable to neighbors and the school district, as it enabled the school to take students who might otherwise have attended overcrowded neighborhood high schools like WPHS.

Following the URP model, the WPC planned to use resources at the universities and newly formed science center to benefit UCHS students. Science center and university experts would act as consultants on the curriculum, and students would undertake hands-on projects at the labs. The WPC anticipated that its innovative school would be eligible for grants from the National Defense Education Act (1958), which funded science education, and later the Elementary and Secondary Education Act (1965), which supported "regional educational laboratories."[68] As the plan for UCHS evolved, it began to take on more aspects of progressive education. The school would emphasize science but also eliminate disciplinary boundaries, focus on experiential learning, and feature open architecture conducive to group projects.[69]

As details of the new school's design and curriculum emerged, it became clear why UCHS could not be both an educational laboratory and a solution to the school district's overcrowding problems. The kind of free-range schooling UCHS advocates were touting would require a favorable student-to-teacher ratio. The new building would thus have to operate at half its capacity of three thousand students.[70] A 1961 WPC report to the board of education also showed that the corporation hoped to manipulate the school's feeder pattern to draw more students from university- and hospital-affiliated families. This report called for excluding students from what it termed "outside areas" to promote "general community morale" and "a healthy school environment."[71] The school board, led by Superintendent C. Taylor Whittier and still dominated by tyrannical business manager Add Anderson, named in Chapter 2, responded unenthusiastically to the WPC's proposal.[72]

Neighborhood residents and school district administrators agreed that building a new school in the area should be a priority, but more to relieve overcrowding than to introduce a new kind of instruction. The current high school that served the neighborhood, WPHS, was overfull to the point where students were split into morning and afternoon shifts.[73] The Lea School, a feeder to WPHS, was similarly overcrowded.[74] Neighbors were understandably unenthusiastic about a school that would serve mainly more affluent, White, university-affiliated students while existing neighborhood schools remained inadequate. They wanted new schools in their neighborhood but also assurances that the schools would not be segregated.

When reformers ousted the board of education's old guard in 1965, however, UCHS's prospects improved. The new board was stocked with friends of the WPC. A nominating committee that included Penn president Gaylord Harnwell selected former mayor, political reformer, and WPC board member Richardson Dilworth as its president. New members included Elizabeth Greenfield, wife of the financier who had backed Philadelphia's political reforms during the 1950s and whose banking interests had supported Society Hill redevelopment.[75] That the new board was more open to input from Philadelphia's universities was evidenced by one of its first actions: the appointment of a panel to explore the use of community resources to help public schools. Members included President Harnwell and the deans of the education schools of both Penn and Temple.[76]

A Gathering Storm

WPC school interventions purported to serve the public good but were problematic on multiple levels. The corporation provided generous funding to URP projects at the Lea School but began to publicize results long before there was a chance to assess their effectiveness. It selected a capable leader—Rebecca Segal, who was genuinely successful at preparing students for college—for its Motivation Program at WPHS. Yet the WPC's focus on publicizing the program and particularly its ability to attract White students to the school indicated that making broad-based improvements in West Philadelphia's public education offerings was not its main goal.

From the university perspective, a shortcoming of WPC interventions was their reliance on uncompensated effort by faculty members. Contributors to URP, like Penn GSE professor Mary Coleman, were asked to serve on planning committees and develop curricula but given neither extra pay nor professional recognition for their work. As detailed in Chapter 4, these faculty would complain that they were being exploited—that the WPC was using their intellectual talents for purposes of which they did not approve and making exaggerated claims of the success of its programs.

In the case of UCHS, the corporation was set on creating a public school that the public had not asked for. One of its architectural consultants, the Group for Planning and Research, suggested expanding the Drew School, an extant, overcrowded middle school in the Black Bottom. In a 1963 document outlining its case for the redevelopment of that neighborhood, the WPC retorted that a science high school was "a much stronger use" of the land:

> In such close proximity to a science center of unusual potentialities for education, we feel an extraordinary opportunity exists to provide scientific education at secondary school level for Philadelphia youth. In other words, we can think of no finer, broader community use of this area than as a location for a Philadelphia Public High School for Science and Technology.[77]

Yet the science center was years away from being realized in a way that would support the kind of lab-based experiential learning it was touting. "Broader community use" was aimed at the narrower community of well-educated professionals the corporation wanted to attract.

The WPC couched its plans in the high-minded rhetoric of "The Great City." It claimed to have "thrift" and "prudence" in mind, bringing new jobs and new industries to the city and expanding its lagging tax base. It purported to place "inside authority"—the will of the people—before the interventions of outsiders. A close look reveals the inconsistencies of its professed aims. A prudent development plan for a research center would have been based on the needs of prospective tenants, who were happy to locate in a science tower. In its original siting, the tower would have also made practical use of underutilized land. Instead, the WPC opted for a sprawling complex of buildings based on wide-eyed projections of future growth and requiring the displacement of thousands of residents. An educational program that responded to the will of the people would have fully addressed overcrowding and academic deficiencies at existing schools before proposing new ones. The WPC's signature project, UCHS, sidestepped those issues. Overall, the corporation's initiatives seemed more aimed at attracting new residents to the neighborhood than serving current ones.

The thread that united these projects was land use. First, there was the need to preserve the value of land in predominantly White areas of West Philadelphia by showing that these areas had high-quality schools. Second, there was the desire to clear and consume land in areas the corporation and its patrons deemed the worst slums in the area. We cannot know for certain the motives of Leo Molinaro and his collaborators when they chose to locate the proposed high school precisely in the Black Bottom neighborhood. It is clear from the map, however, that locating both the high school and research centers there fulfilled the 1959 WPC report's call for a continuous corridor of university-related land uses.[78]

The undeniable ties between school improvement efforts and the desire to remove less well-off Black people from the area put the WPC on a collision course with its neighbors. As we see in the next chapter, Black Bottom residents vigorously protested the plan to replace their homes with a school that did not appear to serve their children. Standing on the morally dubious proposition that it could help the neighborhood by ejecting neighborhood residents, the corporation's plan would falter.

4

CONFLICT AND DISILLUSIONMENT

Black Power and the School Reform Agenda

Through the 1960s, conflict bubbled up nationally and in Philadelphia. The war in Vietnam brought protest to campuses and suspicion of the military-industrial complex that supported university research. Following the overturn of Jim Crow segregation in the South, African Americans throughout the nation confronted racial discrimination. In the School District of Philadelphia (SDP), they called for an end to segregated and inferior schools, teachers who would nurture Black students' academic abilities, and a curriculum that would recognize the contributions of Black people to society. The turmoil of this era exposed contradictions in the school-building plans of the West Philadelphia Corporation (WPC), which professed to create a better learning environment for all residents but favored some over others.

The appointment of a new board of education in 1965 and the hiring of Mark Shedd as school superintendent in 1966 enabled the 1960s zeitgeist to take root in the SDP. As previously noted, Shedd embraced various forms of progressive education and heeded calls for equality for Black students. Though he made strides in the hiring of Black administrators, Shedd's experiments ultimately did little to alleviate the system's greatest problems: inadequate facilities and pervasive racial segregation.[1] This failure would become especially evident in the ensuing controversy over the WPC's push to create University City High School (UCHS).

The conditions of overcrowding and segregation present in the SDP since the early twentieth century reached a nadir during the mid-1960s. Secondary schools such as Gratz, Overbrook, and West Philadelphia High School (WPHS) were serving more than twice the number they had been built for, to the point that students were made to attend in shifts. Gratz, for example, had been built for two thousand students in 1930 but housed forty-three hundred by 1970.[2] At other schools, the district erected "temporary" classrooms, many of which still exist today. The overcrowding was viciously uneven, affecting schools in predominantly Black neighborhoods much more than White. Black school activist turned board of education member George Hutt recalled how these problems affected his family: when his neighborhood elementary school was overfull, his daughter was refused admission to a half-empty nearby White school.[3] Though similar problems plagued other urban school districts, these issues were particularly pronounced in Philadelphia, which at the time had the highest dropout rate of the ten largest U.S. cities.[4] As noted in Chapter 2, the settlement of the discrimination lawsuit *Chisholm v. Board of Public Education* did little to alleviate the inferior treatment of Black students people in the SDP.[5]

Protest on the Parkway

While the NAACP had attempted, with limited success, to fight school segregation in the courts, a more militant generation of Black students used direct action to push the school district to change its culture. On the morning of November 17, 1967, a group of thirty-five hundred students from at least thirteen different high schools marched on the SDP offices at 21st Street and Benjamin Franklin Parkway. The demonstrators demanded more Black representation in the curriculum and teaching staff. Evidence shows that the protest was peaceful at first but boiled over when police commissioner Frank Rizzo ordered more officers to the scene. By the time the confrontation ended, fifty-seven protesters had been arrested and twenty individuals hospitalized.[6] A confrontation erupted between the police chief and the superintendent that exposed larger racial and cultural rifts in the city. According Superintendent Shedd, in the aftermath of the demonstration, the two had a tense meeting in which Rizzo declared, "Get those fucking black kids back to school. This is my town. No softie from the outside is going to come in and screw it up. If you don't keep those kids in school, I'm going to run your ass out of Philadelphia."[7] The incident showed how the school district had become a lightning rod for cultural as well as racial conflict in the city. Rizzo's naming of Shedd a "softie from the outside" drew on a vein of resentment against liberal elites presumed not to understand the values of ordinary Philadelphians.

In the aftermath of the November 1967 protest, Shedd and Board President Dilworth supported the student demonstrators and made concessions to their demands. With Dilworth's backing, the superintendent nominated well-known militants for school staff positions and required teachers to attend the previously mentioned sensitivity retreats organized by Terry Borton and Norman Newberg.[8] Certain programs initiated in response to the march were successful. For example, the district created the Office of African/African American Studies to strengthen schools' ability to educate students about African American history and culture. Philadelphia Educators to Africa (ETA) was created by a group of thirty-eight educators who embarked on a six-week tour of West Africa under the auspices of the newly formed office, sharing their knowledge with others after returning to Philadelphia. ETA has served as a resource to teachers since its founding in 1971.[9]

Not all factions in the school district were pleased with the changes. As noted, many found the sensitivity retreats confrontational, and the teachers' union objected to the charges of racism against WPHS teacher George Fishman.[10] Facing opposition from conservative forces, Shedd and Dilworth dialed back the more confrontational aspects of their program. Eventually, Shedd's efforts at democratization and curriculum reform were derailed by an entrenched district culture of top-down management, a budget crisis, and infighting between Dilworth and the mayor at the time, James Tate.[11] The 1967 school demonstration proved to be a pivotal moment in a growing conservative backlash in Philadelphia, which led to the election of "law-and-order" police chief Frank Rizzo as mayor in 1971. Rizzo used Shedd as a scapegoat to appeal to conservative White voters, making his ouster a campaign promise. According to historian Jon S. Birger, "when white voters began to draw a link, albeit a mistaken one, between social unrest and school reforms aimed at empowering blacks, the prospects of Dilworth and Shedd declined dramatically."[12]

Community Protest against the WPC Agenda

WPC plans to leverage urban renewal programs to displace neighborhood residents sparked community resistance. The turmoil that ensued when these plans were unveiled delayed their implementation and derailed efforts to change public education in the neighborhood. Residents turned out in large numbers to a 1962 community meeting at the Drew Elementary School organized by the Redevelopment Authority (RDA), the agency empowered to acquire land on behalf of the WPC. Though the RDA was ostensibly seeking their feedback, neighbors understood that relocation was a done deal and vented their hostility against the displacement that was about to occur.

Residents followed up with organized resistance, demanding greater compensation for those who were to be displaced and asking that Black businesspeople have a role in housing construction plans for the relocation.[13]

As previously noted, WPC plans for redevelopment of the Black Bottom contained two core elements: a science research park, the University City Science Center (UCSC), and the experimental UCHS, which was to have ties to universities and hospitals in the area. Though the WPC disguised its hand by acting through the impersonal mechanisms of the RDA, the City Planning Commission, and federal urban renewal programs, the controversy increasingly drew WPC leader Leo Molinaro into a personal struggle with his nearby neighbors. A committed urbanist whose belief in racial integration led him to enroll his own sons at the nearly all-Black WPHS, Molinaro was shaken by the community's accusations of racism against the WPC, an organization in which he had invested his energy.

Much of Molinaro's effort from 1963 had been devoted to advising the RDA and SDP on the building of UCHS, especially on where it should be located. Molinaro requested that the RDA and SDP increase the amount of land for the new high school from 9.2 to 16 acres based on the need for outdoor athletic facilities. The required condemnation of nearly seven additional acres of residential properties in Unit 3 netted many owner-occupied houses in an area previously considered for conservation under section 220 of the Housing Act of 1954[14]—a departure from the city's "penicillin not surgery" approach to slum clearance.

A pivotal moment came in May 1963, when forty residents organized as the Citizens Committee of University City Redevelopment Area Unit 3 staged a sit-in at the office of Mayor James Tate to protest the WPC plan. The protesters were able to wrest concessions from the city and RDA, which promised to spare as many homes as possible and make their group a consultant on Unit 3 redevelopment plans.[15] Led by Robert Coleman and John H. Clay, the group moved to formalize its relationship with the RDA. Clay formed the University City Citizens Development Corporation (UCCDC) and drafted but never finalized a consulting contract with the RDA.[16] An enraged Molinaro denied that the Black Bottom was a neighborhood. He expressed as much—and insinuated that Clay had ulterior motives—in a May 20, 1963, memorandum to the WPC board, City Planning Commission, and RDA, quoted earlier and given full treatment here:

This area has never had any "neighborhood" identification, or organization. It was from the beginning, marginal in use and occupancy. *All* of the land from which protests have come (34th to 38th Streets; Market Street to Lancaster Avenue) is currently zoned for industrial and commercial uses. None of it is zoned for residential use. In other words, this is not a fine neighborhood which has been neglected and can now be restored. . . .

Almost two years ago, Mr. Clay came to the Corporation and made it clear that he intended becoming active in a speculative way for profit in Unit #3 and wanted "inside information." Since there wasn't any such information, of course, he left in an unfriendly mood.[17]

The word "marginal" is critical here. Certainly, the area designated by the RDA as Unit 3 and known by residents as the Black Bottom was on the margin: between university and city, industrial and residential, run down and inhabitable. As theorist Katherine McKittrick points out, Black space has long existed on the margin. Those who lived in the Black Bottom prior to its destruction described it as a rough-hewn but colorful area with thriving businesses, gathering places, and a rich history. Molinaro stated correctly that the area was zoned for industrial and commercial use, but that did not negate the fact that it was home to many people.

As noted, the neighborhood had irreplaceable cultural significance. Per Walter Palmer's recollections in Chapter 1, the Black Bottom was alive with the sounds of jazz emanating from the many bars along Market Street. Andre Black recalled that the Divine Tracy Hotel on 36th Street not only offered low-cost meals to community members but also provided accommodations to famous African Americans, like Duke Ellington and Billie Holiday, who were denied lodging elsewhere in the city.[18]

Former residents also described a place in which neighbors looked out for one another. Jerry Davis, for example, told a story about a blind neighbor named Mr. Walt leading him to safety during a powerful storm:

Mr. Walt was like a surrogate father to me, and he did *not* let his total blindness slow him down. He was a living example to Jerry and all others in the neighborhood. He had his cane; he came across the street that day to my house because I was up on the third floor in bed since I was not feeling well. And he said, "There's a storm coming through; it's going to be bad. You gotta come over here." So I went over to his house. God's providential care that I did. Long story short, the storm—tornado—came through, flattened our house, and the bed that I was on in the third floor had all the bricks and the chimney on it. So I wouldn't be here! Plain and simple, Mr. Walt saved my life. There is no question about that![19]

According to Davis, the Black Bottom gave residents a sense of security, a feeling that others would help them in times of need: "By definition, we were poor, but we never *felt* poor. Because you had love, and if you didn't have enough for a meal you could get two or three eggs from next door or a few doors down, and give the eggs back when you get the eggs to give back."[20] The neighborhood cohesion Davis and others described is exactly the type Jane Jacobs sees as a feature of well-preserved urban spaces, where neighbors look out for one another.[21]

Unfortunately, the Black Bottom's social cohesion was unknown to Philadelphia's powers that be. Residents lacked the WPC's close connection to city hall. As noted in Chapter 1, many remained loyal to the Republican party at a time when Democrats were ascendant. Moreover, they had no civic association representing them on the WPC board. Black Bottom residents were not privy to discussions initiated by Edmund Bacon, the Greater Philadelphia Movement, and Penn planners like G. Holmes Perkins, charting a course for the city's redevelopment. Confronted by a juggernaut of well-connected and well-financed forces determined to remake the neighborhood according to their wishes, the Black Bottom community was at a disadvantage.

Members of Clay's protest group also lacked architecture training, a necessity for anyone attempting to field alternate redevelopment plans. When Molinaro saw the UCCDC's first redevelopment proposal to the city in August 1964, he wasted no time pointing out its weaknesses to RDA officials. In a memo to RDA executive director Francis J. Lammer, President Harnwell conveyed Molinaro's complaints about the plan's lack of specificity on such basics as how many units would be available and, more importantly, about its lack of aesthetic sophistication:

> We found the site plan lacking entirely in any form or function; among the glaring design deficiencies were: (1) Disorganized public spaces with no apparent purpose; (2) No visible attempt to relate the residential plan to adjoining streets and structures.[22]

In case the RDA was unwilling to dismiss the UCCDC proposal based on design flaws, however, Molinaro had a backup plan. Days earlier, he had written to Harnwell asking the Penn president to use his connections to derail the UCCDC's financing. The letter exhibited Molinaro's willingness to make underhanded use of the university's power:

> The attached letters [requesting loans from two area banks] are the latest attempt by the John Clay group to gain financial support for their proposal in the so called [sic] compromise area in Unit #3. It is important that we find some discreet way of conveying our ideas to

the two lending institutions who have been approached. If we can explain the matter to the two banks, I believe they will suspend any further discussion with the Clay group.[23]

In the letter, Molinaro suggested that WPC board member and Penn vice president for coordinated planning John Hetherston, who was friendly with an officer of one of the banks involved, and WPC board member Harold Batten, a founder of the Greater Philadelphia Movement and powerful business leader, use their influence to stop the loans. Acknowledging the underhandedness of his request, Molinaro ended with the caveat, "Obviously, the matter will have to be treated completely confidentially."[24]

Though the UCCDC provided additional details on its plan, the RDA rejected it because the rehabilitated housing it offered was too expensive for area residents. The UCCDC made a second proposal that called for the demolition of many existing homes and the construction of high-rise apartments. As this plan contradicted the group's stated intention of neighborhood preservation, Molinaro wasted no time condemning it as well. In a May 3, 1965, note to Myles Standish, executive director of Philadelphia's Commerce and Industry Council, Molinaro lashed out, attacking not only Clay's plan but also his integrity. The attacks followed up on Molinaro's earlier insinuations in a May 20, 1963, memorandum that Clay was shady. The emphasis here is original:

> 1. For two full years, the RDA has awaited Clay's long promised plan to "save people's homes"—now he comes up with total clearance; 2. He is now in big trouble. Many of the people are on to him and demanding an accounting. His own two properties in Unit #3 are within one step of the sheriff. He cannot find financing for his scheme so he's going to create a big fuss, *again*; 3. He is dead wrong when he says the RDA wants demolition of the area. *He* wants it and the Authority is telling him to rehabilitate or get out of the picture. His sole basis for being selected as developer was his insistence on rehabilitation. If it's to be new construction, it should be opened to competitive bidding.[25]

Intent on convincing his colleagues that Clay was up to no good, Molinaro shortly thereafter ordered a background investigation of the attorney's business dealings. Dated May 17, 1965, the report did indeed show that Clay was a shady character. Notably, he had made $10,000 for himself in the purchase of a building for a nonprofit where he was employed and testified as a government witness in the loansharking case against Philadelphia mobster Joseph Bruno.[26]

In response to the RDA's rejection of its second proposal, the UCCDC's parent organization, the Citizens Committee of University City Redevelopment Area Unit 3, filed suit against the city council, FHA, Urban Renewal Administration, UCSC, City Planning Commission, WPC, and RDA for civil rights violations. In September 1965, Citizens Committee member Franny Robinson wrote a letter to U.S. president Lyndon Johnson detailing accusations of racism against the city, the RDA, and the WPC in their plans to displace local residents. The letter shows that, though they had not seen the organization's founding documents from 1959, Black Bottom dwellers well understood the WPC's raison d'être: "We know that the land is a valuable piece of land and that the institutions want this for the wives of their professors and other business people; we know that White people feel that this land is too valuable for Negroes to live on." In the letter, Robinson averred that Molinaro had openly stated the WPC's intent to replace the African American residents with "professors and their wives" at a 1965 meeting. She ended her missive with a none-too-subtle threat to riot if officials dismissed the UCCDC proposal: "If we do not hear from you . . . we will call the people together to determine what action should be taken. We would not like for this to be another Los Angeles."[27]

Stung by these accusations, Molinaro wrote back directly to Robinson, with Housing and Urban Development secretary Robert C. Weaver in copy, denying racist intentions on his part:

> At no time did I say we wanted to remove Negroes for white professors and their families. At no time did I say Negroes should go to any other part of the city. This is extremely important to me because I personally believe in integration in housing and education. . . . Not only do I believe in these matters on the basis of personal conscience but I practice them in my daily life.[28]

Indeed, Molinaro considered himself an integrationist, a principle he put into practice by enrolling his sons, Max and John, in predominantly Black West Philadelphia public schools. Malcolm Bonner, one of the African American interviewees cited in the discussion of the Universities-Related Program (URP), named John Molinaro as one of his best friends while the two attended the Lea School and WPHS. He recalled visiting Molinaro regularly at his home in the University Mews on 45th Street in West Philadelphia. A glance at the school's 1968 yearbook shows that Molinaro's son was an active member of the student body, participating in the debate team and, as shown in figure 4.1, the swim team.

Leo Molinaro saw no conflict between his actions as leader of the WPC and his professed antiracism. In his response to Robinson's letter, he wrote:

Huley Barnett, Frank Brown, Jerry Montgomery, John Molinaro, Del Adams.

Figure 4.1 WPHS swim team, 1968. John Molinaro is second from right. (*WPHS yearbook, courtesy WPHS Alumni Association.*)

> It is totally inaccurate and unfair for you to accuse me and our program of any racial discrimination. The seven acres in the area you are concerned with is better suited for public school buildings which will benefit thousands of children, Negro and white, rather than a handful of residents.[29]

Because he believed, naively, that the changes he was implementing in West Philadelphia—particularly the creation of an elite high school—would serve Black and White people equally, he discounted the harm the demolition of the Black Bottom would cause. He had not grown up in that neighborhood. He had not experienced the discrimination in housing, employment, and education that Franny Robinson and her neighbors had, nor had he experienced the neighborhood culture and community cohesion described by Palmer, Hill, Wilmore, and the Davis Brothers. To Molinaro, Unit 3 was a nonspace, and he could not comprehend why—beyond one group's scheme to profit from urban renewal funds—residents would put up such a fight to keep their homes in that area.

Molinaro's ability to believe that he was helping his Black neighbors while destroying their neighborhood is an example of the "epistemology of ignorance" Charles Mills speaks of as a feature of the Racial Contract that underlies American society. The WPC leader refused to see that Black residents had built a community in this marginal area, having fled the Jim Crow South or been excluded from more desirable parts of the city. He would not admit that historical discrimination would prevent Black Bottom residents from fully benefiting from projects such as the science center and high school. Their displacement was the goal of the project, even if not made explicit.

After city council approved the demolitions in April 1966, the Citizens Committee withdrew its suit but took up the matter with the NAACP and CORE. According to one account, these organizations persuaded the newly established federal Department of Housing and Urban Development (HUD) to suspend the urban renewal grant that was to fund the demolitions, threatening violent protest if the money was released. HUD ultimately restored the urban renewal grant when the RDA promised to provide land in the neighborhood to resettle displaced residents. Historians John Puckett and Mark Lloyd have suggested that there was a connection between the decision to restore funding and Penn's award of an honorary degree to HUD secretary Robert C. Weaver at the 1966 commencement. Whether or not this factor was decisive, Penn's extensive institutional and interpersonal network won the day.[30]

HUD's release of the $12 million in urban renewal funds cleared an important financial hurdle for the UCHS project. However, the demolitions could not proceed, and the school could not be built without SDP approval. Molinaro therefore launched an all-out effort to win over the board of education. He called on high-ranking WPC supporters, including leaders of the Southeastern Pennsylvania Economic Development Corporation, Greater Philadelphia Chamber of Commerce, Provident Mutual Life Insurance, and various West Philadelphia civic associations, to testify at a September 21, 1966, school board hearing. Prior to the hearing, he redoubled his attacks against Clay, describing him in a September 14, 1966, memorandum to the WPC board as "an unscrupulous Negro promoter who does not even live in the area but owns two properties for speculation on Market Street."[31] Molinaro's acolytes spoke eloquently at the meeting. Lea School Home and School Association member Robert S. King justified the school's location in Unit 3 as "the very heart of University City where it can take advantage of the excellent scientific, technical, and academic resources now under development in that area."[32] Allen S. Goldman, vice president of the Spruce Hill Community Association, dismissed the arguments of neighborhood protesters and implied that a larger and more "responsible" group of Black residents was eager to benefit from the new school.[33]

The new school won board of education approval shortly thereafter, and President Harnwell wrote glowing letters of thanks those who had testified.

Members of the Clay group did not attend the hearing. The demolitions proceeded through 1967, though turmoil in the SDP would delay the construction of UCHS until 1971.

Molinaro's victory came at a cost. A neighborhood survey released in September 1966, when the board of education hearings were taking place, belied the notion that responsible residents supported the clearance of the Black Bottom for UCHS.[34] More negative publicity emerged in Penn's student newspaper, the *Daily Pennsylvanian*, in 1967. A series of articles entitled "The Quiet War" revealed the plight of those displaced by the WPC's redevelopment plan.[35] It showed that, according to HUD documents, the demolitions resulted in the displacement of 467 non-White and 107 White families—most of whom were renters and impoverished. In all, 2,653 people, 2,070 of whom were Black, were forced to move, many to the neighborhoods of Southwest Philadelphia, Mantua, and Wynnefield. The neighborhood's population plummeted from 4,603 residents in 1960 to 654 in 1970.[36]

University City High School Falters

As the clearance of the Black Bottom proceeded, it appeared that the WPC plan to create a science-focused high school would be realized. Richardson Dilworth, who had recently been appointed president of the reorganized board of education, initiated a major building program to take place over the next five fiscal years, and voters approved a $60 million bond issue in May 1966.[37] Shortly after, reformer Mark Shedd, whose ideas for progressive education seemed to align with the vision for the school, was selected as school superintendent. But what was that vision? How would UCHS function as an elite science school, a laboratory for progressive education, and a release valve for school overcrowding in West Philadelphia?

Initially, there was much overlap between WPC and school district ideas for education. Soon after taking office in October 1967, Shedd addressed the WPC, praising its impact on the city and its plan for UCHS. Throughout that year, the corporation had laid the groundwork for the construction of the new school by rolling out its vision to the board of education and the community at large. It had proposed an enrollment structure in which 75 percent of the student body would be from West Philadelphia and the remaining 25 percent from the rest of the city via a magnet program.[38] The WPC had also received an endorsement from the Greater Philadelphia Chamber of Commerce, which stated in a report that local companies were "unanimous in urging the establishment of a high school of science and mathematics as a source of scientifically oriented youth who would become the scientists of tomorrow." Addressing the criticism that such a school would be exclusive, the report asserted that the school would "offer opportunities, rather than barriers, to culturally-disadvantaged children from the minorities."[39]

At its third annual community conference, the WPC presented a proposal written by project consultant Clifford Swartz, a State University of New York, Stonybrook physics professor, on the kind of education envisioned for UCHS. His description included a laundry list of progressive educational ideas. Among them were the lowering of boundaries between courses, disciplines, and grade levels; pass-fail grading; projects rather than tests as assessment tools; and experiential learning. To facilitate these innovations, the plan proposed a radically open school architecture:

> The interior of the school building would look much more like a library or science museum than a normal school. There would not be many of the standard corridors and classrooms because, in general, there would not be classes. There would be seminar rooms, group workrooms and even lecture halls because, although learning progress would be individualized, a considerable amount of student time would be spent on group projects or activities.[40]

Swartz's vision aligned well with the progressive ideas of many West Philadelphia parents and reformers in the school district. In many respects, it resembled Mark Shedd's Pennsylvania Advancement School.[41] Significantly, the Swartz proposal laid the groundwork for a packet-based system of independent study in which students worked at their own pace outlined in a set of printed materials.[42] Though written by a physics professor and intended for a science-focused school, the Swartz proposal said curiously little about how science was to be taught.

By the time the vision for UCHS coalesced in 1968, reformers at the SDP had begun to encounter resistance. As mentioned, rising political figure Frank Rizzo exploited the 1967 student protest to rally opposition against the Shedd administration's progressive agenda. Rizzo began to tighten the screws on Shedd, allegedly tapping his phone and having him followed.[43] The politically savvy police chief made good use of Shedd as a scapegoat, blaming the superintendent for youth violence and cementing the support of White conservative voters.[44]

As also noted, some union members took offense to Shedd's handling of the protest, sensitivity retreats, and treatment of teachers like George Fishman, whom they thought was the victim of reverse discrimination.[45] The union became increasingly resistant to Shedd's progressive ideas. Philadelphia Federation of Teachers (PFT) leader Celia Pincius complained, "We've gone through one experiment after another. I have not seen one program that will effect results for all 300,000 school children in Philadelphia."[46]

The SDP was one of seventeen sites to receive a grant from the U.S. Office of Education to participate in Educational System for the Seventies (ES '70), which would develop the packet-based curriculum planners hoped to use in the school.[47] Rather than cooperate with UCHS planners on the implementation of this curriculum, however, the teachers' union threw up roadblocks. It disallowed the selection of department heads based on knowledge of the progressive curriculum, instead insisting that they be chosen based on seniority.[48] By the time the new building opened in fall 1971, only thirty of the sixty teachers needed to offer ES '70 had been trained.[49]

From the start, the WPC had touted access to the universities as one of UCHS's main advantages and a reason for its location. UCHS students would visit labs, and Penn professors would provide curriculum support. As planning for the school proceeded, however, these benefits evaporated. President Harnwell informed program leader George Love in 1968 that UCHS students would not be able to take courses at Penn—nor would they receive preferential treatment for admissions. Provost David Goddard told Love in 1970 that Penn faculty would not be compensated for working with UCHS students, and any instructional time would not be counted as part of their course load.[50] This lack of cooperation by Penn was a major blow to the school's overarching concept.

Another setback was the resignation of WPC executive vice president Leo Molinaro in April 1968. As mentioned, Molinaro left the WPC to work for developer James Rouse, with whom he shared a vision of how to create an ideal American community. Molinaro would assist Rouse in the development of Columbia, Maryland, which planning historians have identified as a beginning point of the global trend toward "new urbanism."[51] However flawed, Molinaro's vision had brought key players together behind UCHS, and his absence at this critical juncture would further hamper its creation.

The Problem of Enrollment

In the years leading up to UCHS's opening in 1971, the question of who should attend became a major issue for the school's planners. According to James "Torch" Lytle, who would serve as principal of the high school from 1995 to 1998, "a sort of last-minute decision was made to not have University City operate at a science magnet school but rather to make it a neighborhood high school."[52] Not actually last minute, this decision was the result of community resistance to building an exclusive school on land cleared with federal dollars. Parents at the WPC's third annual community conference worried that the school would cater to the children of university elites and that their children lacked the requisite preparation in math and science to meet the school's admission standards.[53] In a survey conducted at the WPC's fifth annual community conference (1969), neighborhood respondents indicated that they preferred the new school's enrollment to come from ten neighborhood K–8 or 6–8 schools.[54] These schools, which were underresourced, would not provide the kind of preparation needed for the WPC's original vision of a science-focused high school.

Nor would this feeder pattern enable the school to offer the progressive curriculum its planners increasingly favored. Taking children from the ten neighborhood schools proposed would result in an enrollment of nearly five thousand students.[55] Although the school building could accommodate three thousand, planners recommended that enrollment be set at half that number or less to provide adequate supervision for students' independent learning activities. A member of a committee deciding on the school's enrollment policy wondered, "Can the West Philadelphia University City High School (UCHS) open with only 1,250 pupils and hold seats open, while children in other schools are being educated in overcrowded conditions?"[56] Ultimately, the school's enrollment policy was favorable neither to supporters of a progressive education nor to neighborhood parents concerned about overcrowding. An additional drawback was that it pulled students from different areas whose rival gang affiliations created a violent atmosphere in the school.

A Paltry Budget

With the rise of the Dilworth-Shedd administration in the SDP, it had been expected that there would be plenty of money for capital projects and especially for progressive schools like UCHS. As Shedd came under attack by conservative forces after the 1967 student protest, however, the public's appetite for school funding waned. In May 1969, a divided electorate rejected a $90 million bond issue that would have provided generous funding for the building of new schools. According to Birger, working-class White residents, led by media reports and Rizzo's angry rhetoric to believe that the school district had been turning over most of its resources to Black Philadelphians, were instrumental in defeating the measure.[57] The SDP's fiscal shortfall threatened the budget for UCHS; only an all-out effort by the school's supporters would convince the district to maintain some of its commitment to the school.[58] On behalf of the WPC, Harnwell personally asked Dilworth to maintain funding, and a coalition of home and school associations and other community groups agitated for the same.[59] With school district funding in jeopardy, the community called for increased support for UCHS from Penn. In April 1969, the Friends and Parents of the Lea School asked Harnwell to pledge support.[60] However, the Penn president, who was receiving an increasing number of requests to fund various school projects in West Philadelphia, was unwilling to do so.[61]

An Inauspicious Beginning

The construction of UCHS was delayed, first by the Black Bottom community's resistance to land clearance and then by SDP funding shortfalls. The school was launched in 1971 as a "comprehensive" (general purpose) high school with a magnet program attached.[62] Because the building had not been finished in September of that year, classes were held at a former oncological hospital at 33rd and Powelton Streets, a building owned by Drexel University.[63] When the building finally opened in 1972, it was segmented both architecturally and in terms of curriculum. The cast-concrete structure was divided into pods for students assigned to different academic programs, including one for the magnet program.[64] While a small number of students from university-affiliated families enrolled initially at UCHS, these numbers quickly dwindled, and the school became a highly segregated and deeply troubled institution.

One student enrolled in the magnet program was Carol Williamson, who as noted had attended the Lea School from K–6 and the prestigious Julia R. Masterman School in grades 7–8. Due to her accelerated status, Williamson was the very first person to graduate from UCHS. While the most typical choice of high school for a student of Williamson's caliber would have been the Philadelphia High School for Girls, Williamson recalled that she chose UCHS because, as the daughter of two educators, she was seeking something more "exciting and adventurous."[65] The strong preparation she received at Masterman enabled her to proceed at a faster pace, with an expected graduation date two years later.

Williamson followed an independent study curriculum under the guidance of UCHS teachers and occasionally Penn or Drexel professors. She utilized the previously mentioned ES '70 packets, which she said were an attractive part of the school program.[66] With titles like "Critical Thinking," "Structures and Systems," and "Conflict," the guides encompassed broad swaths of content, from history to political thought to math and science, and were designed to unite many types of thinking—visual, verbal, logical, quantitative—in a single set of projects. By breaking down disciplinary boundaries, encouraging students to learn by doing, and teaching critical thinking, the packets embraced well-known tenets of progressive education. The cover of one such packet, which Williamson used as a student, is reproduced in figure 4.2.

Initially, Williamson had a good experience at UCHS, enjoying the freedom and novelty of her self-study curriculum. With time, she became aware that the different groups the school served were not well integrated. She realized that students enrolled in the magnet program were mostly White and that the school had not been designed with nonmagnet students in mind:

Figure 4.2 Cover of ES '70 learning packet "Critical Thinking." SDP, 1970. (*Carol Williamson, personal collection.*)

It really worked great for a while but what happened was when the building opened there was overcrowding at other schools. So kids who had not thought, "Oh this is great this is what I want to do" were force-transferred there. . . . And so I think that turned out to be awkward. I don't think there was any animosity or anything. But there was just this, you know, kids who wanted more traditional [education] for whatever reason—and go at your own speed, go to the library, and that kind of thing wasn't working for them.[67]

Williamson observed that the willy-nilly assignment of nonmagnet students to UCHS created tense and sometimes dangerous situations for those students. The student body included members of the Moon gang, a group from outside the neighborhood that would sometimes encounter a local gang at dismissal time. Though she was never threatened, Williamson reported that when a gang confrontation was imminent, teachers would caution the magnet students to leave through the back door. Magnet program staff protected their students in other ways as well. Williamson noted that during a 1972 teachers' strike, the program's administrator, Shelley Pavel, who was paid by the University of Pennsylvania, arranged for magnet students to take calculus classes at Drexel and English classes at Penn.[68]

The experience of Lea School graduate Pat Spann, who also attended UCHS during its early years, gave a sense of what the school was like for nonmagnet students. Spann was placed in the school's Business Academy, which she said was intended to move students into the working world by splitting their time between work and study. According to Spann:

> So we would be in school from nine to twelve [o'clock], and then we would go off to our jobs. That's when I started working a five to ten shift at Fidelity Bank. And then some of my classmates were working other places, some were working at Sears, one was working at Rohm and Haas [a chemical company], I remember one was working at a pharmaceutical company.[69]

Graduating from this program, Spann went straight to work rather than enrolling in college. As of this writing, she has held administrative assistant positions at Penn for over forty years, first in the English Department and later in Psychology.[70]

Spann recalled that her curriculum was focused on office skills useful at the time, such as typing and shorthand. Being a business student isolated her from the rest of the school: "Like I said, I was there for a few hours a day and I would leave and go to work. I didn't really interact with anybody that wasn't in the Business Academy for the most part." Outside of her unit, she remembered very little of school life or of the school offering any special educational experiences. As a business student, she spent little time in the library.[71] Though hands on, the curriculum Spann experienced was nothing like the Deweyan learning-by-doing approach, which intended concrete learning as a gateway to critical thinking and problem solving. Instead, she was offered vocational education.

UCHS's planners touted it as a school that would offer a progressive, science-focused curriculum to a wide range of students. It opened as a bifurcated institution that offered its special curriculum to a privileged group and sheltered them from the problems faced by the rest. During the 1970s, Penn would turn its attention from WPC educational initiatives to more pressing internal problems. The energy behind school experiments like UCHS waned, and few students from outside of the neighborhood were attracted to the school's magnet program.

URP: Public Relations to Public Embarrassment

Taking on the task of improving Philadelphia's public schools, the WPC found itself in over its head. The problems it faced were too entrenched and widespread to be handled by an organization whose primary mission was real estate redevelopment. Though started with generous funding, URP was soon under pressure to support every school in the area, not just the ones university and hospital affiliates were likely to attend. Correspondence between university officials, members of the public, and Penn faculty from the years 1969–1971 shows widespread disappointment at the lack of progress in the program.

Community Discontent, Faculty Ire

In a letter to Harnwell, the home and school association chair from the Drew School, located near the epicenter of the Black Bottom demolitions, vented her frustrations: "We met with you on several occasions at which time we asked for help to improve the status of Drew School. You offered your services but only verbally. Now we demand action."[72] Parents and school administrators at the Lea School shared these frustrations. Said one Lea administrator in a letter to Harnwell, "We have worked hard for years at the Lea School to improve it and the results have been discouraging. Our school is dying in the middle of a huge university complex. The University must realize that we can no longer cope with the overwhelming Lea problems nor our parents' fermenting discontent."[73]

In September 1964, Penn President Harnwell had informed Robert L. Taylor, president of the *Philadelphia Evening Bulletin*, that the URP was serving eight thousand students at four elementary schools and WPHS; the experimental reading and math curricula, as well as the science enrichment the program had introduced at Lea, were now being introduced at other schools.[74] By 1968, that number had increased to seven.[75] From an early stage, the coalition of university members the WPC had recruited to run these programs showed signs of discontent. In March 1966, for example, Graduate School of Education (GSE) professor Mary Coleman conveyed to her dean, Morris S. Viteles, that she felt overwhelmed. Of the three universities involved in the program, only Penn had an elementary education program, and therefore she was URP's sole curriculum specialist. Coleman echoed the recollections of former students that programs such as language instruction were a far cry from what the WPC touted in its publicity campaigns. "The teachers," Coleman said, "have an impossible class load, running from one room to another, meeting different age groups and teaching different languages."[76] The education professor suggested that public relations concerns were driving the URP: "It is obvious that the name of the University is now being used to attract people to this area under false pretenses." She went on to say that GSE was hurting its reputation by committing to a program that had grown too quickly and without proper planning.[77]

The testimonies of those who attended the Lea School at the time mirror Coleman's viewpoint. None remembered an extensive world language program. Former Lea student Brenda Bonhomme said that in fifth grade, a language instructor from Penn briefly taught Russian, "but it didn't last very long."[78] Outside of Lea's library, on which the WPC spent significant funds, the former students had few recollections of facilities or resources that were different from those of other public schools.[79] Some remembered visitors from Penn or Drexel at the school but found them distant and their activities superficial. Brenda Bonhomme described the visitors as "these smiling adults—that kind of appeared and said, 'Oh, this is some kind of project.'" The projects, she said, were "little passing activities that would come and go."[80]

Concerns about the effectiveness of URP and the viability of the WPC project spread through the Penn faculty. The corporation had been promising professors and staff members that University City would be a "New Athens" since the early 1960s, but little of that promise had materialized, especially in education. With public protest of WPC-initiated land clearance mounting, faculty sensed growing ill will toward the university from its neighbors. The lackluster results shown in Penn GSE's 1968 appraisal of URP at the Lea School in 1968 brought faculty discontent to a head.

In an October 1968 statement to the university council calling for an overhaul of URP, faculty member James F. Ross decried the "complete failure of the loose affiliation of the Lea School and the University to come to anything":

> The University Committed itself, publicly, politically, and financially, to the renewal of University City. . . . Yet, from a family point of

view, the most important element in a residential community is lacking: adequate primary, elementary and junior level education. This situation obtains after more than five years of well-publicized promises that the university would stimulate and innovate education in University City.[81]

Seemingly outraged on the community's behalf, Ross condemned URP as a "propaganda-oriented disillusioning and disingenuous label designed to give the University credit for an effort it has never undertaken."[82] The philosophy professor declared, however, that if resources were stretched, the university should put the needs of its own constituents first:

> I am well aware of the potential disturbance within the larger community should we have to adopt an explicit priority for faculty families, but there are practical consequences of the faculty's problem upon the University. A number of faculty, if they cannot be assured of rapidly and enormously improved educational facilities for their children, will be forced to leave the University. What Associate Professor with four children can afford 4000 a year tuition to Friends' Select [an elite Quaker school]?[83]

Though he expressed regret at Penn's inability to "renew" the community as promised, Ross thought community needs did not warrant further expenditures. Instead of URP, he proposed Penn create a private, progressive school for its university affiliates and subsidize tuition for families that enrolled children there. This was necessary, Ross thought, for Penn to attract and keep international-caliber faculty members.[84] The tendency of professors like Ross to lament the mistreatment of the community but ultimately put their own interests first was a pattern that would reappear during the creation of the Penn Alexander School (PAS) in the twenty-first century.

Faculty concerns reached President Harnwell's ears as well; he wrote of the URP in 1969 that "a number of projects and programs have been undertaken with varying success. In retrospect, it seems that the visibility of the program has far exceeded its actual impact on the schools involved."[85] Harnwell called for a wider study of the program by a faculty committee. Completed in January 1970, the report recognized that the high expectations the university had set with the URP had fueled public discontent and obligated Penn to improve it:

> The committee finds that despite its ambitious goals, the program has languished and is now ineffective. Nonetheless, community expectations remain high and there is considerable pressure . . . to urge

the University [to] make good its vague public promises. . . . The committee considers that it is in the best interest of the University to expand, coordinate, and intensify the UR program to a level where it is effective in improving the quality of public education in University City.[86]

According to the report, funding of not less than $200,000 ($2,065,000 in 2025 dollars) would be required to make the URP viable. Penn was in no shape, however, to provide such funding. In a follow-up letter, Harnwell noted, "The financial recommendations [of the committee] will present some problems in view of the difficult budgetary situation which the University faces."[87] Penn's growing budget deficit, which had reached $5 million by 1970, was the nail in the coffin of URP.[88] A 1971 WPC report would note that the corporation had withdrawn its support for the program, citing as its reason: "Too many schools claimed to be associated with it and requested that programs be carried out for which funds were insufficient."[89]

The report of the faculty committee Harnwell had appointed to review the URP decried the apparent shallowness of WPC efforts. It noted that the corporation, as of 1970, was still promoting URP as one of University City's assets to convince Penn faculty to live in the neighborhood and "mollify an increasingly critical community, without being willing to invest more than minimal amounts of program-committee personnel, money, or administrative help."[90] Committee members captured the quagmire Penn had created by initiating a program without fully understanding the responsibilities it was undertaking:

> The revitalization of the University City community has not kept pace with institutional development and the external relations of the University in consequence have deteriorated. The increasing disparity between the growing size, wealth, and power of the University, of Drexel Institute, and of the Science Center and the relatively declining economic and social condition of the University City community (partly resulting, for some residents, from condemnation of their residences to make way for institutional expansion) has in fact resulted in open confrontation in demonstrations, protests, and demands.[91]

A Missed Opportunity

The one part of URP that was successful, the Motivation Program, had become disconnected from the WPC and Penn. By 1970, Rebecca Segal was operating the program at Bartram, Overbrook, and Kensington High Schools—

far away from University City—with the help of foundation grants and federal ESEA Title 1 funding.[92] Those who worked with Segal praised her effectiveness in dealing with district bureaucracy. According to Gloria Moskowitz, who began as cultural coordinator of the Bartram Motivation Program in 1967:

> First of all she was a fighter. She fought for everything, and she knew . . . she knew all the principals, and my principal adored her. Most people were afraid of her, but he adored her; she was such a fighter for these kids. She was very modern, even though she was older.[93]

Moskowitz described how, with Segal's blessing and the support of principal Lou D'Antonio, she developed the Motivation Program at Bartram into a school within a school, eventually moving into a separate building as the Bartram Motivation Center. Moskowitz and fellow teacher Jack Weber recalled the freedom they had in their setting to try new ideas, something that was unheard of within the otherwise rigid SDP.[94]

Segal's independent thinking and Penn's waning interest likely led her to sever ties between the Motivation Program and the university. As noted, the use of Penn resources was, in the earlier years, a hallmark of the Motivation director's emphasis on introducing high school students to college-level work and a reason why alumni like Glenn Bryan, Norman Brown, and K. Rose Samuel-Evans thought the program was so effective. Yet the program was increasingly hitting barriers in its efforts to arrange courses and activities on the Penn campus. Correspondence from the Philadelphia Board of Education to Penn in 1970 requested that forty Motivation Program students from WPHS be enrolled in a special math course, a section of the first-year English class, and a first-year elective course, all at the university. Penn reluctantly agreed to the request but reduced class meetings from three per week to one. A board of education document complained that the reduced meetings were "one quite negative educational aspect of this Program" and a "continuing disjointedness" in the program's setup. Correspondence between Rebecca Segal and Penn President Martin Meyerson's assistant for external affairs, Frank M. Betts III, shows that Penn was unwilling to grant a similar request for free tuition for Motivation Program students wanting to enroll in a Penn class.[95]

By the early 1970s, the Motivation Program had drifted out of Penn's orbit. With her own funding sources and the support of the school district, Segal was free to carry on the work wherever and however she pleased. As Penn's interest in supporting the program waned, so did any public memory that the university, through the WPC, had birthed the Motivation Program. This lack of connection was apparent in the comments of the Motivation Program teachers and students I interviewed, who had no inkling of the program's connection to Penn.[96]

Too Much Motivation?

As noted, the Motivation Program was intended to increase college attendance by students from West Philadelphia schools—and it was quite successful in that endeavor. One destination for college-bound Motivation Program graduates was Penn. University administrators were sensitive to criticisms by the community of the paltry numbers of students—particularly African Americans—from the neighborhood. According to a 1968 *Daily Pennsylvanian* article with the not-so-subtle title "Subtle Hatred of University's Guts Is Displayed by Neighbors," Penn named Billy Adams, an African American who had previously taught at Bartram High School, as an assistant dean of admissions as part of a push to recruit more local high school graduates.[97] Historian Stefan Bradley notes that Penn also implemented a race-conscious admissions policy that resulted in an increase of admissions of Black students from 62 in 1968 to 150 in 1969.[98] In 1968, WPHS Motivation Program coordinator Eileen Brown, along with counselor Jettie Newkirk, began working with Adams to increase the number of WPHS students admitted to Penn; Adams supplied Brown with a written promise to accept a group of twenty-six students meeting Penn's qualifications. These students would be eligible to attend for free under the Mayor's Scholarship Program, an arrangement Penn had with the City of Philadelphia that covered tuition for up to 125 Philadelphia high school graduates. Brown identified twenty-six such students and, expecting that their enrollment at Penn would be guaranteed, did not have the group visit or apply to other colleges.[99]

What appeared to be a bounty turned into a disaster when students' notification letters arrived: Penn had accepted only six of the twenty-six. Brown immediately met with Penn's dean of admissions, hoping to obtain a compromise. She recalled saying to him, "Let's go through all of the nonaccepted students and see if there are any others that you feel that you can accept, and if not, you work with me to get them into other colleges." According to Brown, he replied, "Absolutely not. We're not doing anything else. We accepted six. The rest of them are rejected; there's nothing that could be done." The dean's intransigence resulted in a month of confrontation between Penn and the community. At first, Brown and neighborhood groups—including one led by the Reverend Marshall Shepard, pastor of a nearby Black church—attempted to negotiate with Penn's administration. Brown described a string of "the most horrible, horrible, horrible meetings" in which President Harnwell said little while Vice Provost John A. Russell, whom Brown described as a "a real killer," dug in his heels. She remembered Russell saying, "Yes, I understand that the West Philadelphia community is our local community, but you have to realize that the University of Pennsylvania is an international institution."[100] For Brown, Russell's remark embodied the conflict between Penn's stated goal of improving educational opportunities in the surrounding community and its elitist identity as an Ivy League school. The contradictions in Russell's rebuke mirror those in James Ross's critique of URP: when push came to shove, interest in attracting top professors and students from the outside overrode Penn's stated intent of doing right by its neighbors.

With meetings with Penn administrators yielding no results, the community turned to public protest. Eileen Brown recalled that after community members picketed alumni events, Penn relented and agreed to accept the twenty-six students. According to Brown and counselor Jettie Newkirk, when the students matriculated, the Penn community did not embrace them:

> They went in '68. The next year, the students were complaining and coming back to us and to Eileen indicating that they were not being treated very well at Penn. They were not doing well academically; they were falling behind, and nobody seemed to care. They felt very isolated, and so we decided that we would try to do something about it. Well, we couldn't get anybody to listen to us as the counselors.[101]

Malcolm Bonner, one of the students in the cohort of twenty-six, recalled that they were given "marginal" status and treated differently from other students.[102] Angered by this situation, Reverend Shepard again staged a demonstration. According to Newkirk, protesters widened their demands, calling for an end to what they believed was a racist climate at Penn. They asked for academic supports for the twenty-six students from WPHS, an end to the students' isolation, termination of the president, and the appointment of a Black vice president. Penn did not accede to these demands, and as Brown recalls, not one of the cohort of twenty-six graduated.[103]

Protest on Penn's Campus

As neighbors' outrage against Penn administration and the WPC grew, so too did students', though not for all the same reasons. Like many U.S. colleges and universities during the 1960s, Penn saw growing opposition to the Vietnam War on its campus—and consequently, to any involvement with the military. During the 1950s, President Harnwell had set up the Institute for Cooperative Research (ICR) to administer secret defense projects, and the university had embarked on research on biological weapons. The ICR aroused little ire during the 1950s, but as opposition to Vietnam mounted in the 1960s, Harnwell had Penn's military-related projects moved to the University City Science Center (UCSC). Controversy erupted as students became aware of the UCSC's role in both defense research and the displacement of neighborhood residents.[104] Up to that point, the atmosphere at Penn had been relatively calm compared to campuses like Columbia and Berkeley, where student demonstrations had turned violent. A 1968 *Time* magazine article about Penn, for example, described a cooperative relationship between administration and student activists resulting in greater student participation in campus governance. Harnwell boasted that under his leadership a "quiet revolution" had taken place, resulting in students sitting on the university forum alongside faculty and administration and a student panel adjudicating disciplinary cases.[105]

Not all students and community members agreed that Penn's accommodations had resulted in a more just relationship between the university and its neighborhood. Mocking Harnwell's "quiet revolution" was the *Daily Pennsylvanian*'s earlier exposé from January 1967 entitled "The Quiet War in West Philadelphia." The week-long series had documented the displacements then underway in the Black Bottom.[106] At the same time, Black students on campus were increasingly vocal in denouncing instances of racism in the surrounding community. Historian Stefan M. Bradley describes how, in 1968, students affiliated with Penn's Students' Afro-American Society (SAAS) staged a protest at a bank near Penn campus that reputedly refused to hire Black workers. Samuel Cooper, a founding SAAS member, recounted how he and a White friend staged a test there in which they each inquired about a job. Cooper was told there were none available, but the White friend was hired. Incensed by the blatant discrimination, Cooper led a group of students in blockading the bank. A police confrontation ensued from which he and his fellow protesters narrowly escaped. Eventually, the bank relented and changed its hiring practices.[107]

The controversy over both University City redevelopment and defense research came to a head in February 1969, when activist groups organized a protest culminating in a six-day sit-in at College Hall, Penn's main administrative building. Among the protesters were two factions of the Students for a Democratic Society (SDS): a moderate group and the more hardline SDS Labor Committee. Led by Penn student Ira Harkavy, the moderate group edged out the radicals and negotiated a settlement with university administrators and Penn trustees, brokered in part by Penn professors Lee Benson and Michael Zuckerman. In the compromise, Penn formed the Quadripartite Commission (QPC), a body to address protesters' demands, so called because it included four groups: students, faculty, Penn trustees, and community. A key part of the QPC's agenda was the creation of low-income housing in the Black Bottom, the demolition of which had largely been completed by 1967. The trustees pledged to create a housing development fund of $10 million, equivalent to $84.4 million in 2025. As we see in the next chapter, the commission accomplished little. Disagreement arose over whether the trustees had committed to paying $10 million out of university funds or helping the community raise that sum from outside donations. Members also squabbled over the body's makeup, which favored the university over the community, and over who should represent the community. By 1971, the body had dissolved.

What the protest did accomplish was the creation of bonds of trust between a core group of students and neighborhood leaders. During the sit-in, Harkavy had been the liaison with community leaders, including Young Great Society founders Herman Wrice and Andrew Jenkins and founders of Renewal Housing Incorporated Lorenzo Graham and Reverend Edward Sims. Hearing their concerns, Harkavy made it one of his group's demands that a portion of the UCSC properties be turned over to that organization for development. During the standoff between Harkavy's group and the more radical SDS Labor Committee at the sit-in, Black Bottom activist Walter Palmer came to Harkavy's aid by discrediting a pro-Labor Committee agitator who claimed to represent the Black Panthers. Harkavy would continue to cultivate the friendship and support of these community activists as a leader of the university's engagement efforts during the 1980s.[108]

From the beginning, the WPC's educational programs were riven by contradictions. Advertised as creating better schools for all, the corporation's URP more often led to carve outs for some. The programs, promoted as having the support of top faculty members, overstated participants' commitments, leading to the conclusion that URP was mostly public relations. The one WPC program that contributed to neighbors' academic success, the Motivation Program, created a debacle when Penn disdained those neighbors in its own halls. Rescinding offers of admission to the cohort of WPHS Motivation Program graduates, Penn showed its fear that accepting a large contingent of local Black students might undermine its elite status. The WPC's most ambitious effort, UCHS, stood on land it had seized to remove neighbors it said the school would help.

Amid 1960s turmoil, the WPC's educational agenda collapsed. Neighborhood protest delayed the clearance of land in the Black Bottom and derailed the UCHS project. Conservative backlash against Superintendent Shedd's reforms further thwarted the project, and the school that opened bore little resemblance to the boutique progressive school the WPC had proposed. The corporation's URP satisfied neither community nor faculty desires for better public schooling, leading to calls for its overhaul and expansion. Broke and weary of community involvement, Penn and its proxy WPC instead abandoned URP. Penn President Harnwell would resign in 1970, and his successor, Martin Meyerson—who as a city planning professor had spurred the creation of the WPC in 1956—would turn his attention to setting Penn's house in order. West Philadelphia was left to fend for itself.

5

Dark Years in West Philadelphia

The 1970s and '80s saw Philadelphia's reputation sag. Reactions against liberal elites in city government and school administration sent the demagogic Frank Rizzo to the mayor's office; he promised to be tough on crime and rid the educational system of the "outsider influence" of White liberals and Black people.[1] White outmigration to the suburbs continued, diminishing the city's overall population, which had peaked at just above 2 million in 1950, to approximately 1.5 million by 1990.[2] Faced with teacher strikes and budget deficits, Rizzo-appointed school superintendents proved ineffectual. Despite the mayor's tough stance and police background, crime increased, leaving residents feeling unsafe on the streets. The city's malaise was especially evident in West Philadelphia, where the thwarted West Philadelphia Corporation (WPC) plan had cleared large swaths of land but produced little new development. The failure of the WPC's Universities-Related Program (URP) left students dangling and a whole school, University City High School (UCHS)—whose building had displaced so many Black Bottom residents—in a neglected state. The body intended to resolve town-gown differences over these failures, the Quadripartite Commission (QPC), dissolved not long after it was formed, having accomplished little.

From this nadir, a new liberal leadership emerged both in the city and the universities. It employed new rhetoric and tactics—but its plan to save the city again rested on leaving behind the industrial economy in favor of cultural and intellectual capital. This leadership did little to reverse the city's increasing segregation and poverty.

Research Parking Lot

Leo Molinaro's pie-in-the-sky promise to build the University City Science Center (UCSC) as a world-class urban research park yielded lackluster results. A planned FDA laboratory never materialized. A tenant attracted in 1969, the Monell Chemical Senses Center, remained one of the UCSC's only major research and development labs into the twenty-first century. Its first large-scale project, a high-rise building on 36th and Market Streets, was originally built by the federal government for nonscientific purposes, as regional administrative offices of the Department of Labor, HUD, HEW, and Office of Economic Opportunity. By 1970, the UCSC was losing $30,000 per month.[3] The UCSC's fortunes shifted under the leadership of its second president, Randall Whaley, who by 1987 had brought 107 startups to the center, employing more than six thousand people. Yet many of these businesses were short lived, and to maintain its budget, the UCSC would continue to lease office space for nonscientific purposes.[4] Penn was shielded from the UCSC's financial losses because the center was legally part of neither the university nor any other West Philadelphia institution.[5] Moreover, as a nonprofit entity, the university was relieved of paying taxes on the land it had acquired and cleared at U.S. government expense. For some forty years, the UCSC sat on mostly undeveloped parcels left behind by demolitions. Vacant land paved over as parking lots along Market Street was, ironically, a new form of urban blight.

In the wake of UCSC failures, fraying university-community relations, and Penn's changing financial picture, the WPC withered. As noted, Penn was in the throes of a budget crisis the extent of which was revealed when Martin Meyerson replaced Gaylord Harnwell as president in 1970. Harnwell continued to serve as WPC board president after his presidency at Penn ended, but Meyerson, who had instigated the WPC's founding in 1956, showed little interest in the body and attended few of its meetings.[6] Penn continued to be the key institutional player in the WPC through the end of the 1970s, providing the largest single share ($40,000) of the organization's budget of $145,000 in 1979–1980. Acknowledging the community's misgivings about the WPC, the university attempted to reform the institution by adding community members to its board. A 1977 amendment to the corporation's bylaws provided for two classes of membership: active and associate, with the active members being the universities and hospitals and the associates local nonprofit, business, and educational leaders.[7] As it gave no voting rights to associate members, this structure hardly differed from the existing two-tiered board and did little to change the perception that the WPC represented the institutions, not the community. Not until Sheldon Hackney succeeded Meyerson as president in 1981 would Penn reconfigure the WPC into a body that invited more community input—and renew its interest in the affairs of its neighborhood.[8]

A Failed Promise of Community Development

The 1969 sit-in at Penn ended when the university gave community members a voice in future redevelopment through the QPC. The organization's charter began on a contrite note: "The Trustees declare a policy of accountability and responsibility that accepts the concerns and aspirations of the surrounding communities as its own concerns and aspirations."[9] Though not an apology, the statement suggested that Penn had hitherto failed to include the community in its plans and was instituting the QPC by way of making amends. But which community members would be heard, and how much?

The body was called the Quadripartite Commission because it was to represent four constituencies: students, faculty, community members, and trustees. With five representatives from each group, the QPC's numeric makeup was skewed toward the university, a fact that would spur conflict. Community representatives included the leaders of organizations from Mantua, the predominately Black neighborhood just north of where the Black Bottom had once stood. Among them were Herman Wrice of the Young Great Society, Andrew Jenkins of Mantua Community Planners, and Lorenzo Graham and Reverend Edward Sims of Renewal Housing Incorporated. As noted above, during the 1969 sit-in, Ira Harkavy had cultivated cooperation and friendship with them.[10] Yet, minutes from QPC meetings between April 1969 and February 1971 show that these neighborhood leaders quickly began to express dissatisfaction over how well the community was represented in the body.[11]

The charter pledged material support to the QPC's mission, both by funding the organization's operations at the rate of $75,000 per year (more than $630,000 in 2025) and by establishing a "community renewal" fund of $10 million. The ambiguous language in which this commitment was expressed, along with the QPC's lopsided makeup, would contribute to the organization's downfall:

> In keeping with the principle of accountability and responsibility of the University to the surrounding community the members of the Board of Trustees individually and collectively agree to concert their efforts through the corporations, businesses, institutions and agencies to which they have access, to develop the funds and funding sources needed for community renewal programs with the goal of establishing a community development fund with resources of $10,000,000.[12]

What community members and students read as a payment of $10 million, trustees read as a pledge to raise $10 million.

The QPC's one accomplishment was to develop a vision of better development in West Philadelphia. This vision was revealed to the public at a presentation at Penn's architecture school on three successive Saturdays in September and October 1969. The presentation was in the form of a planning charrette—a working session in which a planner proposes ideas and the client gives feedback—except that the client was the West Philadelphia community. It was more inclusive than presentations the city had made in the early 1960s, which laid out the WPC's plans as a fait accompli. And it was more equitable in its approach than Bacon's Better Philadelphia because those making the proposals were not members of the architectural elite but rather representatives of community groups affected by the designs.

The QPC asked representatives from the Young Great Society, an organization based in Mantua, a neighborhood adjacent to the Black Bottom, to produce the charrette. Together with another community group, the Mantua Community Planners, the Young Great Society had formed the Architecture and Planning Center (APC) to produce neighborhood development plans and renovate houses. Historian Stefan Bradley writes in *Upending the Ivory Tower: Civil Rights, Black Power, and the Ivy League* that the Mantua Community Planners sought to prevent houses in its neighborhood from being labeled "blighted" and taken by urban renewal.[13] Operating under its auspices, the APC completed thirty such rehabilitation efforts in 1969 and expected to finish nearly 120 by 1970.[14] Its staff included university faculty and students as well as community members—including Forrest Adams, mentioned in Chapter 2 as a trained planner and leader of the Mantua-Powelton Minischool. Thus, the staff who prepared the charrette were experienced in the field and part of the neighborhood for which they were designing.

The plan produced did not discard the WPC effort to create a science incubator in West Philadelphia but improved on it by accommodating neighborhood residents. In the preface to the booklet that accompanied the charrette, Adams and his collaborators expressed the intent to ask the City Planning Commission and current owners of land in Unit 3 to modify their plans in a way that would allow those living in the neighborhood to remain there:

> The goal of the Charette was to reconcile the community's needs for additional low-income housing with existing institutional commitments in the area. Upon approval by the Commission, the final planning study will be published and formal changes in the Redevelopment Plan for Unit 3 sought.[15]

What followed was a forty-six-page document filled with maps, photographs, renderings, data tables, and explanations that outlined a plan to create four hundred units of affordable housing in scattered sites within and on the borders of Unit 3.[16] As well as addressing housing scarcity, the charrette's goals included demonstrating a "cooperative relationship of institutional and residential uses of the area's land" and suggesting ways the universities and hospitals could "invest their resources in attempting to solve some of the problems of the surrounding neighborhoods."[17] Notably, the document's professionalism shielded it from the kind of criticism Leo Molinaro had leveled at the alternative plan the University City Citizens Development Corporation (UCCDC) had offered in 1963. With trained planners on staff, the APC created a proposal aligned with contemporary practices in architecture and design, emphasizing such concerns as the compatibility of new structures with existing ones and the transitions between neighborhood spaces. As its creators had no profit-making interest in the design, the proposal was not subject to conflict of interest accusations like those Molinaro had made of UCCDC leader John Clay.

By a vote in January 1969, Penn's board of trustees indicated its agreement with the principles outlined in the APC planning document.[18] It made no specific commitment to turn over parcels of land for low-income housing development. However, Penn's administration was, by this point, disappointed with the UCSC's lack of progress in finding research and development clients for the land it had cleared in the Black Bottom. The university recognized that the demolitions had come at great cost to its reputation, and it was under pressure to make good on the WPC's promise to bring benefits to the community. It therefore proposed that some Unit 3 parcels under the control of Presbyterian Hospital and the UCSC be turned over to low-income housing use. When the UCSC balked, members of the QPC pushed back. Under threat of a community-wide protest, Penn pressured the UCSC to go along with the plan.[19] Unfortunately, the QPC dissolved in 1971 with the promise of affordable housing unfulfilled.[20]

The catalyst for the city to finally build a low-income housing project on the UCSC parcels, ironically enough, was Mayor Frank Rizzo's reactionary housing policy. Rizzo vehemently opposed the building of housing projects for Black people in White neighborhoods, yet he did not want to forgo federal housing grants. Building a project in a part of West Philadelphia that was largely empty was likely a more palatable way to use those dollars than building one in, say, South Philadelphia, where his largely working-class White supporters lived. The city advanced the plan to build the University City Townhomes in the 1970s, and the seventy-three-unit project was finally initiated in 1981. In an arrangement with the city, the UCSC leased land to a private developer, IBID, for $1, and IBID used federal dollars to build the townhomes. This arrangement continued until the federal housing contract expired in 2021; despite great opposition by the community, the land was sold off for market-rate development.[21]

The QPC design charrette was an opportunity missed. Its proposal incorporated appropriately designed affordable housing into the existing WPC plan for research facilities and schools, which would have enabled Black residents to live in the neighborhood and benefit from University City jobs and educational opportunities. The charrette also modeled true engagement in the city planning process, allowing community-based planners to have input alongside elite planners. Instead of the four hundred housing units proposed, the community got seventy-three in a plot isolated both visually and geographically from other structures in the neighborhood.

Outreach to Engagement

The 1969 protest and QPC process that grew out of it did not repair the damage inflicted by WPC-initiated displacements. The QPC did, however, facilitate connections between student protest leader Ira Harkavy and community leaders like Walter Palmer, Andrew Jenkins, Herman Wrice, Lorenzo Graham, and Edward Sims. After returning to Penn to earn his Ph.D. in history, Harkavy would parlay those connections into a new, more equitable approach to university-community relations. Where the WPC-era efforts were one-way, with Penn reaching out to offer help to a less-privileged community, Harkavy engaged the community in dialogue, developing programs around community members' stated needs and interests. A focus on engagement rather than outreach would be the hallmark of Harkavy's work at the Netter Center for Community Partnerships, which became a nationwide model for civic engagement at universities.

Though in the 1970s, Penn diminished the WPC's role as a redevelopment mechanism, the university would later seek ways to continue the forays into community relations the corporation had made in the 1960s. In its efforts to retool the local school system, the WPC had posited an expanded role for the university in which professors and students moved beyond the ivory tower and into the neighborhood. The founders of the WPC had made this idea manifest by planning, during the early 1960s, "a series of Town and Gown seminars on new civic responsibilities of higher education":

> Higher education in America traditionally has been conceived as instructional and research functions carried on outside the context of urban life. A great majority of institutions of higher learning in America have self-consciously avoided identification with the city, physically, and with the civic arts and sciences, intellectually. . . . The

University of Pennsylvania is exceptionally well-qualified to undertake general sponsorship of this project. . . . It needs only be stated
that this project would aid immensely the West Philadelphia area.[22]

Tainted by the organization's inequitable redevelopment schemes, the WPC's
high-minded goals bore no fruit. Yet in the 1980s, Penn would find a way of
parlaying these ambitions into a new structure disconnected from those
schemes. In 1983, Penn president Sheldon Hackney reconstituted the WPC
as the West Philadelphia Partnership, an advisory body with community
representation.[23] That year, Hackney also created the Office of Community
Oriented Policy Studies in Penn's School of Arts and Sciences and made Ira
Harkavy its leader.[24]

Harkavy organized the first "academically based community service"
(ABCS) course in 1985, cotaught by President Hackney and historian Lee
Benson, which expanded on the idea of service learning. In a traditional
service-learning course, the student completes a community project alongside their academic investigation; ABCS made that project the focus of the
investigation. Students were asked to reflect on what they had learned in the
field and develop a new understanding of how to attack societal ills. It was
a social science course with a dose of John Dewey's "learning by doing."[25]

The course's first cohort crafted an idea for a youth organization, the
West Philadelphia Improvement Corps (WEPIC), that would offer its services to neighborhood associations and community leaders under the West
Philadelphia Partnership umbrella.[26] This approach underwent a sudden
and extreme test in the summer of 1985, when the MOVE bombing and fire
shook Philadelphia. A militant group that blended Afrocentrism with a
back-to-nature philosophy, MOVE had barricaded itself into a row house in
the West Philadelphia neighborhood of Cobbs Creek. To break the siege, the
police department deployed an explosive device that set the house ablaze.
Firefighters stood by, allowing the flames to consume two entire blocks.
Eleven MOVE members died in the conflagration, and hundreds of residents
were left homeless. Said Steve Harmon, a neighborhood resident interviewed
by the New York Times, "Drop a bomb on a residential area? I never in my life
heard of that. It's like Vietnam."[27] Lois Gelfand, a student at Penn at the
time, recalled the experience of being on campus while the city seemed to
be on fire: "We were sitting in front of the library and we saw the smoke and
then all of our friends were getting calls from people all over the world—'are
you okay?'"[28] The incident cast Philadelphia under an international spot-
light—revealing the depth the city had fallen in allowing neighborhoods to
deteriorate and the power of the police to go unchecked.

In the wake of the MOVE bombing, the WEPIC crew went to work in
nearby schools—first Bryant Elementary School, later Turner Middle School

and West Philadelphia High School (WPHS).[29] A key factor in WEPIC's ability to work successfully in these schools was Harkavy's connection to well-placed teachers, including Marie Bogle at Bryant. Marie's husband, Robert Bogle, was president of the *Philadelphia Tribune*, the Black newspaper that under E. Washington Rhodes's leadership had spoken out against school segregation and discrimination. Marie Bogle introduced Harkavy to principals and teachers at other schools, enabling the program to grow quickly.[30] Penn students trained and worked with K–12 students on projects ranging from landscaping to community health care to the restoration of a pipe organ in one of the school buildings. Over the next several years, WEPIC acquired grants for projects from federal, state, and local sources.[31] This model, in which university and school students collaborate on projects tied to faculty research and supported by grant funding, would become the hallmark of the ABCS approach.

ABCS blossomed with Anthropology 310, "Nutrition, Health, and Community Schools," which resulted in neighborhood-wide efforts to improve health. Taught by nutritional anthropologist Francis E. Johnston, the course had Penn students gather data on public school students' diet and health and map their food sources. Based on the information gathered, participants crafted several interventions including vegetable and fruit stands, fitness nights, and ultimately, the production and sale of healthy foods by the K–12 students. These interventions spawned the Agatston Urban Nutrition Institute (AUNI), a donor-funded project that continues to this day.[32] Meanwhile, Harkavy and his staff encouraged other professors to offer ABCS courses, morphing the WEPIC idea into the Center for Community Partnerships, renamed the Netter Center in 2007 after donors Barbara and Edward Netter.[33] The ABCS idea was at the forefront of a push during the 1990s for civically engaged college campuses. This movement reached a pinnacle in 1999, when the Campus Compact brought fifty-one college presidents together to endorse civic engagement.[34]

Certain ABCS courses attempted to deal with fallout from the destruction of the Black Bottom. Two examples from 1998 to 1999, both arts focused, were Billy Yalowitz's spring 1998 course "Community Performance in West Philadelphia" and Andrea Zemel's "Community, Collaborative, and Public Art." Penn students in these courses collaborated with public school students from UCHS, whose principal at the time was James Lytle. Mentioned in Chapter 2 as a member of the 1960s reformist administration of Mark Shedd, Lytle would later teach at Penn's Graduate School of Education (GSE). His tenure as UCHS principal was a glimmer of hope in the otherwise troubled history of the school. Yalowitz and Zemel attempted to honor the memory of the Black Bottom by having students create theater and artwork based on stories collected from former residents. Yalowitz's course developed *Black*

Bottom Sketches, performed by residents and students at the UCHS auditorium, the nearby Metropolitan Baptist Church, the Annenberg Center for the Performing Arts at Penn, and the studio of PBS affiliate WHYY.[35] In the first iteration of Zemel's course, her students and their UCHS collaborators created *Gatekeepers*, a pair of sculptures mounted on plinths flanking the school's entrance.[36] In the class's second iteration, the group created the mosaic *Black Bottom Memorial Wall* based on history they learned from Yalowitz's *Black Bottom Sketches*.[37]

Though the art these two UCHS-based ABCS courses created belied WPC leader Leo Molinaro's claim that the Black Bottom had no "neighborhood identification," the courses did little to alter the fate of that community or of the ill-conceived UCHS. The political and socioeconomic forces behind the Black Bottom's destruction and the subsequent gentrification of West Philadelphia were too great to be repelled by a pair of art projects—or, for that matter, the myriad other ABCS programs, no matter how well conceived or executed. As we see in a subsequent chapter, UCHS was closed in 2013 and its sculptures removed. Many of the other sites Netter designated as University Assisted Community Schools, too, have since closed. Nevertheless, with the ABCS model of engagement, Penn had discovered a formula for relating to the community that was more credible than the WPC-sponsored outreach of the 1960s. ABCS courses were disconnected from real estate development. They were carried out on the initiative of faculty members rather than at the behest of university administration. The organizer of the program, Ira Harkavy, was a trusted figure who had taken the community's position in the 1969 protests. The ABCS model showed that a university could make serious efforts to improve public education and deal with social problems.

Rock Bottom

The ten-year period following the 1985 MOVE bombing was a low point for West Philadelphia's reputation. Citywide economic decline and White flight had taken hold. In West Philadelphia, the UCSC had failed to deliver on the WPC's promises of jobs and economic development. Hopelessness in the neighborhood fueled the crack epidemic, leading to a spate of street crime.[38]

Such problems were regarded as a fact of life by residents, Black and White. Teresa Esch, who worked as a technician in Penn's Department of Biochemistry and Biophysics from 1988 to 1990, said that car break-ins were so common near her apartment on 41st and Pine Streets that residents would leave their cars unlocked and glove compartments open to avoid having their windows broken.[39] Jacqui Bowman, a resident who was born in the UK and moved to Philadelphia in 1993, said that when she announced her intention to live in West Philadelphia, her husband's colleagues at Penn's school of veterinary medicine said, "You've got to be mad; you can't live there." When she was appointed research associate at the Penn Museum in 1995, she recalled that on her walk from 46th and Spruce Street to campus, a stretch at 43rd Street made her "really nervous."[40] This stretch is where the highly sought-after Penn Alexander School (PAS) is today.

Notably, the areas these individuals described as dangerous were in the Spruce Hill section of West Philadelphia, which, as mentioned, was a predominantly White and middle-class area. It is likely that the neighborhood had declined since the WPC first tried to stabilize it by promoting homeownership and school attendance there. This decline mirrored that of the entire city, which during the period 1980–2000 lost 10 percent of its population. The loss was racially skewed, with 30 percent of the city's White residents exiting during this period.[41] As in the 1950s, hope came with the rise of a new city government—and in West Philadelphia, a new approach to university-community relations.

The administration of Mayor Ed Rendell (1992–2000) ushered in a fresh approach to running the moribund city. Where New Deal–oriented mayors Clark and Dilworth had used federal urban renewal dollars to make redevelopment projects profitable for private developers, Rendell championed a neoliberal approach, relying on tax incentives, deregulation, and private investment. The new mayor also spurred the creation of the Center City District (CCD), a business improvement district that provided services in central Philadelphia such as security patrols, trash cleanup, enhanced public spaces, and a public relations campaign to promote commerce and tourism.[42] Essentially a shadow government that used contributions from businesses to supplement less-than-adequate city services, CCD ran under the umbrella of the nonprofit Central Philadelphia Development Corporation (CPDC). CPDC was, in fact, a renamed version of the Old Philadelphia Development Corporation (OPDC), the entity that had supported the redevelopment of Society Hill during the 1950s and 1960s.[43]

As had happened decades earlier, crime spurred the powers that be in West Philadelphia to act alongside their Center City counterparts. A pair of murders in West Philadelphia—Penn math Ph.D. candidate Al-Moez Alimohamed in 1994 and Penn biophysics research assistant Vladimir Sled in 1996—caused an uproar in the university community. A group known as Penn Faculty and Staff for Neighborhood Issues (PFSNI) called on recently appointed Penn president Judith Rodin to address underlying problems it believed were the cause of increased crime. Rather than merely beefing up campus security, PFSNI demanded "strategic financial involvement and engagement of academic resources to assist the revitalization of West Philadelphia."[44] In a 1993 report, this group called for the creation of "a viable public-school alternative within the local neighborhood."[45]

The Rise of the West Philadelphia Initiatives

As in the late 1950s, Penn's administration took its cues from its brethren in city government. Responding to neighborhood pressure, Rodin formulated a series of market-oriented interventions, the West Philadelphia Initiatives (WPI), that resembled Rendell's neoliberal program. Penn converted empty land acquired under urban renewal in the 1960s into retail and entertainment complexes. Together with Drexel University, Amtrak, and other neighborhood players, the university created its own business improvement district, the University City District (UCD). Like the CCD, the UCD improved the condition of streets and public spaces, creating an inviting environment for businesses and residents. It deployed a force of unarmed "ambassadors" to give residents a greater sense of security on the streets. It launched shuttle bus services to supplement existing public transportation, which was often viewed as inadequate and unsafe. Among its most successful interventions was the improvement of green spaces, including the neighborhood's largest recreation area, Clark Park. Through the efforts of nonprofit partners such as UC Green and Friends of Clark Park, the WPI converted a shadowy and neglected space into a neighborhood focal point.[46] As the author can attest, before WPI took hold, drugs and crime were rampant in the park. Jacqui Bowman, who as mentioned moved to the neighborhood in 1993, recalled, "We would go to the playground, and you know, there might be like drug paraphernalia around."[47] By the end of the first decade of the twenty-first century, the park was teeming with activity with weekly farmers markets, fairs, and outdoor performances and had up-to-date playground equipment for families with young children.[48]

In promoting the WPI, Rodin donned the mantle of urban idealism. She began her memoir of the endeavor, *The University and Urban Revival: Out of the Ivory Tower and into the Streets*, with a quote from Jane Jacobs extolling the virtues of diversity in a city. She referred throughout the book to the urbanist practices Jacobs championed, such as mixed-used development and an "eyes on the street" approach to fostering neighborhood civility. Noting that she was a product of Columbia University in the 1960s, she stated her opposition to that institution's strong-arm development tactics, which led to the disastrous 1968 protests. She declared vehemently that WPI did not mean neighborhood takeover and that Penn "would never again expand" into contiguous areas and displace their residents.[49]

The reason Rodin could declare that Penn would never again expand, however, was that there was already land aplenty from the WPC's 1960s expansions. By building on that land and making no substantive efforts to retain West Philadelphia's Black population, Penn was consummating the WPC agenda. The WPC's statements of intent from 1960s and Penn's from the 1990s were markedly similar. In its founding document, the WPC declared,

> The WPC establishes as a core purpose—a community which holds and attracts institutional and cultural facilities, compatible industrial and commercial uses, standard and marketable residential areas served by adequate schools, parks, churches and shopping.[50]

Rodin's description of WPI intentions also emphasized neighborhood amenities: "We would encourage retail development by attracting new shops, restaurants, and cultural venues that were neighborhood friendly. We would improve the public schools." Rodin claimed that her interventions were different because her administration was "committed to a spirit of seeking true partnership." Recall, however, that the WPC also sought partnership, cultivating relationships with community organizations and conducting studies to discern neighbors' preferences. Like the WPC, the WPI regarded some partners as more critical than others.

An aspect of Rodin's WPI that was different was its emphasis on market-based interventions: "We would spur economic development by directing university contracts and purchases to local businesses, many of which we would help to initiate." She set up, for example, buy and hire West Philadelphia programs that she said reversed Penn's track record of purchasing "hundreds of millions of dollars" per year on goods and services but little from local businesses and workers. Her administration found use for the yet-undeveloped land acquired under urban renewal in the 1960s, creating a supermarket, movie theater, bookstore, and hotel on areas used as parking lots. Rodin's key market investment was in housing for Penn employees. Her administration revived a moribund mortgage guarantee program that enabled university affiliates to purchase homes at favorable interest rates with low down payments. Where in the past, the program had enabled buyers to choose homes in Center City, under Rodin, it focused exclusively on West Philadelphia.[51] Penn professors and staff could obtain loans of up to $21,000 for principal and closing costs and an additional $7,500 for home improvements. These loans were forgiven over seven years if the buyer continued to live in the house. So successful was the program at jumpstarting the housing market that in 2004, Penn scaled it back.[52] I utilized the mortgage guarantee program to purchase a house in University City.

Despite rhetoric promising not to repeat past wrongs, Rodin-era development initiatives did much to advantage predominantly White university affiliates and little to boost Black people who had been set back by those wrongs. The mortgage guarantee program is a key example. As the neighborhood's Black residents were less likely to be employed at Penn and much more likely to be renters, they were generally excluded from the program. All told, the WPI's market-based initiatives were an example of what Keeanga-Yamahtta Taylor has called "predatory inclusion." In this situation, Black people are theoretically included in market-based opportunities White people have long enjoyed, but nothing is done to correct setbacks from previous racial injustices. The result of predatory inclusion is typically that Black people fall further behind.[53] In the case of West Philadelphia, past university actions, which dealt Black people out of the prosperity of the postindustrial economy, contributed to the setbacks.

Thus, market economics became the powerful tool Rodin needed to fulfill the promise, made by Edmund Bacon in 1947 and reiterated by the WPC in 1959, of creating University City as an area "compatible" with educational and medical institutions. Cheap land in hand, Penn could make targeted investments in neighborhood amenities and expect returns in the form of increased property values. With those gains, it was only natural to expect responsible residents to flock to the neighborhood. Absent the WPC-era bulldozers, few people realized that other residents were being displaced. Few acknowledged that the inability of Black people to afford the area they once called home was the legacy of centuries of oppression—first slavery and Jim Crow, then redlining, and ultimately urban renewal displacement. The remake of the neighborhood appeared to result from the ebb and flow of market opportunities.

Shops, restaurants, clean streets, and parks would not suffice to bring that influx of responsible residents to West Philadelphia. To attract better educated and more affluent families, Rodin knew, like the WPC before her, that she would have to change the schools. The WPC had failed miserably at that task, but Penn had since learned much about university-community relations that could help it succeed. It knew, for example, that faculty had to be willing participants. They had to view community engagement as an integral part of their research and teaching rather than an extra burden given by administration. It knew too that the school district had to be a willing partner rather than an obstruction. And it knew that any effort to change the schools would have to avoid the appearance of creating boutique learning for Penn affiliates while leaving the rest of the system in a sorry state. Taking advantage of these learnings and of a favorable political and economic climate, Penn embarked on a round of school interventions that would succeed beyond expectations.

6

A Jewel in Gentrification's Crown

Without a doubt, the key accomplishment of the Rodin-era initiatives was the creation of a university-partnered public school that would become one of the best in the state. It would also cinch the gentrification of the university area of West Philadelphia. In the wake of this school-building project, the neighborhood would see a spike in property values and rental rates unmatched by any other area of the city. It would actualize the 1960s agenda of the West Philadelphia Corporation (WPC) in a way that Leo Molinaro, WPC executive vice president, could never have imagined. After the creation of the Sadie Tanner Mosell Alexander University of Pennsylvania Partnership School (PAS), university planners would never again have to worry that Penn would be surrounded by a "band of blight," as Edmund Bacon and Martin Meyerson feared during the 1940s and 1950s.

To create from whole cloth a good-quality urban public school, the 1990s Penn administration could not err in the way the WPC had in its 1960s school initiatives. The dreams of making H. C. Lea a destination school for university- and hospital-affiliated parents and of creating a progressive, science-focused University City High School (UCHS) had failed on account of reluctant faculty and staff participation, poor relationships with the Philadelphia Federation of Teachers (PFT), mishandling of enrollment policies, and inconsistent funding.

While not without mistakes, the creation of PAS avoided these pitfalls. Dean of Penn Graduate School of Education (GSE) Susan Fuhrman supported the project and selected associate dean Nancy Streim, who had years of experience in the field, to spearhead the school's development. Streim believed that the school would be a model, a "demonstration of how a university could work together with the school system."[1] Other faculty, including social policy and practice professor Dennis Culhane, contributed extensively to the project.[2]

Penn gained the cooperation of the PFT, which allowed teachers to be picked based on the planning group's criteria rather than on seniority, as was customary. Of the PFT officials with whom Streim worked, she said that "they wanted to demonstrate that they were forward thinking and open-minded and that their union contracts could accommodate innovation."[3] The university secured a $325 million planning grant from the Pew Charitable Trusts and fronted the $19 million needed to construct a new building, with the understanding that the state would reimburse Penn and the SDP would lease the land for the nominal amount of $1. Penn also agreed to provide a subsidy of $1,000 per pupil ($700,000 per year total), later raised to $1,330.[4] With strong staffing and generous funding, PAS had the makings of a successful town-gown partnership.

The university's funding of PAS came during the height of economic desperation for the SDP. As education scholar Camika Royal has shown, conflict with state authorities exacerbated the district's economic woes, which had emerged in the 1970s and intensified in the following two decades. The administration of Superintendent David Hornbeck, who began his tenure in 1994, was marked by huge budget shortfalls that reached $115 million by academic year 1995–1996. Appalled by the funding gap between Philadelphia and other districts in Pennsylvania, which at that time averaged $1,500–$2,000 per pupil, Hornbeck denounced the state's funding system as "slavery" and "apartheid." With the legislature and governor's office in the hands of Republicans, the liberal superintendent's outbursts backfired. By 2001, Hornbeck was ousted and the bankrupt district turned over to state control.[5] Hornbeck's miscalculations bore some resemblance to Mark Shedd's from thirty years earlier, which resulted in a similar confrontation with conservative forces. This time, however, they worked to Penn's advantage. A district administration in need of cash and good news was eager to cooperate with the Ivy League school on what seemed like a promising school-building project.

Despite having absorbed lessons from previous school-building experiences, the creation of PAS in the twenty-first century would ultimately divide neighbors as much as WPC projects had in the twentieth. A sign of this tension was the unease I encountered when asking questions about the school. I approached many parents who, like me, had sent their children to PAS during its early years. Most were eager to talk at first, but when I reviewed interview transcripts with them, many rescinded their participation. None of the Black parents I interviewed agreed to be included in the book, some expressing worry about reprisals from Penn. All conveyed an awareness that they were entering a minefield where giving the wrong response could earn them the label "gentrifier"—or worse.

Whose School Is It?

In her book *The University and Urban Revival*, Rodin gave a blunt account of the displacements the WPC had caused and promised not to repeat them. She also recounted the failure of the University City Science Center (UCSC) to produce real economic benefits in West Philadelphia. She did not, however, mention the Universities-Related Program (URP), and she described UCHS as a "public-school initiative with which [Penn] had been involved to a limited degree."[6] As we saw in Chapter 4, it was Penn, through the WPC, that had generated the idea for UCHS—and UCHS that provided a pretext for Black Bottom demolitions. Nevertheless, in their creation of PAS, Rodin and her team showed an uncanny awareness of the problems the WPC had encountered with its school interventions and employed careful calculations to avoid them. PAS planners would not be caught red-handed trying to exclude anyone from their school or splitting the school in two, with one track for university affiliates and another for the rest. They would create a school that appealed to university families, but it would not be a university school.

Rodin and her team rejected the idea of creating a private school. They could have expanded the University City New School, a private, progressive school that served many Penn-affiliated families. Since 1975, this school occupied a space on the 4200 block of Locust Street, on the campus of the former Philadelphia Divinity School in the Spruce Hill Neighborhood. Though it drew many students from Penn faculty families, the New School was diverse in its racial and socioeconomic makeup.[7] During the late 1990s, the university offered tuition assistance in the amount of $2,000 to faculty, staff, and hospital employees whose children attended the school.[8] With its progressive curriculum and subsidized tuition, it was exactly the type of school proposed by the university council during the 1960s as an alternative to the WPC's floundering URP. Despite the risks involved in abandoning this well-liked private school, PAS planners were willing to return to the idea of intervening in the public school system.

Because the New School was located precisely where PAS was to go, opening one school meant closing the other. Jacqui Bowman, mentioned in the previous chapter, was a Penn-affiliated parent who sent her son to the New School before PAS was created. She said of the school, "We loved it, so

obviously we were not the happiest when we heard Penn Alexander was going to displace it."[9] In supplanting the New School, the PAS planners knew
they would have to incorporate enough of its progressive program and diversity to lure its constituents.

They would also avoid creating a laboratory school. They rejected any
school concept that appeared to serve Penn's GSE or Penn-affiliated families
more than the general population.[10] And they declined to reintroduce interventions at the nearby Lea School. Recall that these 1960s and 1970s initiatives, including the WPC's URP and the parent-led programs like the Lea
Learning Lab, resulted in the carving out of separate tracks or programs for
privileged groups.

Like the WPC before it, Rodin's team involved community members and
organizations in planning the project. It organized three committees to
shape PAS: one concerned with the building, another with the curriculum,
and a third with community programming. Nancy Streim chaired the third
one, the education committee.[11] According to historians Puckett and Lloyd,
these committees were racially but not socioeconomically diverse.[12]

Also like the WPC, Rodin's planners listened most closely to representatives from the neighborhoods they wanted to preserve and improve. Recall the
language from the WPC employee appraisal of community relations coordinator Barry Freeman: "In areas of University City where rehabilitation will
be more prevalent, as opposed to redevelopment (such as the Spruce Hill
Area) it will be desirable to develop more intensive forms of involving residents in the process." The PAS team, and the WPI in general, was similarly
attentive to the needs of Spruce Hill. Its elegant Victorian homes were in decline in the 1990s, and, as noted in the previous chapter, it saw an increase
in crime. Rodin referenced a plan developed by the Spruce Hill Community Association that described the neighborhood as "a quintessential Philadelphia place that overflows with the greatest American architecture" as
key to the formation of the WPI.[13] Spruce Hill was a critical asset in the minds
of Penn's administration.

PAS parent Keally McBride, then a postdoctoral fellow at Penn and later
a visiting professor at Temple, was on the Spruce Hill Community Association zoning committee during the early 2000s. She recalled a taut relationship between Penn and the association:

> What was mostly happening at Spruce Hill zoning committee . . .
> was we had some kind of oversight over Penn's development, which
> is unbelievable from my perspective now. Different architects and
> planners from Penn would have to come and pitch, "This is what we
> want to build." And we had to sign off on it.[14]

It is not surprising, then, that Nancy Streim included Spruce Hill Community Association president Barry Grossbach on the PAS education committee—just as the WPC had included Grossbach's predecessor, Joseph Moloznick, on its board.[15] Behind the actions of the 1990s-era Penn administration was the same motivation that underlay the WPC's: stabilize the areas where university- and hospital-affiliates lived, stave off encroaching blight.

Since the school was purported to be for everyone, where it would draw its student body from was a critical decision. Planners selected social scientist Dennis Culhane, a professor at Penn's School of Social Policy and Practice, to research neighborhood populations and recommend a boundary. A specialist in housing policy with extensive knowledge of data analytics, Culhane was also a West Philadelphia resident who had enrolled his own children in the New School. Through his work as director of Penn's Cartographic Modeling Lab, Culhane had access to SDP data on all families living in the neighborhoods adjacent to the university, including those that enrolled their children in public schools and those that did not. He used this data to make a recommendation about which blocks to include to fill the seven hundred seats available in the new school. The most important constraint on the selection, he said, was the SDP's rule that no block adjacent to an existing school could be selected.[16] The process of setting the catchment boundaries did not play out without controversy. In comparison, however, to the prolonged indecision regarding the feeder pattern for UCHS during the 1960s, decisions about PAS's enrollment were taken with strategic acumen.

Penn planners understood that if their efforts resulted in a racially segregated school, the project would fail. According to Streim, "If the lines were going to be drawn so that it was just Spruce Hill, which was primarily White, we weren't interested." There was also a worry that the school would fail if not enough Penn families chose to enroll their children there. Regarding the racial mix of the school, Streim said,

> The literature suggested, at the time, that it would be beneficial to have in the neighborhood of 30 percent White families in order to hold on to the diversity. That if it tipped too far in one direction, then whoever was in the small minority would opt out. If it were only 10 percent White or 15 percent White, then most White families wouldn't choose to go.[17]

Culhane vehemently denied that any such measures had been used to eliminate Black families from the enrollment boundary: "I never heard any interest in reducing the number of Black students who would be in that school. . . . I only heard those kinds of statements or comments from critics of the school who were not involved in the process." He averred that, if an area was ex-cluded from the catchment, it was because of the district rule that no block in one school's catchment be directly in front of another school—or, in some cases, because a block contained such a large population of families with children that it would have exceeded the available seats. Yet Culhane did not deny that the planners desired a certain racial balance in the PAS popula-tion: "We were most definitely hopeful that it was majority Black."[18]

Parents in the community were also concerned about the school's racial balance. Penn's 1990s planners came to the same realization as the WPC in the 1960s regarding constituents' preference for diversity. Recall the results of the 1963 WPC study, which found that "our sample leans towards hetero-geneity in their ideal neighborhood community."[19] The Penn planners cor-rectly intuited among their mostly White, progressive-minded faculty and staff a desire to send their children to a diverse school. Many, in fact, had moved to West Philadelphia specifically so their children could experience diversity.[20]

Among those parents, there was still discomfort about sending their chil-dren to a school where they would be in the minority. Jacqui Bowman en-rolled her son at PAS in grade 5, after he experienced a multicultural envi-ronment at the University City New School and a public school in California. Bowman said of his experience at PAS, "I think it was quite challenging for the few White kids. I think they felt a little separate. Because they were only a handful in each year at that point." Her daughter, however, who enrolled as a kindergartener, had fond memories of the class makeup at PAS. Bow-man said that it did not even register with her that she was the only White child in her grade 1 class.[21] Another parent from the early years was Rosemary Ford, who was born in the UK and came to Philadelphia to study law at Penn. She recalled that when her daughter enrolled at PAS in 2006, six out of twenty of her grade 4 classmates were White.[22] Any reservations these parents had about the population mix did not stop them from enrolling their children at PAS.

Anticipating that the decision to build the school would be controversial, Penn officials announced it jointly with the SDP and PFT at Penn GSE on June 18, 1998, so that Penn faculty, the news media, neighborhood organiza-tions, and the public would receive word at the same time. In Culhane's view, discussions of the catchment boundaries were quite civil, and his explana-tions of their limitations—the one-block buffer with other schools and the need to not include more children than the school could hold—adequately addressed neighbors' questions. Others had different recollections. In Stre-im's account, "all hell broke loose" when Penn announced its intent to create PAS, a view corroborated by historians John Puckett and Mark Lloyd and recorded in Judith Rodin's memoir on the subject, *The University and Urban*

Revival. According to Streim, "there were any number of nighttime meetings at people's living rooms and in churches where . . . people had a gazillion questions."[23] Rodin recalled,

> No topic was more charged than that of the catchment area, and conversations about it could be overheard everywhere. There were all kinds of meetings, many in private homes with just a small group of residents, some of them held in secrecy. . . . Sometimes the educational issues got lost in the clamor, and the conflict occasionally seemed to be more about who would benefit financially from the inevitable rise in property values in the catchment area than about who would benefit educationally.[24]

That Penn officials witnessed residents arguing about who would be in the catchment—and that the arguments were not just about whose children would go to school where—dispels any doubt about whether Penn was aware that PAS was connected to gentrification.

Some community members took the position that PAS should be a citywide school with enrollment by lottery rather than a neighborhood school—ensuring, on a lasting basis, that it would serve a wider range of students. When the University City Community Council, a coalition of six neighborhood associations, voted to support the lottery plan, the lone dissenter, the Spruce Hill Community Association, withdrew from the group. Penn's decision to make PAS a neighborhood school aligned with Spruce Hill's position. Despite Streim's assertions to the contrary, the catchment was almost entirely within the association's boundaries (see fig. 6.1). The decision provides further evidence that, where neighborhood improvement initiatives were concerned, Spruce Hill was, in the 2000s as in the 1960s, the university's most important constituency.[25]

Asked to join mayor-elect John Street in a West Philadelphia meeting on education, Rodin encountered stiff criticism from those in attendance, who were deeply suspicious of Penn: "Some were quite vocal in their feelings about Penn, arguing that nothing Penn had ever done for the schools in West Philadelphia ever worked, that we were such do-gooders but only did what we wanted to." Had she read the 1960s reports mentioned in this book, such as the 1968 Penn GSE appraisal of Lea School, she would have understood what they meant by "nothing Penn had ever done for the schools in West Philadelphia ever worked."[26]

The catchment PAS planners settled on was, in fact, predominantly Black as of 2000. At that time, the racial makeup of the area was 56 percent African American, 18 percent White, 20 percent Asian, 5 percent Hispanic, and 1 percent Native American.[27] However, the school was located in the

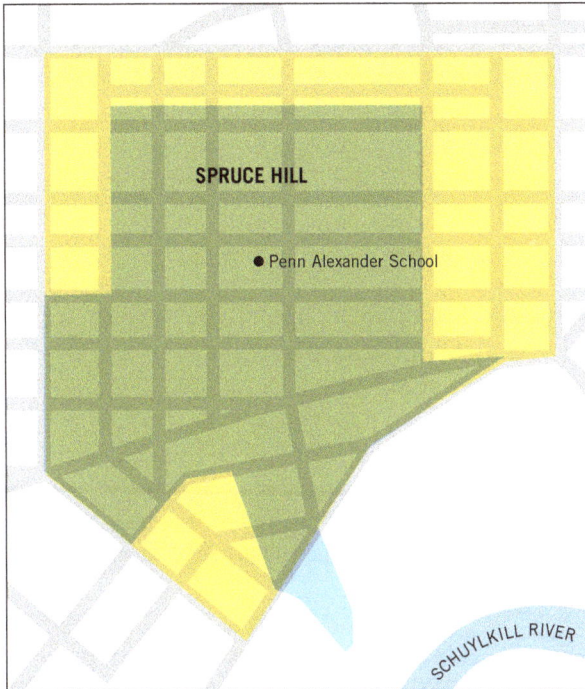

Figure 6.1 Spruce Hill Community Association and PAS catchment. Yellow represents the community association's boundaries, blue, the PAS catchment. Areas of overlap are in green. Blocks to the east not in the catchment are largely student housing. Blocks to the west are directly in front of the H. C. Lea School. (*Map by the author.*)

center of Spruce Hill, on the site of the former Philadelphia Divinity School, in the block bounded by 42nd, 43rd, Locust, and Spruce Streets, owned by Penn since 1977.[28] This location was near St. Mark's Square, described by Carol Williamson in Chapter 2 as "its own little bubble"—a predominantly White area. As gentrification spread to the periphery of Spruce Hill, the catchment's population makeup was bound to change.

In making the case for this location—and dismissing critics' calls for Penn to contribute to existing schools rather than build another one—PAS planners argued that a new, architecturally innovative building in a safe area would better support the school's mission as a "demonstration" school. Moreover, they argued that the new school, which was to function as a community gathering space, would host adult education and recreational activities in the evenings and would therefore not be cut off from its neighborhood.[29] In that regard, PAS planners invoked the concept of the community school, introduced by John Dewey and realized on a wider scale by Frank J. Manley in Flint, Michigan, during the 1930s, funded by the Charles Stewart Mott

Foundation. As noted, Ira Harkavy was an advocate of this model, promoting it at various sites in West Philadelphia where his Center for Community Partnerships was active. Rodin expressed wide-eyed ambition for PAS as a community school, not only hosting "vocational, recreational and adult education programs" but also serving as a "town hall where the community could come together to explore and debate issues and visions of the future."[30]

Footing the Bill

Stable funding would be of critical importance to PAS's success. According to Nancy Streim, to build the $19 million school, the university used its assets to leverage state and city money:

> There was a turnkey arrangement between Penn and the city and the state that the school was going to be built by Penn, for the city, using state dollars, and Penn would front the money, and the state would reimburse the cost of construction, and Penn would own the land but lease it to the school district for a dollar.[31]

The arrangement was not unlike those of the WPC era, wherein Penn's investment in campus expansion projects was matched by federal and state dollars with the stated intent of helping the community. Unlike the WPC, however, Penn in the Rodin era made a long-term commitment to subsidize PAS's operations. Initially, that commitment was $1,000 per student for seven hundred students—a total of $700,000 per year. Streim later raised grant funds on top of the money Penn contributed and garnered in-kind contributions of faculty time. In all, she claimed, the per-student subsidy was closer to $2,000 per pupil per year. The baseline subsidy has continued to the present day; it had climbed, by 2018, to $1,330 per pupil.[32]

As noted, the SDP's woes were Penn's opportunity. Throughout the budget crises of the 1990s, neoliberal elements in the city had proposed charter schools and private funding as remedies for underfunding and underachievement in the SDP. At the time, many of Philadelphia's low-achieving schools were being turned over to private management, often by corporations whose commitment to profit making seemed to exceed their interest in students.[33] In contrast to such radical schemes, Penn's proposal to create a university-funded, district-managed school seemed quite benign, and perhaps that is why it met with few objections. Interestingly, the per-pupil subsidy of PAS, which Streim estimated at $2,000, closely matched the average per-pupil funding gap between the SDP and districts statewide of $1,500–$2,000—the funding gap that Superintendent Hornbeck had so loudly protested to state government. Penn proposed to do in its own backyard what

Hornbeck would have liked to do throughout the SDP: create an urban school with suburban funding levels.

Off to a Good Start

Groundbreaking for PAS took place in March 2001, and the first classes met that fall in the former divinity school while the building was under construction. Selected by a building committee that included community members as well Penn design dean Gary Hack and Penn Facilities and Real Estate Services vice president Omar Blaik, PAS's architect Roy Strickland was internationally known for his work on schools and public spaces. In contrast to the dreary corridors and closed-off spaces of many Philadelphia schools, PAS's central atrium was open and light filled, permitting flexible gatherings as well as traditional classroom learning. The building's architecture (fig. 6.2) was an asset to the school's climate and curriculum[34]—unlike the WPC's school-building experiment, UCHS, in which design became an impediment to discipline.

For the PAS planners, there was a risk that the more affluent, mostly White parents in the neighborhood would not choose PAS for their children. Planners worried that the stigma of the urban public school—no matter how

Figure 6.2 Penn Alexander School. (*Photo by the author.*)

well funded—was so great that many who professed support for such schools would be unwilling to enroll their own children in them. This sentiment is captured in a statement by an SDP official, cited in Maia Cucchiara's *Marketing Schools, Marketing Cities*, about a similar effort to attract affluent families to Center City Philadelphia schools: "I'm willing to dedicate my entire life to this sort of experiment but I'm not going to screw up my kid's education as part of this experiment."[35] Though they ultimately did enroll their children in the school, the PAS parents I spoke to expressed concern about exposing their children to inferior education. Jacqui Bowman, who hailed from the UK and had no direct experience with the matter, was at first reluctant to try PAS because of what she had heard about urban U.S. public schools: "I think that primary concern was that the reputation of the public-school education was that it wasn't as good as it could be."[36] Yet there was also a feeling among these progressive-leaning parents that public education was a just cause. Combined with the knowledge that Penn had had a hand in the creation of PAS, this sentiment was a powerful incentive to choose the new school. It helped tip the balance for Rosemary Ford when she was deciding whether to try PAS or keep her daughter at the Philadelphia School, a private school where her daughter had had an unsatisfactory grade 3 experience. Ford said of her decision, "I believe in public education, period, so I felt like a bit of a hypocrite having my child in private school."[37]

In the end, the knowledge that Penn was making an all-out effort with PAS was enough to convince progressive White parents that the school was a good bet. By the fall of 2004, PAS had a full complement of students from grades K–8. Parents like me moved to West Philadelphia to enroll their children in the school. Another like me was Carola Lelieveld, originally from the Netherlands and living in New York City at the time PAS opened. Lelieveld's husband had family in Philadelphia, and the pair decided to relocate after hearing about PAS. The move aligned with their preference for a diverse, urban neighborhood:

> When we lived in Brooklyn, we really knew we didn't want to move to the suburbs, and we wanted to stay in a city. And it was a factor. But the main thing was that we knew there was going to be a school there and that West Philadelphia was fairly—actually, at the beginning, very—diverse.[38]

The school would quickly gain recognition as one of the top public schools in the state and the nation. As of 2004, 70 percent of its K–5 students were proficient in reading and math, according to standardized test results.[39] In 2016, PAS was awarded a National Blue Ribbon by U.S. secretary of education John King, one of ten Philadelphia-area schools and 329 nationally to win the award. It would win again in 2021, one of seven in the area and 325 nationally.[40] The university and SDP had demonstrated that they could jointly create a quality K–12 school as measured by conventional student achievement criteria.

Teaching Staff and Leadership

As noted, the planners of PAS scored a victory when the PFT allowed them to control the hiring of staff. The school's organizers included parents from the neighborhood on the committees charged with interviewing candidates.[41] Though not every staffing choice was to everyone's liking, the committees clearly chose a capable group. One parent who was generally happy with the teaching staff was Rosemary Ford. As noted, she moved her daughter to PAS after an unsatisfactory grade 3 experience at the private Philadelphia School. She said her child had a "fabulous" experience with grade 3 teacher Alexis Adorno and fond recollections of middle school social studies teacher Chadd Johnson, math teacher Cara Crosby, and science teacher Richard Staniec. The latter encouraged her to enter numerous science competitions, which Ford said improved her child's public presenting skills.[42] Other parents also mentioned these teachers as outstanding. Certain parents remembered kindergarten teacher Penny Silver as one of the best in the school. Keally McBride was effusive about her children's fondness for Ms. Silver:

> And they both had Ms. Silver for kindergarten, and they loved her. They absolutely loved her. I can still remember them talking, much further on, maybe middle school or something, they were like, "Yeah, basically we learned so much in kindergarten it all felt like you were repeating until fourth and fifth grade."[43]

McBride reported that though her children "both had really great kindergarten years," the quality of teaching thenceforth was inconsistent. One had "a really mean first grade teacher and a kind of inept second grade teacher."[44] Jacqui Bowman also found the teaching quality uneven, noting that her daughter's grade 4 teacher was "the best she's ever had" but that her son's grade 5 teacher was "absolutely appalling."[45] Despite these variances, no parent I spoke to found teaching at PAS deficient overall.

Parents' opinions of school leadership also varied. As noted, Penn chose Sheila Sydnor—a Black woman who was a product of the SDP, the WPC-initiated Motivation Program, and Penn GSE—to be the principal. Rosemary Ford appreciated the principal's personal involvement with the school:

"Sheila Sydnor . . . would greet every student every morning by the big glass door. I thought that was a lovely touch. It meant that the students knew her even if they didn't really talk to her other than that."[46] Jacqui Bowman spoke highly of Sydnor's no-nonsense approach to discipline:

> I think she was great. And she was the heart and soul of that place. . . . She just did it all right. She was the right person. She was good with the kids. She was tough with the kids. There was a famous time when, I can't remember which year it was, but there were two kids fighting in the playground, and she just came and pulled them off. I mean she was just really the classic, tough love.[47]

Others were less pleased with Sydnor's approach. Keally McBride, for example, remembered being rebuffed when she approached Sydnor about being more involved in the school: "She gave me the straight-arm. She was kind of like, 'We don't want parents in here messing things up. We don't want parents in here having opinions.'"[48]

It is possible that the undemocratic aspects of Sydnor's leadership style were rooted in long-standing district culture. As we saw in Chapter 2, this authoritarian tendency could be traced to the administration of Superintendent Brumbaugh in the early 1900s, with its emphasis on standardized testing and social efficiency. It was perpetuated by such tyrannical figures as Add Anderson, whose nearly thirty-year rule kept the SDP in the dark ages. It resulted in brusque treatment of parents, as we saw in reports from Rochelle Nichols-Solomon in Chapter 2. A more generous interpretation is that Sydnor's approach was protective. She was following in the footsteps of groundbreaking Black school leaders like Ruth Wright Hayre, who saw the tough love approach as necessary to shield children from a hostile environment. She maintained high expectations in both discipline and academic performance, especially for Black children, in a system that often discounted students' abilities. Either way, Sydnor acted like a typical SDP school leader, leaning toward the strict and away from the permissive.

Progressive versus Traditional Schooling

Sydnor's no-nonsense leadership was one way in which PAS resembled a conventional neighborhood school. According to Streim, it was

> not the goal that it be the kind of lab school where GSE would be trying . . . new things. That is not to say that we didn't want to do those things, but Susan [Fuhrman] very specifically believed in Penn Alexander being a part of the School District of Philadelphia.[49]

Insofar as the PAS curriculum resembled, for the most part, that of other K–8 schools in the district, the planners achieved that goal. PAS did not reconstitute the progressive University City New School in the form of a public school. This choice had positive and negative consequences from the perspective of parents.

For those who wanted a traditional school, PAS fit the bill. One who appreciated the PAS curriculum was Rosemary Ford, whose daughter had a bad experience at the progressive Philadelphia School prior to enrolling in PAS. According to Ford, "She told me 'I want a desk, I want grades.'" Ford reported that her daughter "thrived" in PAS's more structured learning environment when she entered the school in grade 4.[50] Keally McBride would have preferred a more progressive approach. She felt that PAS would have benefited from a closer relationship with Penn GSE:

> I think everyone was really disappointed that the School of Ed didn't seem more involved in Sadie Alexander than they were. I think the promise had been that it would be more like the University of Chicago Lab School or something, where there would be more interaction, more pushing the envelope with innovative teaching.[51]

Though McBride criticized the school in this regard, she found that teachers like Penny Silver—in whose classroom she volunteered—struck a balance between discipline and freedom:

> After lunch, she [Penny Silver] would read them stories and she would let them sleep if they needed to. And there was still a sense of, "Yes, you need to learn the rules and not disturb your classmates. But who you are and what your needs are still being noticed and attended to."[52]

The PAS approach to curriculum and learning was not experimental, nor was it advertised to be. Nevertheless, most parents I spoke to found the culture of the school to be child centered, which, together with strong academics, made for an effective learning environment.

Parental Influence

The question of how much parents should be involved in their children's school is complex. Such involvement anchored progressive schools like the Walnut Street Center and the Mantua-Powelton Minischool to their community and was part of their founding philosophy. In the latter case, parents helped not only with teaching but also with the construction of the school. Yet there has been concern about affluent White parents exerting disproportionate influence or making their intervention in an urban school's curriculum and administrative policies a precondition for enrolling their children there. In her 2014 book *When Middle-Class Parents Choose Urban Schools*, sociologist Linn Posey-Maddox documents the case of an influx of middle-class, predominantly White families in an urban California school. Parents of these families launched fundraising initiatives that brought new amenities to the school, but their interventions made the Black families who were already there feel unwelcome and unheard.[53] In the 2020 *New York Times* podcast "Nice White Parents," journalist Chana Joffe-Walt profiles a group of privileged newcomers who felt it was their prerogative to push curriculum changes at a Brooklyn public school that was courting their children. This case resembles that of West Philadelphia in that it had an antecedent in the 1960s, when an effort to draw White families to the school had failed.[54]

Closer to home, sociologist Maia Cucchiara found that not long after the creation of PAS, Philadelphia's Center City School Initiative (CCSI) pushed the SDP make significant changes at a group of Center City schools to appeal to a target group of upper-middle class parents. Launched in 2004, the CCSI pushed changes to curriculum, facilities, and staffing, including the replacement of a Black principal who was an SDP insider with a White one who hailed from the suburbs.[55] In these cases, parental influence was disproportionate, with a small group forcing changes not in the interests of the general school population. How did parental involvement in PAS compare to these examples?

At PAS, multiple groups and individuals exerted influence for different reasons. An example was the math curriculum. During the school's planning phase, Penn and the SDP agreed to use the TERC Investigations, an approach developed during the 1990s with National Science Foundation support.[56] Certain parents challenged the use of this curriculum but were rebuffed. Unable to change it, these parents formed an after-school math enrichment club led by Angela McIver, who at the time was a doctoral student in math education at Penn GSE.[57] She eventually turned the club into an entrepreneurial venture called Trapezium Math, which offers online enrichment programs for elementary students.[58] Jacqui Bowman, who had a Ph.D. in biological anthropology from the University of Cambridge in England, was part of a separate parent group that wanted a stronger math curriculum:

> There was a group of us parents who were really concerned about the standard of the math teaching. A lot of us were scientists. A lot of us ... knew how important it was to get a good grounding in mathe-

matics. And so we pushed back a lot on that. Didn't have any effect, so we ended up just doing supplementary tutoring for our children.[59]

Other parents had no problem with the way math was taught at PAS. For example, Rosemary Ford believed that strong math preparation at the school enabled her daughter to earn a high enough score on her state exams to gain admission to the prestigious Julia R. Masterman magnet school. And though she had one of her daughters participate in Angela McIver's math club, Carola Lelieveld was generally pleased with the PAS math curriculum: "Especially for my younger daughter, who was a math major, I think she got really good basic education in math at Alexander."[60] With so many opinions about the math curriculum, it would not be accurate to say that one group of parents exercised disproportionate influence. Penn and the SDP stuck with the curriculum they had proposed, and people who disliked it found workarounds.

Another area where parents tried to influence the curriculum was the visual art program, which, because of budget cuts, was scaled back not long after the school opened.[61] Jacqui Bowman, who worked at the Penn Museum and later served as director of the University City Arts League (2005–2007), was among those disappointed with the visual arts offerings. An arts committee she joined helped find grant money to partially restore arts instruction in the school. As head of the Arts League (a position that, as noted in the Introduction, I held in 2008–2009), Bowman also organized after-school visual arts classes that served PAS children. Located across the street from the school, the Arts League was a convenient location for such activities.[62] And though the school's visual arts program was limited, its performing arts curriculum was strong. Bowman, for example, said that her children enjoyed music class; her daughter played cello and was a member of the chorus.[63] If the quality of arts teaching at Penn Alexander was mixed, it did not lead parents to withdraw their children from the school. As with math, those who were not satisfied with the curriculum tended to supplement it with out-of-school programs.

Whatever involvement parents had at PAS, the force most responsible for shaping its curriculum was Penn. Having gained the support of the SDP and the teachers' union and garnered generous funding, PAS planners were able to create a school with a curriculum that closely matched their intentions. And that curriculum was, by and large, a conventional one. As Streim said, the intent was not to create a specialty school. The planners made the bet that, when Principal Sydnor turned down parents' requests to customize the curriculum, most would keep their children in PAS. They won that bet. This was a public relations victory for Penn: it allowed it to claim that it had created a regular public school, not one for Penn affiliates.

The way Penn catered to those affiliates was by drawing catchment boundaries that ensured they would be able to attend. As mentioned, Penn declined to allow admission by lottery, which would have netted a significant number of students from the outside. Instead, it made PAS a neighborhood school whose catchment was coterminous with Spruce Hill, where Penn affiliates were most likely to live.

An Urban Village?

As noted, the planners intended to make a community hub, not just a school. They hoped it would become a center for adult education, community meetings, recreation, and the arts. And they hoped it would be a diverse school, where students of different racial and socioeconomic backgrounds would get along. Did PAS achieve these goals?

According to Nancy Streim, objections from the teachers and practical limitations of the building's design prevented PAS from becoming a community school: "We didn't pull that off, and the community organizations that had imagined using the building for their own programming, we couldn't build the kinds of spaces they needed. So [for] a community arts organization, we didn't have a big art studio that could meet their needs. We didn't have an auditorium that was going to work."[64] Parent Keally McBride recalled that Principal Sydnor's opposition also hampered the realization of the community school vision:

> So we went to the school and asked if we could even have a meeting there, and they were like, "No." I had been told, and I never went to Ms. Sydnor directly, but I had been told, she said she didn't want anyone messing with her school after hours. She didn't trust the community to be able to use the space.[65]

PAS did offer activities that brought together families whose children were enrolled. These included book fairs, pizza nights, and ice-cream socials. PAS parent Carola Lelieveld remembered that PAS "had a number of events during the school year where we met all the parents, things like Father's Day, Tea, or cooking rice dishes from all over the world."[66] Numerous parents recalled that the school plays were popular and well attended.[67] Jacqui Bowman remarked on how the chorus was a community-building experience, not just a musical one: "So many kids did it, and it was a really big part of the school, especially in grade 5. Basically everyone was in it."[68] Many parents, especially those who had grown up in the suburbs, highlighted the benefit of having the building in walking distance. They would sometimes take turns escorting each other's children to school, helping to build community.[69] Even if it was unsuitable as a community school, the siting of PAS built community.

Parents gave mixed opinions about how tolerant a place PAS was. Some reported that relations between people of different races and classes were not ideal. Numerous Black parents spoke to me confidentially about how they were mistreated by White parents, especially those in high-level professional or academic positions.[70] Keally McBride, who is White, felt that the school reflected the racial politics of Philadelphia as a whole: "I think what the kids experienced was that the Black kids ended up being disciplined more."[71] There were also concerns that tracking was being used to divide students in the middle grades, much the way it had been at the Lea School during the era of URP forty years earlier. Recall Malcolm Bonner's observation in Chapter 3 that the highest track at Lea was populated mainly by White students—some of whom, in his view, did not merit placement there.

Not every aspect of race and class relations at PAS was negative. White parents reported that their children rose to the challenge of getting along with students of other backgrounds.[72] Rosemary Ford recounted that her daughter, who was initially intimidated by the Black girls in her class, came to understand their communication style:

> At first, she was nervous around her Black classmates . . . because they had their own culture and were more street-savvy. She said, "And they thought of me as this goody-two shoes." In the bathroom, they'd be like, "Come on, say a swear word." But if she said something like, "No, I'm not going to do that," they'd accept it. It wasn't bullying; it was more like goading.

Ford said that by the end of her time at PAS in grade 7, her daughter felt completely comfortable with everyone in her class.[73] As mentioned, some Black parents to whom I spoke were treated badly by White parents. The report from Ford suggests that the children at PAS were better at race relations than the adults.

Was PAS an exceptional school? Not every aspect lived up to the promises its planners made. As noted, some parents took exception to aspects of the curriculum or the principal's leadership style. Not every teacher was well liked. Race and class relations were less than perfect. And the school building never lived up to its promise of becoming a community hub. Yet the parents with whom I spoke all found many aspects of the school praiseworthy, and almost all found that it compared favorably with other schools their children attended—including private schools and highly competitive magnet schools.[74] Recall that Rosemary Ford's daughter preferred PAS to the private Philadelphia School when she transferred in grade 4 because its more traditional learning environment suited her learning style. When she moved to the elite Julia R. Masterman School in grade 8, she found it to be a "zoo" with respect to the language and behavior of students.[75] The ultimate gauge of the school's success was whether parents would keep their children enrolled. In this regard, the school did well. With one exception, the parents I spoke to did not feel the need to pull their children from PAS, and many students stayed on through grade 8. One reason for the failure of Penn's 1960s effort to make H. C. Lea a destination school was that more affluent, university-affiliated parents tended to shift their children to private or magnet schools after grade 5. There was no such problem at PAS.

Anecdotal evidence of parents keeping their children in PAS is backed by the numbers. Where planners initially feared that PAS's enrollment would be insufficient, within a few years, there were more students than could be accommodated. Parents queued up overnight to register children for the PAS kindergarten class. As the school became more popular, the university had to crack down on families claiming to live in the catchment when they really lived elsewhere. In response to enrollment pressure, the university renegotiated its agreement with the SDP to add another kindergarten class, offering to pay the teacher's salary and cover the subsidies for additional students.[76]

The school PAS planners created was not perfect, but it did not need to be. To succeed in the goal of making University City a stable home for their constituents, they needed only create a school that was on par with a typical suburban public school or one of the area private schools. By conventional measures such as test scores, PAS achieved this goal. Its facilities, too, were at least as good as the other options. Where curriculum and discipline were concerned, PAS landed in the middle: neither so freeform as to be labeled chaotic nor so strict that its teachers and administrators could be called compassionless. Moreover, the planners succeeded in deflecting community perception that they had created a boutique progressive school for university affiliates. In its use of conventional curricula, approach to discipline, and limits on parental involvement in school governance, PAS resembled a regular SDP school. These choices risked alienating some university-affiliated parents, but ultimately, they did not lead to a loss of enrollment. PAS planners avoided the conflict the WPC created when it offered UCHS as an experimental school at a time when the city was asking for high-quality conventional schools.

With the school as its focal point, the surrounding neighborhood came into its own. Families seeking a place with diversity, shady streets, public transportation, shops, restaurants, and, above all, good public education could find all these things in the part of West Philadelphia just west of the Penn campus. That the neighborhood had become a comfortable, safe place to raise children and a place of social connection was a view the parents I spoke to shared. For Keally McBride, whose book *Collective Dreams* contains a chapter titled "Community in Practice" that extols the virtues of West Philadelphia at that time, social connection was the key factor. Like so many Americans who grew up in places where there was no community or whose families moved from place to place, McBride craved the sense of mutual support present in the neighborhood:

> So I can remember for me, and I wrote about this in my book, it was after having my own completely peripatetic childhood—this was the exact opposite. And I was really happy to be able to provide that for my children, friends who they could play with all over the neighborhood. It was really easy just to coordinate and run into one another. And when you have such young kids, you really rely on the help of other people and to know that, "Oh, these are the four people that do pick up on Tuesdays." And if my train from Temple broke down or something, I knew that someone . . . I didn't have a cell phone then, but I knew someone would take my daughter home, and I didn't need to worry about it.[77]

Ironically, the sense of mutual support McBride described had existed in the Black Bottom before it was destroyed by the city and the WPC. Recall Jerry Davis's stories about neighbors helping each other in times of need: "If you didn't have enough for a meal, you could get two or three eggs from next door or a few doors down."[78]

Priced out of the Neighborhood

PAS's diversity, fine tuned through the catchment boundary, eroded as gentrification set in. This effect was not noticeable at first but became pronounced after the first decade of the school's operation. According to Culhane, the initial rise in property values that the school and broader WPI program spurred seemed to benefit the entire community. Homeowners in the catchment and just beyond it saw an increase in the equity they had in their property, enabling some struggling residents to pay bills and make overdue repairs. A study Culhane conducted shows that the number of building permits in the area increased significantly between 2003 and 2006. He observed that repairs were being done by a diverse group: "It was by homeowners in these mostly Black parts of the neighborhood. People who were fixing their roofs, redoing their kitchens and what have you. And it was just incredible. And I think we felt that was a really good place because it was like a rising tide that was lifting up boats everywhere." Soon, however, the rise in property values accelerated, and homes that had initially been priced at $200,000 were sell-ing for $300,000 to $400,000. For Culhane, this was unexpected: "I think the home price acceleration surprised everyone, that the neighborhood became attractive to a lot of people who would never have lived in the neighborhood before. And it became Whiter. It became families with . . . higher incomes."[79]

Did PAS planners understand the competitive pressures they were bringing to bear when they created this school? Remarks by Penn officials suggest that they did. As noted, Rodin observed neighbors arguing "more about who would benefit financially from the inevitable rise in property values in the catchment area than about who would benefit educationally."[80] According to Culhane, in anticipation of the rise in housing costs in the neighborhood, Penn attempted to leverage $30 million to preserve two thousand affordable apartments. This deal, to which Penn offered to contribute $10 million if Fannie Mae and real estate firm Trammell Crow did the same, collapsed when the other partners pulled out. With Citizen's Bank as a substitute partner, Penn executed a scaled-back version of the deal, forming the Neighborhood Preservation and Development Fund (NPDF) and purchasing five hundred units in various declining buildings throughout the neighborhood.[81] Meanwhile, housing costs in the area continued to increase, and there was a sharp decline in the Black population in the catchment, as shown in figure 6.3. Said Culhane, "I think a lot of people regret . . . the gentrification at the kind of scale of it has occurred. . . . I think that's disappointing; it's reduced diversity in the neighborhood."[82] Rodin, too, made a tepid admission of the harm WPI programs have inflicted on vulnerable populations, saying that the "tension between gentrification and affordability has increased, and the issue needs constant vigilance."[83]

The neighborhood was not, strictly speaking, becoming Whiter. Figure 6.3 shows a slight decline in the White population and a significant increase in the Asian population. A combination of factors was making it more exclusive and therefore out of reach for low-income Black people. First, the PAS population became Whiter, as the school won over White Spruce Hill parents previously reluctant to enroll their children in a public school. Having earned White approval, the school, and subsequently the surrounding neighborhood, began to attract a higher-income resident. These mutually reinforcing factors caused housing prices to skyrocket.

Rodin and her team could very well have predicted that their investments in the neighborhood would bring an influx of affluent residents and a decrease in affordability. Years earlier, the WPC had anticipated such an influx and even planned for it. A 1959 report to the WPC's founders cautioned them that to fund "brainsville," they might have to attract more than scholars and bohemians:

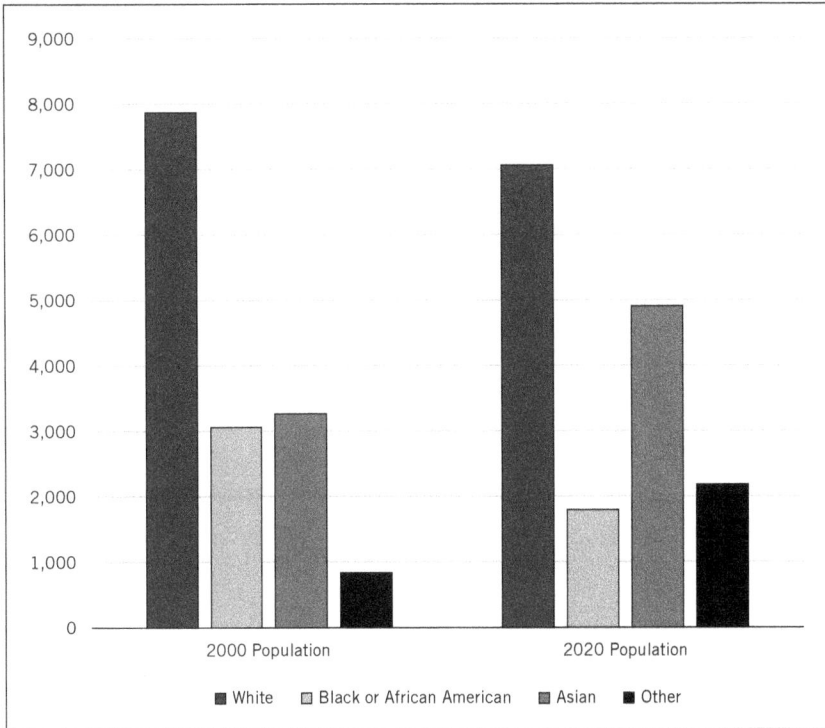

Figure 6.3 Population Makeup of Spruce Hill. (*U.S. Census data, accessed through Social Explorer, www.socialexplorer.com.*)

The numbers and incomes of the faculties, staffs, and students are not sufficient to support the specialty activities and shops that appeal to intellectual tastes and make the area feel like a "University" community (book, music, record, and food specialty shops, and foreign film theatres). Substantial numbers of business people and professionals must be available in the "University" community.[84]

The authors of the report perceived a distinction between the middle- and upper-middle class that was key to their redevelopment plan. Ultimately it was the upper-middle—the professional and managerial—worker that they would have to attract. Contemporary authors writing about the phenomenon of city schools appealing to White parents have also noted this distinction. In her study of Philadelphia's CCSI, which took place on the heels of the founding of PAS, Maia Cucchiara noted that the underlying agenda was to attract "mobile capital and professional class residents." She described these residents as being decision-makers and those who have the knowledge to "shape institutions."[85] Writing about a similar example in a California city, Linn Posey-Maddox also described the parents enrolling their children in an urban school as belonging to the "professional and managerial" class.[86]

The WPC would have been able to see, from the redevelopment of Society Hill unfolding during the planning stages of University City, the role of outside investment in jumpstarting the process. As noted in Chapter 1, the urban pioneer families restoring Society Hill's historic homes needed loans from financial institutions—as did the consortia undertaking major development projects. When local resources were insufficient, planners would call on outside investors, as in the case of the I. M. Pei–designed Society Hill towers, which were financed by metals-extraction giant ALCOA and New York real estate magnate William Zeckendorf.[87]

Such an infusion of cash hypercharges the existing market, pricing residents out of the neighborhood. In 2023, the median household income in Philadelphia was $60,698, meaning a typical family could afford monthly housing costs of approximately $1,500, based on 30 percent of gross monthly income. Median house value in Society Hill was $519,208, according to 2019–2023 census data, yielding a monthly housing cost of more than $3,400.[88] Engineering "back to the city" movements in Society Hill and West Philadelphia, first through government subsidy and later through private investment, amplified inequalities. As a chastened Richard Florida noted in his 2017 book *The New Urban Crisis: How Our Cities Are Increasing Inequality, Deepening Segregation and Failing the Middle Class—And What We Can Do about It*, such movements have resulted in the "plutocratization" of cities. Thriving neighborhoods have become "deadened trophy districts, where the global rich park their money."[89]

A similar mechanism caused the loss of affordability in University City, though its full effect was delayed by forty years. As noted, the mortgage program Penn initiated for its affiliates during the 1960s was largely unsuccessful, but when that program was revived in the late 1990s under the Rodin administration, it was so successful that loan amounts were reduced. Efforts to lure high-powered science and technology firms to the UCSC bore lackluster results during the 1960s and '70s, but the thicket of skyscrapers erected in the former Black Bottom, along with the emerging development of railyards adjacent to the Schuylkill River, show the success of Penn, Drexel, and the UCSC in the long term.

Significantly, in 2015, Drexel attracted Wexford Science + Technology, a firm that touts building "knowledge communities that drive growth," as the developer of "UCity Square," Drexel's moniker for the former Unit 3 and the area that was once at the heart of the Black Bottom. Wexford's portfolio includes such science-focused developments as the Arizona State University–sponsored Phoenix Biomedical Campus, mentioned in Davarian Baldwin's *In the Shadow of the Ivory Tower* as a contemporary example of urban redevelopment that misuses university tax exemptions for commercial purposes and results in gentrification. Drexel also forged a partnership with the Brandywine Realty Trust to develop the Schuylkill Yards, a multibillion dollar mixed residential and research project on land east of the Black Bottom and adjacent to Philadelphia's 30th Street Station.[90]

The success of PAS as a university-assisted public school has emboldened Drexel to embark on its own public school initiatives. As part of the UCity complex, Drexel broke ground in 2019 on the combined Powel Elementary and Science Leadership Academy Middle School (SLAMS), sited on the land UCHS once occupied. Integrating Powel, a well-regarded neighborhood elementary school, with SLAMS, part of a network of progressive, project-oriented schools within the SDP, the campus provides a K–8 public school option for residents in the vicinity of the Drexel campus. Like PAS, Powel-SLAMS received a generous mix of funding from public and private sources and a permanent subsidy from Drexel.[91] Its presence in the former Black Bottom is the ultimate realization of the WPC plan, which called for research, institutional, and K–12 public school uses in that area. With the UCity complex completed, the "band of blight" Edmund Bacon feared would encroach on the universities has been replaced by a band of affluence.

Such development will further accelerate real estate price increases. An inflated market will displace low-income Black residents but eventually also "respectable" faculty, graduate students, staff members, and creative types. Regarding the diversity of University City now, compared to when she first arrived, PAS parent Jacqui Bowman observed,

> It's just a very different neighborhood now . . . it's less international. I feel there's probably less staff. Seems to be more like people who are, you know, techy people and design people and web people and, you know, that kind of profession rather than the professors.

As for the cost of living, she opined, "It's certainly now a very expensive place. There's no way we would buy a house here now. We probably wouldn't be able to afford it."[92]

To illustrate the situation in financial terms, let us consider the case of the Gopniks, the family described in the 1963 *Elaborations* booklet as do-it-yourselfers who enjoyed Penn's myriad cultural amenities, preferred a racially diverse community, and sent their children to the Lea School. How would a similar family fare in today's University City? As mentioned in Chapter 4, the head of the household, Irving Gopnik, was an English professor at Rutgers University in Camden. A Chronicle of Higher Education survey for the 2023–2024 academic year shows that an average professor at Rutgers Camden institution made $126,693. An individual making that amount of money would have a maximum housing expenditure of $3,167, using the recommended figure of 30 percent of gross monthly income. In 2023, the median home value for the census tracts that correspond to Spruce Hill was $533,755, yielding a monthly housing expenditure of $3,504. Thus, in the era of PAS, the Gopnik family would not have been able to afford a mortgage payment for a Spruce Hill home.[93]

By using urban renewal funding to remove citizens it felt were undesirable rather than improve their lot, the WPC, with the City of Philadelphia as its partner, set in motion a chain of events that led to current-day gentrification. Land that was once home to hundreds of mostly African American families was cleared, turned over to the universities and their proxies, and left underdeveloped for decades. As the memory of the former Black Bottom faded, the mega-nonprofits that owned the land sold it to developers, creating high-end retail, office, and residential space and—in a final fulfillment of the WPC agenda—public schools that serve affluent residents in the neighborhood. The University City that has emerged is a magnet for outside investment, with developers like Wexford and Brandywine filling remaining parcels from Unit 3 and the railyards to the east with upscale buildings. Space for lower-income African Americans—and for diversity of any kind—has dwindled.

7

Good Causes, Evil Effects

The buying up of the properties, the building of the student
housing, all of the new stores. But I knew a change was
coming when they built the elevators.[1]

So said activist Rasheda Alexander, referring to elevators constructed
during the 2010s at the 40th Street station of Philadelphia's Market-
Frankford rapid transit line. Alexander was a resident of the University
City Townhomes, a HUD-financed project constructed during the 1980s as
an indirect result of the Quadripartite Commission (QPC) recommendation
that land in the former Black Bottom be set aside for affordable housing. What
we would normally regard as a public good—the installation of elevators to
make a subway station more accessible—was to her a sign that her neighborhood was becoming unfriendly toward Black residents. How did this reality
come to be?

Speaking to neighbors like Rasheda Alexander led me to rethink my
own actions. Projects I thought were laudable, like restoring old homes,
creating opportunities for artists, and sending my child to what appeared to
be an unsegregated public school, bore a racial taint. In West Philadelphia,
these undertakings completed efforts begun in 1960 by the West Philadelphia Corporation (WPC) to turn a neighborhood into a "University City"—
to create a place where everyone was welcome, but people of a certain educational level and professional standing were more welcome. Given the
country's racial history, wherein Black Americans were once forcibly excluded from education and denied the fruits of their labor, it is clear that
Black people were not among that favored group.

Race-Based Displacement

The WPC plan was tied to a racist agenda. From its formation in 1959, the corporation mixed educational improvement with the displacement of Black populations from West Philadelphia. Heeding warnings from the city planning office dating to 1947 and from planning professor Martin Meyerson in 1956, the WPC set its sights on the Black Bottom, a mixed commercial and residential area to the north that had become predominantly Black as the result of the Great Migration. The unwanted elements in this area would spread, planners warned, leaving Penn, Drexel, and the hospitals as islands in a "sea" of blight. Federal funding was available to clear this land, but the WPC needed to show that public interest justified doing so.

Simultaneously, the WPC worked to attract those more affluent, well-educated residents it wanted to see in the neighborhood. Anticipating future urban pioneer narratives, it created slick publications showing energetic, creative-minded residents fixing up houses in newly minted "University City." The corporation promised that the "New Athens" it was creating would also have excellent public education. Its Universities-Related Program (URP), it said, would add rigorous, diverse, and progressive programs to neighborhood schools.

The WPC merged both agendas in its most ambitious educational intervention: the creation of University City High School (UCHS). The centerpiece of a planned science incubator, this science magnet school was appealing to city planners and could serve as justification for the use of federal urban renewal funds. It was also a large enough endeavor to swallow the eighty-three-acre tract of land that was the heart of the Black Bottom. Yet this school would not serve local Black populations, who desperately needed new conventional high schools to relieve overcrowding in existing schools. The idea of removing Black families to create a special school not designed with their children in mind seems blatantly racist—and more so when we consider the long history of mistreatment of Black people by the School District of Philadelphia (SDP). It did not seem so to WPC executive vice president Leo Molinaro, who was mortified when neighbors accused him of racism and quick to point out his dedication to integration. He sent his children to West Philadelphia public schools, even the overcrowded ones.

Racial Contract at Work

Molinaro and his team promoted the idea that a school like UCHS would benefit all residents—and that the investments and tax proceeds from development would help the city. Because of historical racism, Black residents were ill equipped to take advantage of such benefits. Years of unequal schooling—in Philadelphia and in the Jim Crow South, from which many had fled—left their children unprepared for admission to the type of magnet school the WPC proposed. As many were renters, they would not benefit from the WPC's home rehabilitation initiatives. Nor were they likely to be included in the "brainsville" economy the WPC was attempting to develop as a substitute for West Philadelphia's dwindling industries. The self-deception involved in the WPC's dealings is a manifestation of what Charles Mills describes as the Racial Contract. Our nation's founding documents expounded the rights of all humankind but declared Black people not fully human. Slavery persisted for nearly a century, and then a system of legalized segregation denied Black people full citizenship. As Mills has stated, the most salient feature of this system of inequality is the agreement not to discuss it. What we are required to know is not the truth but that which supports the racialized understanding of humanity. Molinaro's incomprehension of the racist nature of the WPC's doings was exactly what the Racial Contract asked of him.

The Rodin administration's measures acknowledged the racism of the WPC plan and proposed corrections. Its West Philadelphia Initiatives (WPI) offered a jobs program and a buy West Philly program. It planned subsidized housing. It engineered the PAS catchment to include Black residents. And it named the school after a Black female civil rights attorney. These corrections, however, were overridden by the injustice of the WPC's removals. The clearance of the Black Bottom enabled the neighborhood to be branded "University City," a high-rent district where banks and developers could count on steady returns and residents on a cluster of high-status public schools. PAS and WPI overall would not have succeeded in the same way had they not been situated in such a White-identified neighborhood. Meanwhile, many of the people who had been displaced were long gone, forced to parts of the city with no plan to build a brainsville.

Building on land the WPC had cleared, adding green space and other amenities, and creating a high-quality public school, WPI spurred an increase in real estate prices unmatched by other areas of the city. Once it was established that PAS was an acceptable school choice for White residents in Spruce Hill, they began to enroll their children in large numbers. Soon, the area became a destination for more affluent families, and the presence of the area's original Black residents—which PAS planners had worked so hard to engineer—declined. Rodin and her team shrugged off such replacement as an unintended consequence. As with Molinaro, their professed ignorance is on script. Per the Racial Contract, she and her collaborators are "unable to understand the world they themselves have made."[2]

PAS's success was arguably the factor that greenlit the massive projects Penn, Drexel, and their development partners launched in the second decade of the twenty-first century. While the WPC's urban research park was never realized, companies like Wexford revived it as an "innovation district," a place that, as Laura Wolf-Powers states, provides employment and amenities for "knowledge workers with a preference for urban lifestyles." She says that in such places, displacement is hard to detect because it is indirect:

> Neighborhoods created in the innovation district mold rarely directly dispossess or displace these [Black] households. Yet the capacity of innovation districts to deliver benefits to them remains constrained, because the developers of these new urban spaces are designing them— physically, economically, and institutionally—around the capital, credentials, and purchasing power of people who already possess high socioeconomic status.[3]

Racism's cumulative effect—from the loss of wealth due to slavery through the loss of opportunity due to discrimination in housing and education— has excluded Black households from such districts.

In mid-twentieth-century Philadelphia, liberal actors who professed an abhorrence of racial division acquiesced to its workings, referring to it through coded language. Speaking of the effect of a particular school building plan, Edmund Bacon said that the "relocation of Kendrick School in the area proposed would introduce large numbers of negro children into the area which may have the effect of reducing the probability of adjacent residential redevelopment." In other words, the appearance of Black people in a neighborhood was regarded as a pox. Taking this prejudice as a given, the City Planning Commission and later the WPC opted to plan for racism rather than challenge it. Though Rodin decried the WPC's racism, her administration did little to counteract the racial bias the corporation had perpetuated. To remove such biased assumptions, we must do away with White Americans' tendency to regard Black Americans as second-class citizens and everything Black as second rate. This will require more than efforts to ameliorate existing disadvantages. It will require more than jobs programs, housing subsidies, demonstration schools, or the naming of institutions after Black people. It will require more, even, than well-thought-out community engagement programs like those of Penn's Netter Center. We need to correct the warped worldview that has been a part of America for centuries.

The Remedy: Reparations

Recent years have seen intensifying discussion of the need to repair the harm done to Black people in the United States. We have also seen concrete examples of reparations made by private institutions and local governments, such as the Jesuit Order's pledge to raise $100 million for descendants of people held in slavery and sold to build wealth for Georgetown University and the Evanston, Illinois, pledge of $10 million in housing grants to victims of redlining during the years 1919–1969.[4] These examples show that reparations, the merits of which have been debated for some time, can be realized in pursuit of justice and racial healing in the United States.

Reparations offer a threefold basis for correcting the damage inflicted on Black residents of West Philadelphia and setting the city on course for equitable development in the future. In their book *From Here to Equality: Reparations for Black Americans in the Twenty-First Century*, authors William A. Darity and A. Kirsten Mullen name acknowledgment, redress, and closure as the appropriate goals of such programs.[5] Acknowledgment by responsible parties would clear the false narratives of the Racial Contract and pave the way for Black Philadelphians to be treated as equal citizens. In the case of West Philadelphia, it would correct the assumption that because Black Bottom residents were not homeowners in a neighborhood with officially recognized boundaries, they had no stake in the development of the area. Redress would provide significant material restitution for the harm done; it would help close the wealth gap created by centuries of racial mistreatment and by the city and WPC, which shut Black Philadelphians out of the wealth creation that has taken place in West Philadelphia since the 1960s. Such a transfer would enable future generations of Black Philadelphians to take advantage of home rehabilitation programs and locate in neighborhoods with desirable schools.

Just as important, it would establish a direct and proportionate connection between what was given and what was taken. With so many empty gestures of apology in the past, real transfer of wealth is the only way to establish the responsibility of parties for their actions. In this way, redress would pave the way for the third part of the process: closure. By incurring a debt for their wrongdoing, White institutions would see their Black neighbors as being *owed* equal treatment. The city and its universities, hospitals, and major corporations would be more likely to plan for a better Philadelphia with input from everyone, not just favored neighborhoods. The mistrust many Black residents hold for predominantly White institutions would diminish. White people would seek solutions to the problems of public education together with their Black neighbors rather than trying to carve out boutique schools in an otherwise failing system.

While reparations cannot guarantee that changes of mind, heart, and habit will occur, a historical example gives us reason to hope. In her book *Learning from the Germans: Race and the Memory of Evil*, philosopher Susan Neiman describes how German reparations for the Holocaust initiated a decades-long process of *Vergangenheitsaufarbeitung*, "working off the past."

The process began with an apology but included direct payments to Holocaust survivors. Though the program was controversial when initiated, Neiman believes that reparations transformed Germany. Today, she notes, the May 8 anniversary of Nazi forces' surrender in World War II is celebrated as a liberation day in Germany. There is no such observance by Southerners of the surrender of Confederate forces at Appomattox.[6] We can only hope that reparations in Philadelphia would cure the kind of myopic thinking that led Leo Molinaro to declare the Black Bottom a nonspace and refuse to acknowledge that you cannot help people by demolishing their community.

Race to the Top, Race to the Bottom

The WPC plan to attract a more "responsible" type of citizen to West Philadelphia grew out of a larger push by the city to do the same. Beginning in the 1950s, Philadelphia drifted from its roots as an industrial city. From that point forward, government, corporate, and nonprofit actors moved independently toward a similar goal: creating a city friendly to knowledge workers. As well as causing race-based displacement, this approach undermined good government and civic cohesion. In Maia Cucchiara's wording, it treated citizens as "unequally valuable."[7]

The tendency to develop for elites was less a matter of intent than a path of least resistance. Philadelphia's reform-era mayors Clark and Dilworth made an effort to revitalize industries. They hired an economist, Kirk R. Petshek, to analyze the city's decline and recommend strategies for forestalling the exodus of factory jobs. The measures Petshek proposed, however stood no chance against the pull of cheap labor in the South and overseas.[8] By contrast, Philadelphia's historic neighborhoods—and its universities and hospitals—were not going anywhere. City planners and university officials used the tools they had to create their "Better Philadelphia." What they devised was a city for the creative and technocratic class.

Planning for Whom?

Ironically, their approach was born of Bacon's early efforts to make a city more accommodating to workers. His work in Flint aimed to create better housing for auto industry employees and, more broadly, to use the built environment to address social problems. He sought community input for his plans, in one instance distributing thousands of response cards to the public and incorporating their ideas into his plans.[9] Ultimately, he was rebuffed by the executives who ran the city's General Motors plants. He learned that to implement an idea, community approval was important, but so was buy-in from the powers that be.[10] He would be more successful in Philadelphia. At a time when the suburbs were in vogue, he gained broad support for his emphasis on rehabilitating the city center. Yet the compromises he made to garner support often sapped the idealism of his original intentions. The designs that were actualized were less bold than the ones he proposed.

Also detracting from the ideals behind Bacon's approach was the cronyism of the people who realized his plans. As noted, Philadelphia's 1950s political reformers were, by and large, Ivy League–educated brahmins. They professed to represent the will of the people but stood aloof from Philadelphians' everyday lives. Clark and Dilworth, the reform mayors who prioritized city planning, were supported by business leaders from the Greater Philadelphia Movement like Harold Batten and C. Jared Ingersoll. The City Planning Commission was led by Penn affiliates like Edward G. Hopkinson, an alumnus, and G. Holmes Perkins, dean of the School of Fine Arts. Gustave Amsterdam, also a Penn alumnus, chaired the Redevelopment Authority (RDA)—and, infamously, a bank that benefited from redevelopment. Penn president Gaylord Harnwell and WPC executive vice president Leo Molinaro were friendly with all these individuals; in correspondence, they would often address each other by first name.[11]

This cronyism prevailed despite mechanisms intended to overcome it. From his days in Flint in the 1930s, Bacon emphasized community input as part of the planning process. In 1943, before joining Philadelphia's City Planning Commission, he helped organize the Citizens' Council on City Planning as a community advisory mechanism for that body. Yet he did not always take the group's advice. According to biographer Gregory Heller, "years later, once he became planning director, Bacon would at times find himself at odds with this very group that he had been so instrumental in creating."[12] Following Bacon's lead, the WPC—and, later, Judith Rodin's WPI—created mechanisms for community input. Recall the WPC's community advisory, its board representation of local homeowners' associations, and the Social Audit of West Philadelphia residents it commissioned. Remember also the three planning committees Rodin's team organized for PAS. These mechanisms were problematic. Organizations such as the Spruce Hill Community Association represented a narrow slice of West Philadelphia's population—and one that overlapped with Penn. The advice it gave the WPC and Rodin administration resembled views they already held. And when community organizations gave dissenting views—such as the preference the four other West Philadelphia neighborhood associations for lottery-based admissions at PAS—Penn disregarded them.

Community input is indeed important for generating innovative ideas and essential to the democratization of the planning process. Yet when incorporated into institutional power structures, it is often overridden by established forces of money and influence. In such cases, it becomes little more than public relations for planning decisions that have already been taken. In Philadelphia in the mid-twentieth century—and at the beginning of the twenty-first century—lack of real community input meant redevelopment benefited the few rather than the many.

Sameness Creeps In

Philadelphia's planners also drifted from urbanist principles in their intolerance of the city's heterogeneous nature. In their booklet *Elaborations on Living in University City*, Molinaro and his team quoted Irwin Gopnik as preferring the city because "living here is at little bit like dipping into a bowl of minestrone. . . . It's always full of surprises."[13] Yet in their assessments of the conditions in the Black Bottom, city planners expressed the desire to be rid of surprises.

A 1962 Unit 3 plan labeled the Black Bottom "blighted" based on such characteristics as "defective design and arrangement of the buildings" and "economically and socially undesirable land uses." Specifically, it found the mixing of industrial, commercial, and residential uses—hotels, auto repair shops, car washes, and machine and metal shops—unacceptable.[14]

By demolishing the Black Bottom, the WPC and its successors in the twenty-first century wiped out much of West Philadelphia's character. Per the accounts of Andre Black in Chapter 4, the hotel the plan found objectionable, the Divine Tracy, played host to such musical greats as Duke Ellington and Billie Holiday when they were denied accommodation elsewhere. The Black Bottom's mixed industrial and commercial establishments provided employment and filled the needs of those who lived there. And its bars showcased great music and entertainment. In *Death and Life of Great American Cities*, Jane Jacobs notes that activity need not be squeaky clean to contribute to safe streets and neighborhood cohesion. A bar, in her view, can fulfill that function as well as a church youth center. "The greater and more plentiful the range of all legitimate interests," she says, "that city streets and their enterprises can satisfy, the better for the streets and for the safety and the civilization of the city."[15] Though Bacon believed in the primacy of downtown renewal over the creation of suburbs, he did not embrace cities' natural heterogeneity. Of the miscellaneous enterprises in the areas north of the Penn campus, he complained, "many of these uses, such as candy manufacturing, auto accessories and rug cleaning, have no connection with the University"—as if candy, cars, and rugs were antithetical to the academic pursuit.

The QPC design charrette offered an opportunity to preserve some part of the Black Bottom amid new development. It proposed to intersperse affordable housing with research labs and university buildings in a way that

Figure 7.1 2022 view of Market Street looking east from 37th Street. (*Photo by the author.*)

would provide continuity with existing neighborhoods and make use of the playing fields of UCHS, which was under construction at the time. This plan was not seriously considered. The low-income housing built on Unit 3, the University City Townhomes, concentrated and isolated impoverished residents.

Even the WPC's original plan for the UCSC complex was better than the development that emerged. Created by the Group for Planning and Research, an architectural team led by Penn faculty member Robert Geddes, the original plan featured buildings of moderate scale with generous green space. Though it accommodated cars, the design provided room for pedestrians and bicycles. Figure 7.1 shows Market Street in its current state, with little green space and oversized, glass-sheathed towers that bear no relationship to the row houses of the surrounding neighborhood.

Relying as they did on the levers of institutional power and the infusion of corporate capital, planners veered from their professed urban ideals. Instead of the city with room for "differences in taste and proclivity" Jane Jacobs calls for, they created pockets of affluent sameness surrounded by expanding blight. Instead of planning for the citizens who were there, they started to plan for ones they wished were there.

Planning for Everyone

As Maia Cucchiara puts it, we are dealing with the question of "the nature of citizenship in an era of market-oriented solutions to social problems."[16] How can a person be accounted a full citizen if the government metes out services to them according to a calculation of their earnings potential or knowledge capital? This is the kind of thinking the WPC engaged in when it said that people in coveted neighborhoods were entitled to "more intensive" consultation about the redevelopment process than dwellers in the Black Bottom. The decision-makers, who were of a certain social set, decided that some citizens were entitled to more consideration than others when it came to the redevelopment process.

Thus, in addition to the reparations called for earlier, which deal specifically with the racial injustices of redevelopment, we must attend to the problems of concentration of power and wealth that derail the urban project. We should be more conscientious about the flow of advice to institutional leaders, ensuring the broader community, not just the cronies of decision-makers, are represented on citizens' committees. We should require leaders to follow such advice and prevent them from using advisory bodies as a public relations ploy. When land lays fallow, either through failed development schemes or the impoverishment of its owners, we should require its speedy and equitable distribution. Vacant land should not be held by institutions—especially wealthy, tax-exempt universities—as they await opportunities for profitable redevelopment. Instead, it should be used for the areas of greatest need, especially affordable housing, which is increasingly scarce.

And we must be vigilant against the abuse of legislation for the public good. The urban renewal acts that enabled the taking of land in the Black Bottom are a case in point of the perversion of a well-intentioned government program. The Housing Act of 1949, which enabled the demolition of decayed housing for the creation of new, affordable housing, became the Housing Act of 1954, which funded the rehabilitation of existing homes. In the case of Society Hill, rehabilitation was not always for the benefit of people in need. In its 1959 iteration, the act allowed the replacement of decayed homes with university development, as in University City. "Public good" became the education of elite students and the provision of housing and schools for their professors.

For those of us who are "knowledge workers with a preference for city living," what is there to be done? How can we atone for having benefited from systemic racism? If we stay in the city, how should we ensure that displacement does not intensify? Daniel Hertz's article "There's Basically No Way Not to Be a Gentrifier" paints a bleak picture. He asserts that locating in a formerly disfavored urban area like West Philadelphia hurts socioeconomically disadvantaged Black residents—but so does moving to an already affluent and segregated suburb:

> Moving to a higher-income neighborhood—one where market and regulatory forces have already pushed out the low-income—means

you're helping to sustain the high cost of living there, and therefore helping to keep the area segregated. You're also forcing lower income college graduates to move to more economically marginal areas, where they in turn will push out people with even less purchasing power.[17]

He does, however, suggest ways to reduce segregation, primarily by mitigating the market forces that perpetuate racial wealth disparities. Returning to policies like rent control, rescinding constraints on the construction of affordable housing, and protecting tenants from eviction due to rising rents would, in his view, help stem rising tide of economic segregation that goes hand in hand with racial segregation.[18]

To these measures, I would add pushing for equitable state funding of public schools so that cities are less reliant on property taxes and therefore less incentivized to develop for the wealthy. In cities dominated by large nonprofits, demanding payments in lieu of taxes (PILOTs) will similarly reduce school budget shortfalls and reduce pressure to increase property tax receipts. I would argue that the most important step is awareness: knowing about the history of racism that contributed to current day disparities in your city and understanding the incentives for institutional leaders to engage in cutthroat competition for elite constituents. Cognizant of these forces, we are better situated to demand that when our leaders plan for a better city, they plan it for everybody.

NOTES

A NOTE ON RACIAL TERMINOLOGY

1. Karen Yin, "Capitalizing for Equality," Conscious Style Guide, 2017, https://con sciousstyleguide.com/capitalizing-for-equality/; see also American Psychological Association, "Racial and Ethnic Identity," Publication Manual of the APA, 7th ed. (Washington, DC: APA, 2020).

INTRODUCTION

1. Samantha Melamed, "The Penn Alexander Effect: Is There Any Room Left for Low-Income Residents in University City?" *Philadelphia Inquirer*, November 1, 2018.

2. Charles W. Mills, *The Racial Contract* (Ithaca, NY: Cornell University Press, 1997), 11–13. Following Mills, I use lowercase for the general "social contract" and uppercase for the special "Racial Contract."

3. Mills, *Racial Contract*, 17.

4. "Better Philadelphia" refers to the exhibition of that name, described in Chapter 1. See Gregory Heller, *Ed Bacon: Planning, Politics, and the Building of Modern Philadelphia* (University of Pennsylvania Press, 2013), 48–53.

5. Davarian L. Baldwin, *In the Shadow of the Ivory Tower: How Universities Are Plundering Our Cities* (New York: Bold Type Books, 2021), 6–9. Throughout the book, Baldwin discusses examples of displacement in cities such as Chicago, New York, Hartford, Baltimore, Phoenix, Philadelphia, and New Haven.

6. The first uses of "University City" predate the formation of the WPC. The organization began using the name extensively in its publicity as soon as it was formed in 1959. See Laura Wolf-Powers, *University City: History, Race, and Community in the Era of the Innovation District* (Philadelphia: University of Pennsylvania Press, 2022), 22–28.

7. Edmund N. Bacon to Raymond F. Leonard, memorandum, November 29, 1947, p. 1, PCA 145.2, box 14 A2914, folder "Redevelopment—University 1946–50," Philadelphia City Planning Commission Files.

CHAPTER 1

1. Ernest Havemann, "The Rebirth of Philadelphia: City Is Living Proof of What Citizens Can Do to Secure Good Government, Civic Renaissance," *National Civic Review* 51 (1962): 538–40.

2. Gregory Heller, *Ed Bacon: Planning, Politics, and the Building of Modern Philadelphia* (Philadelphia: University of Pennsylvania Press, 2013), 90–92; Robert Cozzolino, *David Lynch: The Unified Field* (Oakland: University of California Press, 2014), 21–24.

3. Carolyn Adams, David Bartelt, David Elesh, Ira Goldstein, Nancy Kleniewski, and William Yancy, *Philadelphia: Neighborhoods, Division, and Conflict in a Postindustrial City* (Philadelphia: Temple University Press, 1991), 6, 30–31.

4. Adams et al., *Philadelphia*, 31, 41–42.

5. Nicholas Lemann, *The Promised Land: The Great Black Migration and How It Changed America* (New York: A. A. Knopf, 1991), 3–7.

6. John L. Puckett and Mark F. Lloyd, *Becoming Penn: The Pragmatic American University, 1950–2000* (Philadelphia: University of Pennsylvania Press, 2015), 6; Lee Benson, Ira Harkavy, John Puckett, Matthew Hartley, Rita A. Hodges, Francis E. Johnston, and Joann Weeks, *Knowledge for Social Change: Bacon, Dewey, and the Revolutionary Transformation of Research Universities in the Twenty-First Century* (Philadelphia: Temple University Press, 2017), 90.

7. Adams et al., *Philadelphia*, 11

8. Guian A. McKee, *The Problem of Jobs: Liberalism, Race, and Deindustrialization in Philadelphia* (Chicago: University of Chicago Press, 2008), 12–13. During the 1950s, sixty-nine thousand White Philadelphia residents decamped to the suburbs, a loss of 3 percent of the city's total population. See Puckett and Lloyd, *Becoming Penn*, 90; U.S. Census Bureau data, accessed through Social Explorer, www.socialexplorer.com.

9. Adams et al., *Philadelphia*, 44.

10. Adams et al., *Philadelphia*, 52.

11. Isaac "Ikey" Davis and Gerald "Jerry" Davis, in discussion with the author, John Balzarini, and Walter Palmer, January 21, 2019.

12. Prentice Cole, Jr., in discussion with the author, February 28, 2018.

13. Matthew J. Countryman, *Up South: Civil Rights and Black Power in Philadelphia* (Philadelphia: University of Pennsylvania Press, 2006), 48–58.

14. Roger Miller and Joseph Siry, "The Emerging Suburb: West Philadelphia, 1850–1880," *Pennsylvania History: A Journal of Mid-Atlantic Studies* 47, no. 2 (1980): 107, 117–20.

15. Pearl S. Simpson, "The Black Bottom," in *Black Bottom Picnic* (pub. by author, 2005), 35–36; Miller and Siry, "Emerging Suburb," 103.

16. Miller and Siry, "Emerging Suburb," 106–7; Stephen Salisbury, "Oldest African American Graveyard in West Philadelphia Lies beneath Proposed Apartments," *Philadelphia Inquirer*, January 25, 2018.

17. Cora "Diddy" Hill, Herman "Butch" Wilmore, and Mary Hill Jackson, in discussion with the author, March 6, 2019.

18. Andre Black, in discussion with the author, July 20, 2018.

19. John T. Spencer, *In the Crossfire: Marcus Foster and the Troubled History of American School Reform* (Philadelphia: University of Pennsylvania Press, 2012), 23.

20. Hill et al., discussion.

21. Hill et al., discussion.

22. Puckett and Lloyd, *Becoming Penn*, 89–91.

23. Walter Palmer, in discussion with John Balzarini, January 26, 2018.

24. Davis et al., discussion. Five dollars in 1940 is equivalent to approximately $115 in 2025.

25. Hill et al., discussion.

26. Black, discussion; Hill et al., discussion.

27. Black, discussion.

28. Davis et al., discussion.

29. Vincent P. Franklin, *The Education of Black Philadelphia: A Social and Educational History of a Minority Community, 1900–1950* (Philadelphia: University of Pennsylvania Press, 1979), 63.

30. Edmund N. Bacon to Raymond F. Leonard, memorandum, November 29, 1947, p. 4, PCA 145.2, box 14 A2914, folder "Redevelopment—University 1946–50," Philadelphia City Planning Commission Files.

31. Palmer, discussion.

32. Hill et al., discussion.

33. Davis et al., discussion.

34. Davis et al., discussion.

35. Palmer, discussion.

36. Walter Palmer, in discussion with the author, February 21, 2024.

37. Davis et al., discussion.

38. Black, discussion.

39. Palmer, discussion, January 26, 2018.

40. "A Profile of Basic Marketing Factors in West Philadelphia Corporation Market Area," UPA 4, box 74, folder "West Philadelphia Corporation 1955–1960, IV," UARC. Source: U.S. Census, Registration Commission, City of Philadelphia, City Planning Commission.

41. James Axtell, *The School upon a Hill: Education and Society in Colonial New England* (New Haven: Yale University Press, 1974), 208.

42. John R. Thelin, *A History of American Higher Education*, 2nd ed. (Baltimore: Johns Hopkins University Press, 2011), 30.

43. Craig Steven Wilder, *Ebony and Ivy: Race, Slavery, and the Troubled History of America's Universities* (New York: Bloomsbury, 2014), 6, 7, 10, 11, 53–54, 84–85, 137–38.

44. Harley F. Etienne, *Pushing back the Gates: Neighborhood Perspectives on University-Driven Revitalization in West Philadelphia* (Philadelphia: Temple University Press, 2012), 15–17.

45. Puckett and Lloyd, *Becoming Penn*, 6; Benson et al., *Knowledge for Social Change*, 90. Other examples of socially oriented research at Wharton include an 1893 study exposing corruption among municipal gas suppliers and numerous studies of child labor and utility rate gouging.

46. Puckett and Lloyd, *Becoming Penn*, 17, 25, 26.

47. McKee, *Problem of Jobs*, 5, 18–20.

48. Henry Resnik, *Turning on the System: War in the Philadelphia Public Schools* (New York: Pantheon, 1970), 30; Carolyn T. Adams, "The Greater Philadelphia Movement," in *Encyclopedia of Greater Philadelphia* ed. Charlene Mires (Camden, NJ: Mid-Atlantic Regional Center for the Humanities at Rutgers-Camden, 2016), https://philadelphiaencyclopedia.org/essays/greater-philadelphia-movement/.

49. McKee, *Problem of Jobs*, 18–20.

50. John M. McLarnon and G. Terry Madonna, "Dilworth, Clark, and Reform in Philadelphia, 1947–1962," *Pennsylvania Legacies* 11, no. 2 (November 2011): 26; Jon S. Birger, "Race, Reaction, and Reform: The Three Rs of Philadelphia School Politics, 1965–1971," *Pennsylvania Magazine of History and Biography* 120, no. 3 (1996): 181.

51. Heller, *Ed Bacon*, 5, 12, 23–24, 25.

52. Heller, *Ed Bacon*, 23–24, 26, 30, 38.

53. Heller, *Ed Bacon*, 31–36.

54. Barbara Pressman, in discussion with the author, February 23, 2024.

55. Heller, *Ed Bacon*, 49.

56. Heller, *Ed Bacon*, 48–53. Puckett and Lloyd, *Becoming Penn*, 32; Neil Smith, *The New Urban Frontier: Gentrification and the Revanchist City* (New York: Routledge, 1996), 122.

57. Heller, *Ed Bacon*, 49–53, 54.

58. Heller, *Ed Bacon*, 52.

59. "The Philadelphia Cure: Clearing Slums with Penicillin, Not Surgery," *Architectural Forum*, April 1952, 112–13; Francesca Russello Ammon, "Urban Renewal," in *Encyclopedia of Greater Philadelphia* ed. Charlene Mires (Camden, NJ: Mid-Atlantic Regional Center for the Humanities at Rutgers-Camden, 2016), https://philadelphiaencyclopedia.org/essays/urban-renewal/.

60. Gregory L. Heller, "The Life Experiences That Shaped Edmund Bacon," in *Imagining Philadelphia: Edmund Bacon and the Future of the City*, ed. Scott Gabriel Knowles (Philadelphia: University of Pennsylvania Press, 2009), 42; Francesca Russello Ammon, "Picturing Preservation and Renewal: Photographs as Planning Knowledge in Society Hill, Philadelphia," *Journal of Planning Education and Research* 42, no. 3 (2022): 316.

61. The widely held view among city planning scholars is that the term "gentrification" first appeared in an essay by British sociologist Ruth Glass in 1964. See Ruth Glass, E. J. Hobsbawm, Harold Pollins, W. Ashworth, J. H. Westergaard, William Holford, Margot Jefferys, John A. Jackson, and Sheila Patterson, *London: Aspects of Change* (London: MacGibbon & Kee, 1964), xviii.

62. Neil Smith, "Toward a Theory of Gentrification: A Back to the City Movement by Capital, Not People," *Journal of the American Planning Association* 45, no. 4 (1979): 538–48; Smith, *New Urban Frontier*, 119–39. Smith's finding that the transformation of Society Hill was engineered by and largely for the benefit of big business was seminal in the evolution of thinking about gentrification.

63. Richard Florida, *Cities and the Creative Class* (New York: Routledge, 2005), 35. Florida holds that it was the preferences of this creative class, not any financial incentives by the government, that spurred the growth of certain "creative" cities: "The Creative Centers are not thriving for such traditional economic reasons as access to natural resources or transportation routes. Nor are they thriving because their local governments have gone bankrupt giving tax breaks and other incentives to lure business. They are succeeding largely because creative people want to live there."

64. Smith, *New Urban Frontier*, xiv. See also Franklin, *Education of Black Philadelphia*, 29.

65. Smith, *New Urban Frontier*, 119–20.

66. Philadelphia Office of the Controller, "Mapping the Legacy of Structural Racism in Philadelphia," January 23, 2020, https://controller.phila.gov/philadelphia-audits/mapping-the-legacy-of-structural-racism-in-philadelphia/.

67. Smith, *New Urban Frontier*, 130–34.

68. Smith, *New Urban Frontier*, 119–20.

69. Smith, *New Urban Frontier*, 122–23, 124–25.

70. Edmund Bacon, "Philadelphia Yesterday, Philadelphia Today, Philadelphia Tomorrow," *Philadelphia Inquirer Magazine*, September 10, 1961, 10.

71. Smith, *New Urban Frontier*, 129.

72. Agnes C. Ingersoll, "A Society Hill Restoration," *Bryn Mawr Alumnae Bulletin*, Fall 1963.

73. Smith, *New Urban Frontier*, 123–24.

74. Smith, *New Urban Frontier*, 126, 130–34.

75. Smith, *New Urban Frontier*, 126–28; Ammon, "Picturing Preservation and Renewal," 316–17.

76. Smith, *New Urban Frontier*, 53.

77. Robert Fishman, "The Fifth Migration," *Journal of the American Planning Association* 71, no. 4 (2005): 358.

78. Smith, *New Urban Frontier*, 125. Smith also shows that Society Hill's redevelopment attracted few home buyers from the suburbs; most were already taxpayers in Philadelphia.

79. Ammon, "Picturing Preservation and Renewal," 316.

80. Smith, *New Urban Frontier*, 137–38.

81. U.S. Census data, accessed through Social Explorer, www.socialexplorer.com. According to the 2019–2023 American Community Survey, Society Hill's population was nearly 90 percent White with median income more than $126,000.

82. Katherine McKittrick, "On Plantations, Prisons, and a Black Sense of Place," *Social & Cultural Geography* 12, no. 8 (2011): 949.

83. Leo Molinaro to WPC board of directors, May 20, 1963, UPA 4, box 156, folder "West Phila. Corp. General 1962–63," UARC.

84. Edmund N. Bacon to Raymond F. Leonard, memorandum, November 29, 1947, p. 1, PCA 145.2, box 14 A2914, folder "Redevelopment—University 1946–50," Philadelphia City Planning Commission Files.

85. Bacon to Leonard, November 29, 1947, 1.

86. Bacon to Leonard, November 29, 1947, 4.

87. Bacon to Leonard, November 29, 1947, 6.

88. Bacon to Leonard, November 29, 1947, 6.

89. Pressman, discussion.

90. Bacon to Leonard, November 29, 1947, 6.

91. Bacon to Leonard, November 29, 1947, 7.

92. Margaret Pugh O'Mara, *Cities of Knowledge: Cold War Science and the Search for the Next Silicon Valley* (Princeton, NJ: Princeton University Press, 2005), 60.

CHAPTER 2

1. Sam Bass Warner Jr., *The Private City: Philadelphia in Three Periods of Its Growth*, 2nd ed. (Philadelphia: University of Pennsylvania Press, 1987), 115; Franklin, *Education of Black Philadelphia*, 32.

2. Franklin, *Education of Black Philadelphia*, 33.

3. Franklin, *Education of Black Philadelphia*, 34.

4. Franklin, *Education of Black Philadelphia*, 34–35.

5. Philadelphia Board of Public Education, *Annual Report, 1907*, "Report of the Superintendent," 43, quoted in Franklin, *Education of Black Philadelphia*, 36.

6. Herbert M. Kliebard, *The Struggle for the American Curriculum, 1893–1958*, 3rd ed. (New York: Taylor and Francis, 2004), 76. Social efficiency was an all-encompassing approach that trained students to fit in: to think and act in ways that meshed with emerging industrial age work environments. Moreover, it made use of "a science of exact measurement and precise standards" to assure the public of its efficacy. Among the influences to social efficiency curriculum was scientific management pioneer Frederick Winslow Taylor, whose theories of how to exact efficient work from laborers were applied in schools. Though their doctrine was not explicitly racist, advocates of social efficiency expressed racist tendencies in their writing. Edward A. Ross, for example, glorified the "restless, striving, doing Aryan" in contrast to the "docile Slav or quiescent Hindoo."

7. Michael Clapper, "School Design, Site Selection, and the Political Geography of Race in Postwar Philadelphia," *Journal of Planning History* 5, no. 3 (2006): 241.

8. Ruth Wright Hayre and Alexis Moore, *Tell Them We Are Rising: A Memoir of Faith in Education* (New York: John Wiley & Sons, 1997), 29–30.

9. Hayre and Moore, *Tell Them We Are Rising*, 33.

10. Spencer, *In the Crossfire*, 25.

11. Spencer, *In the Crossfire*, 25.

12. Birger, "Race, Reaction, and Reform," 184–85; Resnik, *Turning on the System*, 31–33.

13. Rochelle Nichols-Solomon, in discussion with the author, November 30, 2017. Her mother, Mamie Nichols, would go on to earn university degrees in social work and counseling.

14. Nichols-Solomon, discussion.

15. Nichols-Solomon, discussion.

16. Anne E. Phillips, "The Struggle for School Desegregation in Philadelphia, 1945–1967" (Ph.D. diss., University of Pennsylvania, 2000), 62, ProQuest (9965544).

17. Phillips, "Struggle for School Desegregation," 93.

18. Phillips, "Struggle for School Desegregation," 81–85.

19. Phillips, "Struggle for School Desegregation," 117–18.

20. William W. Cutler III, "Outside in and Inside Out: Civic Activism, Helen Oakes, and the Philadelphia Public Schools, 1960–1989," *Pennsylvania Magazine of History and Biography* 37, no. 3 (2013): 307; Resnik, *Turning on the System*, 31–38.

21. Resnik, *Turning on the System*, 33.

22. Cutler, "Outside in and Inside Out," 308–9.

23. Cutler, "Outside in and Inside Out," 309–10.

24. Puckett and Lloyd, *Becoming Penn*, 92.

25. Martin Meyerson to G. Holmes Perkins, June 30, 1956, UPA 4, box 73, folder "Community Relations, 1955–1960, The West Philadelphia Corporation I," UARC.

26. Arnold R. Hirsch, *Making the Second Ghetto: Race and Housing in Chicago, 1940–1960* (Chicago: University of Chicago Press, 1983, reprint 1998), 136.

27. Puckett and Lloyd, *Becoming Penn*, 93–96.

28. Stefan M. Bradley, *Harlem vs. Columbia University: Black Student Power in the Late 1960s* (Champaign: University of Illinois Press, 2009), 21, 28, 34–35.

29. Baldwin, *In the Shadow of the Ivory Tower*, 28–29, 133.

30. Puckett and Lloyd, *Becoming Penn*, 100.

31. Draft of press release on the hiring of Leo Molinaro, December 27, 1959, UPA 4, box 73, folder "Community Relations 1955–1960 The West Philadelphia Corporation," UARC. Leo Molinaro to WPC board, April 10, 1968, Acc 350, box 350, folder 42 "Goldie Hoffman," SCRC; Miles Orvell, *The Death and Life of Main Street* (Chapel Hill: University of North Carolina Press, 2012), 184–86. Columbia, Maryland, was one such urban

experiment. It was a planned community of one hundred thousand residents consisting of villages of ten to fifteen thousand, each divided into smaller clusters of twenty-five hundred. Clusters had amenities such as a pool, childcare center, store, playing fields, park, and community room.

32. Draft of press release on the hiring of Leo Molinaro, December 27, 1959.

33. Richardson Dilworth to John Moore, April 27, 1959, UPA 4, folder 73, "Community Relations, 1955–1960, The West Philadelphia Corporation I," UARC.

34. Fact sheet "The West Philadelphia Corporation," fall 1959, UPA 4, box 73, folder "Community Relations, the West Philadelphia Corporation 1955–60 I," UARC.

35. Evaluation report of Barry Freeman's work, 1959–1961, May 1, 1961, UPA 4, box 152, folder "Community Relations Advisory," UARC.

36. Graeme Lorimer to Gaylord P. Harnwell, June 13, 1961, box 152, folder "Gaylord P. Harnwell 1960–65," UARC.

37. Project report "Family Needs in University City Planning: A Study of Factors Affecting the Selection of Neighborhoods by Faculty and Staff of the University of Pennsylvania," June 6, 1963, UPA 4, box 152, "Community Relations II, 1960–65," UARC.

38. Educational Service Bureau, Graduate School of Education, University of Pennsylvania, "Data Relating to Public Schools in the West Philadelphia Corporation Area," June 6, 1960, papers of Ira Harkavy.

39. WPC board meeting minutes, June 7, 1960, Acc. 350, box 350, folder 69, "Board of Directors Meetings, 1959–60," SCRC.

40. In the early 1960s, SDP schools were typically organized into a K–6 (elementary school), 7–9 (junior high school), and 10–12 (high school) scheme, with certain schools (e.g., Lea) comprising grades K–9.

41. William B. Castetter, Frederick B. Davis, and Richard S. Heisler, *The Henry C. Lea School: An Appraisal* (Philadelphia: Educational Research and Service Bureau, University of Pennsylvania, 1968), x; Rebecca Segal, *Got No Time to Fool Around: A Motivation Program for Education* (Philadelphia: Westminster Press, 1972), 92.

42. Miller and Siry, "Emerging Suburb," 107, 117–20. The authors describe how, beginning in the 1850s, developers of West Philadelphia's Hamilton Village built rows of large twin homes that in their outward appearance resembled single mansions. Moderate in price but with features deriving from historical styles (e.g., French and Italian), these houses appealed to middle-class buyers. Developers preserved the residential character of the area through covenants of sale that forbade establishment of manufacturing operations on these properties.

43. Carol Williamson, in discussion with the author, January 19, 2019.

44. Bettie Livermore, "Family Needs in University City Planning: A Study of Factors Affecting the Selection of Neighborhoods by Faculty and Staff of the University of Pennsylvania," June 6, 1963, UPA 4, box 152, "Community Relations II, 1960–65," UARC.

45. West Philadelphia Schools Committee to the Board of Education, January 16, 1963, UPA 4, box 152, FF "Community Relations—West Phila. Corp. Minutes of Annual Meetings I 1960–65," UARC.

46. Gaylord P. Harnwell to Allen Wetter and Mrs. Albert M. Greenfield to Leo Molinaro, Acc. 350, box 27, FF "Board of Education 1963," SCRC.

47. Resnik, *Turning on the System*, 4–5; Birger, "Race, Reaction, Reform," 185–86.

48. Resnik, *Turning on the System*, 106. Scaffolding is part of a field of ideas that centers the learner over the teacher in education. These include John Dewey's experimentalism, which posits trial-and-error effort on concrete tasks as the source of learning rather than memorization of facts. In the field of psychology, Vygotsky pioneered the "zone of

proximal development" to describe the range of skills a child of a certain developmental level can learn with adult guidance. This range is on the margin between tasks the child has already learned and those they are incapable of learning at their present level. See Laura E. Berk and Adam Winsler, *Scaffolding Children's Learning: Vygotsky and Early Childhood Learning* (Washington, DC: National Association for the Education of Young Children, 1995), 25–34; and Penny L. Beed, E. Marie Hawkins, and Cathy M. Roller, "Moving Learners towards Independence: The Power of Scaffolded Instruction," *The Reading Teacher* 44, no. 9 (1991): 648–55.

49. Mark Shedd, "Speech to the Assembled Staff," *Philadelphia*, September 11, 1967, quoted in Birger, "Race, Reaction, and Reform," 171. Birger notes the similarity between Shedd's plea to promote free expression in the classroom and Dewey's vision of a less rigid form of education that nurtures students' imagination and provides a model for democratic society.

50. Resnik, *Turning on the System*, 235–43; Norman Newberg and Adina Newberg, in discussion with the author, February 13, 2019.

51. Newberg and Newberg, discussion.

52. Newberg and Newberg, discussion.

53. Newberg and Newberg, discussion. The book, *The Gift of Education*, analyzes the results of an effort by philanthropy to boost college access for students at an underserved Philadelphia school. Newberg shows the shortcomings of such efforts absent more comprehensive improvements in urban education. He also describes the ways in which the program was successful and suggests paths toward better outcomes.

54. Norman Brown, in discussion with the author, April 25, 2018.

55. Brown, discussion.

56. Jettie Newkirk, in discussion with the author, July 25, 2019.

57. Newkirk, discussion.

58. Newkirk, discussion. Newkirk collaborated with Charles Askew, a school district administrator at the Kennedy Center in Career Education, and English teacher Barry Slepian to create the Benjamin Banneker Urban Center. The project was spearheaded by activist Herman Wrice and supported by a Department of Education grant.

59. Lytle, discussion.

60. Lytle, discussion.

61. Birger, "Race, Reaction, and Reform," 172n20.

62. Birger, "Race, Reaction, and Reform," 172n20.

63. Hayre and Moore, *Tell Them We Are Rising*, 77–78.

64. Birger, "Race, Reaction, and Reform," 168–69.

65. Lillian Weber, *The English Infant School and Informal Education* (Englewood Cliffs, NJ: Prentice-Hall, 1971), 63, 76.

66. "Proposal for a Community School," undated draft, likely 1968, papers of Ira Harkavy.

67. Susan Bank, in discussion with the author, November 21, 2019; Dorothea Camp, in discussion with the author, December 3, 2019.

68. Carol Williamson, in discussion with the author, January 19, 2019.

69. Pat Spann, in discussion with the author, February 11, 2019.

70. Camp, discussion.

71. Rochelle Nichols-Solomon, in discussion with the author, November 30, 2017.

72. Sandra Scarr, Susan Kallenbach, and Elinore S. Prockop, "The Educational Needs of University Families in University City," Fall 1968, papers of Ira Harkavy.

73. "Proposal for a Community School."

74. Nichols-Solomon, discussion.

75. Lois Gelfand and Mildred Gelfand, in discussion with the author, January 21, 2019.

76. Barbara Pressman, in discussion with the author, February 23, 2024.

77. Ruth Bacon, "Notes for a Philosophy Particular to the Walnut Street Center," July 12, 1968, personal collection of former Walnut Street Center teacher Barbara Pressman.

78. Bacon, "Notes for a Philosophy Particular to the Walnut Street Center."

79. Gelfand and Gelfand, discussion.

80. "Let's Go out Together," Citizens Committee on Public Education in Philadelphia, 1969, https://www.youtube.com/watch?v=ikXQu-0Lfmo; Pressman, discussion.

81. Bacon, "Notes for a Philosophy Particular to the Walnut Street Center."

82. Gelfand and Gelfand, discussion.

83. Morris Mendelson, "The Report on the Walnut Street Center," Ad Hoc Committee on Education in University City, October 12, 1969, papers of Ira Harkavy.

84. Pressman, discussion; Gerald A. Goldin, letter to the editor, *Philadelphia Daily News*, July 30, 1977.

85. Mendelson, "Report on the Walnut Street Center."

86. Resnik, *Turning on the System*, 164, 169.

87. Resnik, *Turning on the System*, 163, 165.

88. Resnik, *Turning on the System*, 165–66. The funding amount is equivalent to more than $1.2 million in 2025.

89. Resnik, *Turning on the System*, 164–66.

90. Resnik, *Turning on the System*, 173.

91. Resnik, *Turning on the System*, 171, 178, 183, 185; William C. Nielsen, "The Storefront School," in *Restructuring American Education: Innovations and Alternatives*, ed. Ray C. Rist (New Brunswick, NJ: Transaction Books, 1972), 227.

92. Resnik, *Turning on the System*, 175, 178.

CHAPTER 3

1. *WPC 2nd Annual Report*, 1961, Acc. 350, box 1, folder 2, "Annual Report 1961–62," SCRC.

2. Castetter, Davis, and Heisler, *Henry C. Lea School*, 3; data from the 1960 U.S. census.

3. Brenda Bonhomme, in discussion with the author, August 22, 2024

4. West Philadelphia Realty Board, Spruce Hill Study, Oct. 1961, UPA 4, box 156, folder "West Phila. Corp. external communications, 1961–62," UARC.

5. Amy T. Orr, in discussion with the author, November 21, 2017; Antoinette Gibson, in discussion with the author, May 30, 2019; Williamson, discussion; Cole, discussion.

6. Bonhomme, discussion.

7. West Philadelphia Realty Board, Spruce Hill Study, October 1961, UPA 4, box 156, folder "West Phila. Corp. external communications, 1961–62," UARC; Castetter, Davis, and Heisler, *Henry C. Lea School*, 45; Orr, discussion; Williamson, discussion.

8. Orr, discussion.

9. Universities-Related Program advisory, report on assistance to the H. C. Lea School, March 20, 1964, UPA 4, box 154, folder "Community Relations, West Philadelphia Corporation, Henry C. Lea School," UARC.

10. Report on assistance to the H. C. Lea School.

11. Bonhomme, discussion.

12. Report on assistance to the H. C. Lea School.

13. Report on assistance to the H. C. Lea School.

14. *The Universities-Related Program in the Henry C. Lea School*, January 1964, pp. 2–5, Amy T. Orr, personal collection.

15. *Henry C. Lea School Brochure*, Lea Home and School Association, 1963, Amy T. Orr, personal collection.

16. Bonhomme, discussion.

17. Malcolm Bonner, in discussion with the author, February 12, 2020.

18. Brown, discussion.

19. Semiannual report to the WPC board, 1964, UPA 4, folder 155 "WPHS MP 1963–64," UARC.

20. Barry Freeman, "Evaluation of the College Motivation Program for WPHS Students," UPA 4, box 152, folder "Gaylord P. Harnwell 1960–65," UARC.

21. Freeman, "Evaluation."

22. "Report to the Trustees of the West Philadelphia Corporation Program for the Development of University City," unsigned, 1963, UPA 4, box 156, folder "West Phila. Corp. General 62–63," UARC.

23. Segal, *Got No Time to Fool Around*, 14.

24. Rebecca Segal, editorial on the Motivation Program, *Wall Street Journal*, 1963, UPA 4, box 155, folder "WPC Committee Meetings, 1963–64," UARC.

25. WPC semiannual report on the Motivation Program, UPA 4, box 155, folder "West Philadelphia High School Motivation Program," UARC.

26. WPC press release on the Motivation Program, UPA 4, box 155, folder "West Philadelphia High School Motivation Program," UARC.

27. Brown, discussion.

28. Brown, discussion.

29. Brown, discussion.

30. K. Rose Samuel-Evans, in discussion with the author, October 6, 2017.

31. Samuel-Evans, discussion.

32. Brown, discussion.

33. Samuel-Evans, discussion.

34. Glenn Bryan, in discussion with the author, November 20, 2017; Samuel-Evans, discussion. Bryan, discussion.

35. Segal, *Got No Time to Fool Around*, 167.

36. Samuel-Evans, discussion.

37. Bryan, discussion.

38. "Report to the Trustees."

39. Segal, *Got No Time to Fool Around*, 29.

40. Orr, discussion; Bonner, discussion.

41. Marechal-Neil E. Young and Jack H. Neulight, "The Motivation Program of West Philadelphia High School," UPA 4, box 188, folder "The West Philadelphia Corporation II," UARC.

42. Eileen Brown, in discussion with the author, August 14, 2018.

43. "University City- Proposed Land Use," fall 1959, p. 2, UPA 4, box 73, "Community Relations, 1955–1960, The West Philadelphia Corporation I," UARC.

44. West Philadelphia Corporation, *Elaborations on Living in University City*, back cover, September 1963, box 152, FF "Community Relations—West Phila. Corp. V 1960–65," UARC.

45. WPC, *Elaborations*, 7.

46. WPC, *Elaborations*, 7.

47. WPC, *Elaborations*, 11.

48. WPC, *Elaborations*, 2.

49. WPC, *Elaborations*, 11.

50. WPC, *Elaborations*, 14.

51. Edmund Bacon to Gaylord P. Harnwell, September 18, 1963, UPA 4, box 152, folder "Community Relations—West Phila. Corp. V 1960–65," UARC.

52. Booklet *The West Phila. Corporation—A Word to Our Friends*, 1962, p. 5, Acc. 350, box 1, folder "1st Annual Report," SCRC.

53. "Comments on University City Urban Renewal Area Unit #3," March 19, 1963, p. 1, Acc. 350, box 11, "Unit 3—1962–63," SCRC.

54. Richard Graves to Gaylord Harnwell and James Creese, May 18, 1960, UPA 4, box 74, folder "Community Relations, the West Philadelphia Corporation V," UARC; *WPC Second Annual Report*, October 1, 1961, Acc. 350, folder 1, "Statements sent to Associate Members," SCRC.

55. O'Mara, *Cities of Knowledge*, 170–71.

56. Peter Binzen, "University City Tower Shifted," *Evening Bulletin*, August 30, 1961, Acc. 350, box 1, folder 70, "Board of Directors, General Material Relating to the Board, 1961–1964," SCRC.

57. O'Mara, *Cities of Knowledge*, 60.

58. O'Mara, *Cities of Knowledge*, 170–71; Binzen, "University City Tower Shifted."

59. "University City- Proposed Land Use," 12–13.

60. O'Mara, *Cities of Knowledge*, 170–71.

61. Leo A. Molinaro to G. Holmes Perkins, January 20, 1961, Acc. 350, box 11, folder "Unit 3 Boundaries," SCRC.

62. Fact sheet "The West Philadelphia Corporation."

63. Puckett and Lloyd, *Becoming Penn*, 97; O'Mara, *Cities of Knowledge*, 159.

64. Puckett and Lloyd, *Becoming Penn*, 32–33, 37.

65. Smith, *New Urban Frontier*, 124–25.

66. Resnik, *Turning on the System*, 4–5; Birger, "Race, Reaction, and Reform," 185–86.

67. Puckett and Lloyd, *Becoming Penn*, 60–62.

68. "Questions and Answers Relating to Title IV of the Elementary and Secondary Education Act," May 19, 1965, Acc. 350, box 22, folder "Educational Regional Laboratory 1965 (Archives)," SCRC.

69. Clifford Swartz, "A Design Proposal for the Philadelphia Science-Math 'Magnet' High School," 1968, p. 5, Acc. 350, box 22, "University City High School 1968," SCRC.

70. Jessica Oliff, "University City High School: An Experiment in Innovative Education, 1959–1972," senior thesis paper, University of Pennsylvania, 79.

71. Report prepared for the Board of Public Education, "University City in Philadelphia: An Opportunity for Educational Leadership and Educational Innovation," September 12, 1961, Acc. 350, box 22, folder "Board of Ed—Report of Meeting September 12, 1961," SCRC.

72. Oliff, "University City High School," 14–15.

73. Clapper, "School Design," 245.

74. Orr, discussion; Nichols-Solomon, discussion; Williamson, discussion.

75. Oliff, "University City High School," 24; Conrad Weiler, *Philadelphia: Neighborhood, Authority and the Urban Crisis* (New York: Praeger, 1974), 84–85.

76. Oliff, "University City High School," 24.

77. "Comments on University City Urban Renewal Area Unit #3."

78. "University City- Proposed Land Use" and accompanying map.

CHAPTER 4

1. Resnik, *Turning on the System*, 3; Cutler, "Outside in and Inside Out," 309; William W. Cutler, "Philadelphia, Pittsburgh, and the Historiography of Urban Public Education in Pennsylvania," *Pennsylvania Magazine of History and Biography* 141, no. 3 (2017): 236–37.

2. Resnik, *Turning on the System*, 124.

3. Resnik, *Turning on the System*, 48–50, 124.

4. Resnik, *Turning on the System*, 4.

5. Phillips, "Struggle for School Desegregation," 84–89, 117–19, 129–33.

6. Countryman, *Up South*, 226; Birger, "Race, Reaction, and Reform," 164.

7. Quoted in Joseph R. Daughen and Peter Binzen, *The Cop Who Would Be King: Mayor Frank Rizzo* (Boston: Little, Brown, 1977), 116.

8. Birger, "Race, Reaction, and Reform," 172n20; Norman Newberg, in discussion with the author, February 13, 2019; N. Brown, discussion.

9. Philadelphia Educators to Africa Collection, Charles L. Blockson Afro-American Collection, Temple University.

10. Birger, "Race, Reaction, and Reform," 172n20.

11. Resnik, *Turning on the System*, 113–14.

12. Birger, "Race, Reaction, and Reform," 168–69, 198–99.

13. Puckett and Lloyd, *Becoming Penn*, 107–8.

14. Oliff, "University City High School," 38.

15. Puckett and Lloyd, *Becoming Penn*, 108–9; Oliff, "University City High School," 39–40; Wolf-Powers, *University City*, 30–32.

16. Puckett and Lloyd, *Becoming Penn*, 108–9; Oliff, "University City High School," 39–40; Wolf-Powers, *University City*, 35.

17. Leo Molinaro to WPC board of directors, May 20, 1963, UPA 4, box 156, folder "West Phila. Corp. General 1962–63," UARC.

18. Black, discussion.

19. Davis et al., discussion.

20. Davis et al., discussion.

21. See Jane Jacobs, *The Death and Life of Great American Cities* (New York: Vintage, 1961), chapters 2, 3, and 4, which discuss how, in a well-functioning city, sidewalks promote safety, communication between neighbors, and the socialization of children.

22. Gaylord P. Harnwell to Francis J. Lammer, August 24, 1964, Acc. 350, box 11, folder "Unit #3 (1963–64) Clay Group," SCRC.

23. Leo A. Molinaro to Gaylord P. Harnwell, August 17, 1964, Acc. 350, box 11, folder "Unit #3 (1963–64) Clay Group," SCRC.

24. Molinaro to Harnwell, August 17, 1964.

25. Puckett and Lloyd, *Becoming Penn*, 103; Oliff, "University City High School," 39–40.

26. Background Report on John H. Clay, Acc. 350, folder 11, "Unit 3 (1965) Clay Group (archives)," SCRC.

27. Franny Robinson to President Lyndon B. Johnson, September 14, 1965, Acc. 350, folder 11, "Unit 3 (1965) Clay Group (archives)," SCRC.

28. Leo Molinaro to Franny Robinson, September 20, 1965, Acc. 350, folder 11, "Unit 3 (1965) Clay Group (archives)," SCRC.

29. Molinaro to Robinson, September 20, 1965.

30. Puckett and Lloyd, *Becoming Penn*, 108–10.

31. Leo Molinaro to the WPC Board of Directors, September 14, 1966, UPA 4, box 188, folder "Community Relations (WPC) 1965–1970," UARC.

32. Robert S. King, statement to the Philadelphia Board of Education, September 21, 1966, Acc. 350, box 22, "Public Hearing 1966," SCRC.

33. Allen S. Goldman, statement to the Philadelphia Board of Education, September 21, 1966, Acc. 350, box 22, "Public Hearing 1966," SCRC.

34. Charles W. Campbell, "Neighborhood Attitudes toward Redevelopment and Rehabilitation Investigative Report," Acc. 350, box 22, folder "Public Hearing 1966," SCRC.

35. Lawrence Beck and Stephen Kerstetter, "The Quiet War in West Philadelphia," series of articles published in the *Daily Pennsylvanian*, January 23–27, 1967.

36. Puckett and Lloyd, *Becoming Penn*, 114–15.

37. Oliff, "University City High School," 35.

38. Oliff, "University City High School," 64–65.

39. Newsletter, "University City," vol. 6, no. 3, December 1967, UPA 4, box 188, folder "West Philadelphia Corporation V (Community Relations) 1965–1970," UARC.

40. Swartz, "A Design Proposal," 5.

41. Oliff, "University City High School," 69; Resnik, *Turning on the System*, 59–61.

42. Swartz, "A Design Proposal," 11.

43. Birger, "Race, Reaction, and Reform," 179.

44. Birger, "Race, Reaction, and Reform," 168–69.

45. Birger, "Race, Reaction, and Reform," 172.

46. Philadelphia Federation of Teachers president Celia Pincius, quoted in Birger, "Race, Reaction, and Reform," 192.

47. Newsletter, "ES '70," vol. 1, no. 7, February 1969, Acc. 350, box 22, folder "University City High School 1969," SCRC.

48. Oliff, "University City High School," 106.

49. Report "A Plan for a Demonstration Summer School—1969," Acc. 350, box 22, folder "Campus Summer School 1969," SCRC; Oliff, "University City High School," 102.

50. "A Plan for a Demonstration Summer School"; Oliff, "University City High School," 102.

51. Leo Molinaro to the WPC Board of Directors, April 30, 1968, Acc. 350, box 1, folder "Barkan, Bernard," SCRC; see also Orvell, *Death and Life of Main Street*. Columbia, Maryland, was a planned community of one hundred thousand residents consisting of villages of ten to fifteen thousand residents, each divided into smaller clusters of twenty-five hundred. Clusters would have amenities such as a pool, childcare center, store, playing fields, park, and community room.

52. James Lytle, in discussion with the author, March 13, 2019.

53. Oliff, "University City High School," 67–68.

54. Oliff, "University City High School," 81–82.

55. Oliff, "University City High School," 81.

56. Oliff, "University City High School," 79; Report of minutes, Feeder Committee of the West Philadelphia-University City High School, April 9, 1969, Acc. 350, box 22, folder "University City High School 1969," SCRC.

57. Birger, "Race, Reaction, and Reform," 196.

58. Oliff, "University City High School," 83–84.

59. Oliff, "University City High School," 83–84.

60. Gaylord Harnwell to Chad F. Gottschlich, October 21, 1969, UPA 4, box 257, folder 17, "Office of the President, Community Relations, WPC, Universities-Related School Program," UARC.

61. Oliff, "University City High School," 86–87.

62. Puckett and Lloyd, *Becoming Penn*, 112–14.

63. Carol Williamson, in discussion with the author, January 19, 2019.

64. Lytle, discussion.

65. Williamson, discussion. Girls High School was established in 1848 and is a college-preparatory magnet school. Until 1983, when Philadelphia's Central High School began to admit girls, it was the school of choice for female students seeking an academically competitive curriculum in the SDP.

66. Williamson, discussion.

67. Williamson, discussion.

68. Williamson, discussion.

69. Pat Spann, in discussion with the author, February 11, 2019.

70. Spann, discussion.

71. Spann, discussion.

72. Drew Home and School Association Chair Carolyn Johnson to Gaylord Harnwell, September 10, 1969, UPA 4, box 257, folder 17, UARC.

73. Drew Home and School Association Chair Carolyn Johnson to Gaylord Harnwell, September 26, 1969, UPA 4, box 257, folder 17, UARC.

74. Gaylord P. Harnwell to Robert L. Taylor, September 1964, UPA 4, box 155, folder "West Phila. Corp General, 1964–65," UARC.

75. Castetter, Davis, and Heisler, *Henry C. Lea School*, x.

76. Mary Coleman to Morris S. Viteles, March 14, 1966, UPA 4, box 256, folder 4, UARC; Amy Orr, in discussion with the author, November 21, 2017; Prentice Cole, in discussion with the author, February 28, 2018; Williamson, discussion.

77. Coleman to Viteles, March 14, 1966.

78. Bonhomme, discussion.

79. Orr, discussion; Cole, discussion; Williamson, discussion; Spann, discussion; Dottie Camp, in discussion with the author, 3 December 2019.

80. Bonhomme, discussion.

81. James F. Ross, "Education in the City," statement to the university council, October 25, 1968, p. 2, folder "Ad Hoc Committee on Education in University City," papers of Ira Harkavy.

82. Ross, "Education in the City," 2.

83. Ross, "Education in the City," 3.

84. Ross, "Education in the City," 3.

85. Harnwell to Gottschilch, October 21, 1969.

86. Report of ad hoc Senate committee on URS, January 20, 1970, UPA 4, box 257, folder 17, UARC.

87. Report of ad hoc Senate committee on URS, January 20, 1970.

88. Puckett and Lloyd, *Becoming Penn*, 144.

89. WPC Executive Committee Minutes, May 13, 1971, UPA 4, box 257, folder 11, UARC.

90. Report of ad hoc Senate committee on URS, January 20, 1970.

91. Report of ad hoc Senate committee on URS, January 20, 1970.

92. Segal, *Got No Time to Fool Around*, 92

93. Gloria Moskowitz, in discussion with the author, December 2, 2017.

94. Moskowitz, discussion.

95. Frank M. Betts III, Assistant to the President for External Affairs, to Rebecca Segal, August 9, 1971, UPA 4, box 257, FF 15, University of Pennsylvania Archives, Philadelphia.

96. Moskowitz, discussion; K. Rose Samuel-Evans, in discussion with the author, October 6, 2017.

97. Phil Akrow, "Subtle Hatred of the University's Guts Is Displayed by Neighbors," *Daily Pennsylvanian*, October 14, 1968.

98. Stefan M. Bradley, *Upending the Ivory Tower: Civil Rights, Black Power, and the Ivy League* (New York: New York University Press, 2018), 217.

99. E. Brown, discussion; Newkirk, discussion.

100. E. Brown, discussion.

101. Newkirk, discussion.

102. Malcolm Bonner, in discussion with the author, February 12, 2020.

103. Newkirk, discussion.

104. Puckett and Lloyd, *Becoming Penn*, 127–34.

105. "Power to Participate," *TIME Magazine*, March 15, 1968, 78–79.

106. Beck and Kerstetter, "Quiet War in West Philadelphia."

107. Bradley, *Upending the Ivory Tower*, 219.

108. Puckett and Lloyd, *Becoming Penn*, 129–32; Ira Harkavy, in discussion with the author, November 30, 2017.

CHAPTER 5

1. Birger, "Race, Reaction, and Reform," 213.

2. U.S. Census data, accessed through Social Explorer, https://www.socialexplorer.com.

3. John L. Puckett, "University City Science Center," *Encyclopedia of Greater Philadelphia*, https://philadelphiaencyclopedia.org/archive/university-city-science-center/.

4. Puckett, "University City Science Center and the Black Bottom," *West Philadelphia Collaborative History*, https://collaborativehistory.gse.upenn.edu/stories/university-city-science-center-and-black-bottom.

5. Puckett and Lloyd, *Becoming Penn*, 102.

6. Marion Pond, "Memo Regarding the West Philadelphia Corporation," undated, UPA 4, box 256, folder 15, UARC.

7. Amendment to WPC bylaws, November 29, 1977, UPA 4, box 256, folder 23, UARC.

8. Puckett and Lloyd, *Becoming Penn*, 224.

9. Charter of the Quadripartite Commission, February 23, 1969, box 188, folder "Quadripartite Commission on University/Community Development (Community Relations) 1965–1970," UARC.

10. Meeting minutes, Quadripartite Commission, March 10, 1969, UPA 4, box 188, folder "Quadripartite Commission on University/Community Development (Community Relations) 1965–1970," UARC.

11. Meeting minutes, Quadripartite Commission, March 31, 1969, UPA 4, box 188, folder "Quadripartite Commission on University/Community Development (Community Relations) 1965–1970," UARC.

12. Meeting minutes, Quadripartite Commission, March 31, 1969.

13. Bradley, *Upending the Ivory Tower*, 210.

14. Russell L. Ackoff, "A Black Ghetto's Research on a University," *Operations Research* 18, no. 5 (September–October 1970): 764–65. Ackoff was a faculty representative on the QPC.

15. Architecture and Planning Center of the Young Great Society, "Unit 3 Planning Charrette," October 13, 1969, preface, UPB 101.4, box 23, folder "Quadripartite Commission 1969–1970," UARC.

16. Quadripartite Commission minutes, UPB 101.4, box 23, folder "Quadripartite Commission 1969–1970," UARC.

17. APC of the Young Great Society, "Unit 3 Planning Charrette," 7.

18. Penn Board of Trustees, Executive Board Resolution, November 14, 1969, UPB 101.4, box 24, folder 29 "Quadripartite Commission"; Penn Almanac announcement, UPF 8.5, box 237, folder "News Bureau-Subject Files, Quadripartite Commission"; *Evening Bulletin*, January 18, 1970, UPF 8.5, box 237, folder "News Bureau-Subject Files, Quadripartite Commission," UARC.

19. *Evening Bulletin*, January 18, 1970.

20. Puckett and Lloyd, *Becoming Penn*, 133.

21. Rasheda Alexander and Sterling Johnson, "Frank Rizzo, the UC Townhomes, and the Fight to Save Black Philadelphia," *WHYY*, April 20, 2022, https://whyy.org/articles/frank-rizzo-university-city-townhomes-fight-to-save-black-philadelphia/.

22. "Proposal for a Series of Town and Gown Seminars on New Civic Responsibilities of Higher Education in Urban America," UPA 4, box 74, folder "Community Relations—1955–1960, West Philadelphia Corporation V," UARC.

23. Puckett and Lloyd, *Becoming Penn*, 224.

24. Benson et al., *Knowledge for Social Change*, 97.

25. Lee Benson, Ira Harkavy, and John L. Puckett, *Dewey's Dream: Universities and Democracies in an Age of Education Reform* (Philadelphia: Temple University Press, 2007), 88.

26. Benson, Harkavy, and Puckett, *Dewey's Dream*, 87–88.

27. William K. Stephens, "Police Drop Bomb on Radicals' Home in Philadelphia," *New York Times*, May 14, 1985, 1.

28. Lois Gelfand and Mildred Gelfand, in discussion with the author, January 21, 2019.

29. Benson, Harkavy, and Puckett, *Dewey's Dream*, 97–98.

30. Ira Harkavy, in discussion with the author, November 30, 2017.

31. Benson, Harkavy, and Puckett, *Dewey's Dream*, 98.

32. Benson et al., *Knowledge for Social Change*, 124–25, 128–29.

33. Benson et al., *Knowledge for Social Change*, 115.

34. Matthew Hartley, "Idealism and Compromise and the Civic Engagement Movement," in *To Serve a Larger Purpose: Engagement for Democracy and the Transformation of Higher Education*, eds. John Saltmarsh and Matthew Hartley (Philadelphia: Temple University Press, 2011), 42. For further discussion of the civically engaged campus, see Ernest L. Boyer, "The Scholarship of Engagement," *Bulletin of the American Academy of Arts and Sciences* 49, no. 7 (April 1996): 18–33.

35. John L. Puckett, "The Past Recaptured: Honoring the Memory of the Black Bottom," *West Philadelphia Collaborative History*, https://collaborativehistory.gse.upenn.edu/stories/past-recaptured-honoring-memory-black-bottom.

36. Andrea Zemel, "Fine Arts 349: Community, Collaborative, and Public Art," *Art Journal* 58, no. 1 (Spring 1999): 63–67.

37. Puckett, "The Past Recaptured."

38. Puckett and Lloyd, *Becoming Penn*, 181.

39. Teresa Esch, in discussion with the author, March 29, 2023.

40. Jacqui Bowman, in discussion with the author, February 17, 2023.

41. Maia Bloomfield Cucchiara, *Marketing Schools, Marketing Cities: Who Wins and Who Loses When Schools Become Urban Amenities* (Chicago: University of Chicago Press, 2013), 43–44.

42. Cucchiara, *Marketing Schools, Marketing Cities*, 26–28, 31.

43. Central Philadelphia Development Corporation, *OPDC | CPDC: 50 Years Remaking Center City*, April 2006, iii, https://centercityphila.org/research-reports/opdc-cpdc-50-years-of-remaking-center-city.

44. Puckett and Lloyd, *Becoming Penn*, 251–52; Judith Rodin, *The University and Urban Revival: Out of the Ivory Tower and into the Streets* (Philadelphia: University of Pennsylvania Press, 2007), ix–x.

45. Rodin, *University and Urban Revival*, 42.

46. Puckett and Lloyd, *Becoming Penn*, 257–58.

47. Bowman, discussion.

48. Puckett and Lloyd, *Becoming Penn*, 257–58; Bowman, discussion.

49. Rodin, *University and Urban Revival*, v, 8, 44, 61.

50. WPC press release, April 22, 1959, UPA 4, box 73, folder "Community Relations, 1955–1960, The West Philadelphia Corporation I," UARC.

51. Rodin, *University and Urban Revival*, 92.

52. Rodin, *University and Urban Revival*, 92–93; Puckett and Lloyd, *Becoming Penn*, 259.

53. Keeanga-Yamahtta Taylor, *Race for Profit: How Banks and the Real Estate Industry Undermined Black Homeownership* (Chapel Hill: University of North Carolina Press, 2019), 7.

CHAPTER 6

1. Nancy Streim, in discussion with the author, January 19, 2022.

2. Dennis Culhane, in discussion with the author, April 12, 2022.

3. Streim, discussion; Puckett and Lloyd, *Becoming Penn*, 262.

4. Streim, discussion; Puckett and Lloyd, *Becoming Penn*, 262, 266; Melamed, "Penn Alexander Effect."

5. Camika Royal, *Not Paved for Us: Black Educators and Public School Reform in Philadelphia* (Cambridge, MA: Harvard Education Press, 2022), 82–87.

6. Rodin, *University and Urban Revival*, 33–36, 145.

7. Gregory Richards, "New School Closes Its Doors for the Last Time," *Daily Pennsylvanian*, July 5, 2001, https://www.thedp.com/article/2001/07/new_school_closes_its_doors_for_the_last_time; Elizabeth A. Ratay, "UCNS Head: Time We Spoke Up," letter to the editor, *Penn Gazette*, November 1, 2000, https://thepenngazette.com/letters-62/.

8. "Grants for Penn Parents at University City New School," *Penn Almanac*, July 15, 1997, https://almanac.upenn.edu/archive/v44/n01/newsch.html.

9. Jacqui Bowman, in discussion with the author, February 17, 2023.

10. Rodin, *University and Urban Revival*, 147–48.

11. Streim, discussion.

12. Puckett and Lloyd, *Becoming Penn*, 264.

13. Rodin, *University and Urban Revival*, 43.

14. Keally McBride, in discussion with the author, February 20, 2023.

15. Streim, discussion.

16. Culhane, discussion.

17. Streim, discussion. Streim's colleague Dennis Culhane denied any use of this tipping point literature because it would suggest that the PAS planning team had sought to reduce the number of Black students in the school. Perhaps another reason was the stigma this literature has acquired over the years. First introduced in the 1950s, the idea that a certain proportion of Black residents in a neighborhood triggers White flight seems shameful today because it regards prejudice as a natural law rather than a moral

outrage. For an example, see Morton Grodzins, "Metropolitan Segregation," *Scientific American* 197, no. 4 (October 1957): 33–41. Tipping point literature was used by developer James Rouse in planning his urban community of Columbia, Maryland, in 1968, with Leo Molinaro assisting. For more on Columbia, see Orvell, *Death and Life of Main Street*.

18. Culhane, discussion.

19. Betty Livermore, "Family Needs in University City Planning: A Study of Factors Affecting the Selection of Neighborhoods by Faculty and Staff of the University of Pennsylvania," June 6, 1963, UPA 4, box 152, "Community Relations II, 1960–65," UARC.

20. Julia Crane, in discussion with the author, April 21, 2023; Carola Lelieveld, in discussion with the author, January 31, 2023; McBride, discussion.

21. Bowman, discussion.

22. Rosemary Ford, in discussion with the author, February 17, 2023.

23. Streim, discussion; Puckett and Lloyd, *Becoming Penn*, 265–66.

24. Rodin, *University and Urban Revival*, 156.

25. Puckett and Lloyd, 265–66; Rodin, *University and Urban Renewal*, 155.

26. Rodin, *University and Urban Renewal*, 155.

27. Rodin, *University and Urban Renewal*, 157.

28. Puckett and Lloyd, *Becoming Penn*, 262.

29. Streim, discussion; Rodin, *University and Urban Renewal*, 152.

30. Rodin, *University and Urban Renewal*, 152; Clyde M. Campbell, "Contributions of the Mott Foundation to the Community Education Movement," *The Phi Delta Kappan* 54, no. 3 (November 1972): 195–97. See also Benson et al., *Knowledge for Social Change*, 48, 54–55.

31. Streim, discussion; Puckett and Lloyd, *Becoming Penn*, 263, 266.

32. Melamed, "Penn Alexander Effect."

33. Royal, *Not Paved for Us*, 85–87.

34. Streim, discussion.

35. Cucchiara, *Marketing Schools, Marketing Cities*, 56–57.

36. Bowman, discussion.

37. Ford, discussion.

38. Lelieveld, discussion.

39. Rodin, *University and Urban Renewal*, 159.

40. Kristen A. Graham and Martha Woodall, "10 Philly, Suburban Schools Win National Honor," *Philadelphia Inquirer*, September 28, 2016; Dale Mezzacappa, "GAMP, Penn Alexander in Philly Recognized as National Blue Ribbon Schools," *Chalkbeat*, September 21, 2021.

41. Crane, discussion.

42. Ford, discussion.

43. McBride, discussion.

44. McBride, discussion.

45. Bowman, discussion.

46. Ford, discussion.

47. Bowman, discussion.

48. McBride, discussion.

49. Streim, discussion.

50. Ford, discussion.

51. McBride, discussion.

52. McBride, discussion.

53. Linn Posey-Maddox, *When Middle-Class Parents Choose Urban Schools: Class, Race and the Challenge of Equity in Public Education* (Chicago: University of Chicago Press, 2014), 2–4, 74–77, 108–11.

54. Chana Joffe-Walt, "Nice White Parents," podcast series, *New York Times*, July 23–August 20, 2020, https://www.nytimes.com/2020/07/23/podcasts/nice-white-parents-serial.html.

55. Cucchiara, *Marketing Schools, Marketing Cities*, 75–76, 100.

56. TERC website, https://www.terc.edu/. The organization was founded by Arthur Nelson in 1965 in Cambridge, MA, as the Technical Education Research Centers. It originally focused on math and science in vocational and technical education but has since evolved to encompass all areas of STEM education. See also https://investigations.terc.edu/. The Investigations Center for Curriculum and Professional Development at TERC began development work on math curricula in the 1980s and released the first edition of the Investigations curriculum in 1990 through Pearson Publishing, with funding from the National Science Foundation.

57. Lelieveld, discussion.

58. Lelieveld, discussion.

59. Bowman, discussion.

60. Ford, discussion; Lelieveld, discussion.

61. Ford, discussion; Bowman, discussion.

62. Bowman, discussion.

63. Bowman, discussion; Crane, discussion.

64. Streim, discussion.

65. McBride, discussion.

66. Lelieveld, discussion.

67. Bowman, discussion; Crane, discussion.

68. Bowman, discussion.

69. Lelieveld, discussion.

70. As noted, no Black parents agreed to speak on the record about PAS, though a few agreed to an initial interview. Some expressed worry that criticizing Penn might have a negative impact on their career. None mentioned specific threats of retaliation.

71. McBride, discussion.

72. Crane, discussion; Ford, discussion; Lelieveld, discussion.

73. Ford, discussion.

74. Crane, discussion; Ford, discussion.

75. Ford, discussion.

76. Joann Mitchell, in discussion with the author, April 25, 2022.

77. McBride, discussion.

78. Davis et al., discussion.

79. Culhane, discussion.

80. Rodin, *University and Urban Renewal*, 156.

81. Culhane, discussion; Rodin, *University and Urban Renewal*, 96–97; NPDF website, accessed May 16, 2022, https://altmanco.com/apartments/PA/Philadelphia/N.P.D.F./.

82. Culhane, discussion.

83. Rodin, *University and Urban Renewal*, 179.

84. Report "University City-Proposed Land Use," accompanied by map, no date, p. 3, UPA 4, box 73, folder "Community Relations, 1955–1960, The West Philadelphia Corporation I," UARC.

85. Cucchiara, *Marketing Schools, Marketing Cities*, 15, 16–17.

86. Posey-Maddox, When *Middle-Class Parents Choose Urban Schools*, 9.

87. Smith, *New Urban Frontier*, 126–28.

88. U.S. Census Bureau data, accessed through Social Explorer, https://www.socialexplorer.com. Note that the 30 percent figure for maximum monthly housing costs has

been widely used since 1969. See "Rental Burdens: Rethinking Affordability Measures," *The Edge*, Housing and Urban Development Office of Policy and Research, September 22, 2014, https://www.huduser.gov/portal/pdredge/pdr_edge_featd_article_092214.html.

89. Richard Florida, *The New Urban Crisis: How Our Cities Are Increasing Inequality, Deepening Segregation and Failing the Middle Class—And What We Can Do about It* (New York: Basic Books, 2017), 6–8.

90. Baldwin, *In the Shadow of the Ivory Tower*, 188; Wolf-Powers, *University City*, 95–96.

91. Kristen A. Graham, "With $40M in Public and Private Money, a New Building Is Rising for Two West Philly Schools," *Philadelphia Inquirer*, December 9, 2019.

92. Bowman, discussion.

93. Brian O'Leary and Julia Piper, "How Much Has Faculty Pay Changed Over Time?," *Chronicle of Higher Education*, April 1, 2025. https://www.chronicle.com/article/explore-faculty-salaries-at-3-500-colleges-2012-20; U.S. Census Bureau data, accessed through Social Explorer. https://www.socialexplorer.com.

CHAPTER 7

1. Rasheda Alexander, in discussion with the author, April 30, 2023.

2. Mills, *Racial Contract*, 18.

3. Wolf-Powers, *University City*, 97.

4. Julie Bosman, "Chicago Suburb Shapes Reparations for Black Residents: 'It Is the Start,'" *New York Times*, March 22, 2021, https://www.nytimes.com/2021/03/22/us/reparations-evanston-illinois-housing.html; Rachel L. Swarns, "Catholic Order Pledges $100 Million to Atone for Slave Labor and Sales," *New York Times*, March 15, 2021, https://www.nytimes.com/2021/03/15/us/jesuits-georgetown-reparations-slavery.html.

5. William Darity Jr. and A. Kirsten Mullen, *From Here to Equality: Reparations for Black Americans in the Twenty-First Century* (Chapel Hill: University of North Carolina Press, 2020), 2–3; 264–65.

6. Susan Neiman, *Learning from the Germans: Race and the Memory of Evil* (New York: Farrar, Strauss & Giroux, 2019), 311.

7. Cucchiara, *Marketing Schools, Marketing Cities*, 2.

8. McKee, *Problem of Jobs*, 24–26.

9. Heller, *Ed Bacon*, 23–27.

10. Heller, *Ed Bacon*, 36–37.

11. An example is Richardson Dilworth to Leo Molinaro, February 21, 1967, Acc. 350, box 1, folder 7, "Annual Report 1966–67, 7th Annual Report," SCRC.

12. Heller, *Ed Bacon*, 46.

13. WPC, *Elaborations*, 11.

14. "University City 3 Redevelopment Area Plan," May 18, 1962, Acc. 350, box 11, folder "Unit 3—1962–63," SCRC.

15. Jacobs, *Death and Life of Great American Cities*, 41.

16. Cucchiara, *Marketing Schools, Marketing Cities*, 2.

17. Daniel Hertz, "There's Basically No Way Not to Be a Gentrifier," *CityLab*, April 23, 2014, https://www.citylab.com/equity/2014/04/theres-basically-no-way-not-be-gentrifier/8877/.

18. Hertz, "There's Basically No Way Not to Be a Gentrifier."

Bibliography

ARCHIVES

Philadelphia City Archives
Philadelphia City Planning Commission Files (PCA 145.2)

Temple University Special Collections Research Center
West Philadelphia Corporation Records (Acc. 350)

University of Pennsylvania Archives
Office of the President Records, Gaylord Probasco Harnwell Administration (UPA 4 Harnwell)
Office of the President Records, Martin Meyerson Administration (UPA 4 Meyerson)
University Relations Information Files (UPF 8.5I)
University Relations News and Public Affairs Records (UPF 8.5)
Vice President for Coordinated Planning Records (UPB 101.4)

GENERAL SOURCES

Ackoff, Russell L. "A Black Ghetto's Research on a University." *Operations Research* 18, no. 5 (September–October 1970): 761–71.

Adams, Carolyn, David Bartelt, David Elesh, Ira Goldstein, Nancy Kleniewski, and William Yancey. *Philadelphia: Neighborhoods, Division, and Conflict in a Post-industrial City*. Philadelphia: Temple University Press, 1991.

American Psychological Association. "Racial and Ethnic Identity." In *Publication Manual of the APA*. 7th ed., edited by Emily L. Ayubi and staff. Washington, DC: APA, 2020. https://apastyle.apa.org/style-grammar-guidelines/bias-free-language/racial-ethnic-minorities.

Ammon, Francesca Russello. "Picturing Preservation and Renewal: Photographs as Planning Knowledge in Society Hill, Philadelphia." *Journal of Planning Education and Research* 42, no. 3 (2022): 314–30.

Axtell, James. *The School upon a Hill: Education and Society in Colonial New England.* New Haven: Yale University Press, 1974.

Baldwin, Davarian L. *In the Shadow of the Ivory Tower: How Universities Are Plundering Our Cities.* New York: Bold Type, 2021.

Beed, Penny L., E. Marie Hawkins, and Cathy M. Roller. "Moving Learners towards Independence: The Power of Scaffolded Instruction." *The Reading Teacher* 44, no. 9 (1991): 648–55.

Benson, Lee, Ira Harkavy, and John L. Puckett. *Dewey's Dream: Universities and Democracies in an Age of Education Reform.* Philadelphia: Temple University Press, 2007.

Benson, Lee, Ira Harkavy, John L. Puckett, Matthew Hartley, Rita A. Hodges, Francis E. Johnston, and Joann Weeks. *Knowledge for Social Change: Bacon, Dewey, and the Revolutionary Transformation of Research Universities in the Twenty-First Century.* Philadelphia: Temple University Press, 2017.

Berk, Laura E., and Adam Winsler. *Scaffolding Children's Learning: Vygotsky and Early Childhood Learning.* Washington, DC: National Association for the Education of Young Children, 1995.

Birger, Jon S. "Race, Reaction, and Reform: The Three Rs of Philadelphia School Politics, 1965–1971." *Pennsylvania Magazine of History and Biography* 120, no. 3 (July 1996): 163–216.

Boyer, Ernest L. "The Scholarship of Engagement." *Bulletin of the American Academy of Arts and Sciences* 49, no. 7 (1996): 18–33.

Bradley, Stefan M. *Harlem vs. Columbia University: Black Student Power in the Late 1960s.* Champaign: University of Illinois Press, 2009.

———. *Upending the Ivory Tower: Civil Rights, Black Power, and the Ivy League.* New York: New York University Press, 2018.

Castetter, William B., Frederick B. Davis, and Richard S. Heisler. *The Henry C. Lea School: An Appraisal.* Philadelphia: Educational Research and Service Bureau, University of Pennsylvania, 1968.

Clapper, Michael. "School Design, Site Selection, and the Political Geography of Race in Postwar Philadelphia." *Journal of Planning History* 5, no. 3 (2006): 241–63.

Countryman, Matthew. *Up South: Civil Rights and Black Power in Philadelphia.* Philadelphia: University of Pennsylvania Press, 2006.

Cozzolino, Robert. *David Lynch: The Unified Field.* Oakland: University of California Press, 2014.

Cucchiara, Maia Bloomfield. *Marketing Schools, Marketing Cities: Who Wins and Who Loses When Schools Become Urban Amenities.* Chicago: University of Chicago Press, 2013.

Cutler, William W., III. "Outside in and Inside Out: Civic Activism, Helen Oakes, and the Philadelphia Public Schools, 1960–1989." *Pennsylvania Magazine of History and Biography* 37, no. 3 (2013): 301–24.

———. "Philadelphia, Pittsburgh, and the Historiography of Urban Public Education in Pennsylvania." *Pennsylvania Magazine of History and Biography* 141, no. 3 (2017): 221–43.

Darity, William, Jr., and A. Kirsten Mullen. *From Here to Equality: Reparations for Black Americans in the Twenty-First Century.* Chapel Hill: University of North Carolina Press, 2020.

Daughen, Joseph R., and Peter Binzen. *The Cop Who Would Be King: Mayor Frank Rizzo.* Boston: Little, Brown, 1977.

Etienne, Harley F. *Pushing back the Gates: Neighborhood Perspectives on University-Driven Revitalization in West Philadelphia.* Philadelphia: Temple University Press, 2012.

Fishman, Robert. "The Fifth Migration." *Journal of the American Planning Association* 71, no. 4 (Autumn 2005): 357–66.

Florida, Richard. *Cities and the Creative Class.* New York: Routledge, 2005.

———. *The New Urban Crisis: How Our Cities Are Increasing Inequality, Deepening Segregation and Failing the Middle Class—And What We Can Do about It.* New York: Basic Books, 2017.

Franklin, Vincent P. *The Education of Black Philadelphia: A Social and Educational History of a Minority Community, 1900–1950.* Philadelphia: University of Pennsylvania Press, 1979.

Glass, Ruth, E. J. Hobsbawm, Harold Pollins, W. Ashworth, J. H. Westergaard, William Holford, Margot Jefferys, John A. Jackson, and Sheila Patterson. *London: Aspects of Change.* London: MacGibbon & Kee, 1964.

Grodzins, Morton. "Metropolitan Segregation." *Scientific American* 197, no. 4 (October 1957): 33–41.

Hartley, Matthew. "Idealism and Compromise and the Civic Engagement Movement." In *To Serve a Larger Purpose: Engagement for Democracy and the Transformation of Higher Education,* edited by John Saltmarsh and Matthew Hartley, 27–48. Philadelphia: Temple University Press, 2011.

Havemann, Ernest. "The Rebirth of Philadelphia: City Is Living Proof of What Citizens Can Do to Secure Good Government, Civic Renaissance." *National Civic Review* 51, no. 10 (November 1962): 538–42.

Hayre, Ruth Wright, and Alexis Moore. *Tell Them We Are Rising: A Memoir of Faith in Education.* New York: John Wiley & Sons, 1997.

Heller, Gregory L. *Ed Bacon: Planning, Politics, and the Building of Modern Philadelphia.* Philadelphia: University of Pennsylvania Press, 2013.

———. "The Life Experiences That Shaped Edmund Bacon." In *Imagining Philadelphia: Edmund Bacon and the Future of the City,* edited by Scott Gabriel Knowles, 19–51. Philadelphia: University of Pennsylvania Press, 2009.

Hertz, Daniel. "There's Basically No Way Not to Be a Gentrifier." *CityLab,* April 23, 2014. https://www.citylab.com/equity/2014/04/theres-basically-no-way-not-be-gentrifier/8877/.

Hirsch, Arnold R. *Making the Second Ghetto: Race and Housing in Chicago, 1940–1960.* Chicago: University of Chicago Press, 1983. Reprint, 1998.

Ingersoll, Agnes C. "A Society Hill Restoration." *Bryn Mawr Alumnae Bulletin,* Fall 1963: 13–17.

Jacobs, Jane. *The Death and Life of Great American Cities.* New York: Vintage, 1961.

Joffe-Walt, Chana. "Nice White Parents." Podcast series, *New York Times,* July 23–August 20, 2020. https://www.nytimes.com/2020/07/23/podcasts/nice-white-parents-serial.html.

Kliebard, Herbert M. *The Struggle for the American Curriculum, 1893–1958.* 3rd ed. New York: Taylor and Francis, 2004.

Knowles, Scott Gabriel, ed. *Imagining Philadelphia: Edmund Bacon and the Future of the City.* Philadelphia: University of Pennsylvania Press, 2009.

Lemann, Nicholas. *The Promised Land: The Great Black Migration and How It Changed America.* New York: A. A. Knopf, 1991.

McKee, Guian A. *The Problem of Jobs: Liberalism, Race, and Deindustrialization in Phila-delphia*. Chicago: University of Chicago Press, 2008.

McKittrick, Katherine. "On Plantations, Prisons, and a Black Sense of Place." *Social and Cultural Geography* 12, no. 8 (2011): 947–63.

McLarnon, John M., and G. Terry Madonna, "Dilworth, Clark, and Reform in Philadel-phia, 1947–1962." *Pennsylvania Legacies* 11, no. 2 (November 2011): 24–31.

Melamed, Samantha. "The Penn Alexander Effect: Is There Any Room Left for Low-In-come Residents in University City?" *Philadelphia Inquirer*, November 1, 2018.

Miller, Roger, and Joseph Siry. "The Emerging Suburb: West Philadelphia, 1850–1880." *Pennsylvania History: A Journal of Mid-Atlantic Studies* 47, no. 2 (1980): 99–145.

Mills, Charles W. *The Racial Contract*. Ithaca, NY: Cornell University Press, 1997.

Neiman, Susan. *Learning from the Germans: Race and the Memory of Evil*. New York: Far-rar, Strauss & Giroux, 2019.

Nielsen, William C. "The Storefront School." In *Restructuring American Education: In-novations and Alternatives*, edited by Ray C. Rist, 223–35. New Brunswick, NJ: Trans-action Books, 1972.

Oliff, Jessica Lee. "University City High School: An Experiment in Innovative Education, 1959–1972." Senior thesis paper, University of Pennsylvania, 2000.

O'Mara, Margaret Pugh. *Cities of Knowledge: Cold War Science and the Search for the Next Silicon Valley*. Princeton, NJ: Princeton University Press, 2005.

Orvell, Miles. *The Death and Life of Main Street*. Chapel Hill: University of North Caro-lina Press, 2012.

Phillips, Anne E. "The Struggle for School Desegregation in Philadelphia, 1945–1967." Ph.D. diss., University of Pennsylvania, 2000. Proquest (9965544).

Posey-Maddox, Linn. *When Middle-Class Parents Choose Urban Schools: Class, Race & the Challenge of Equity*. Chicago: University of Chicago Press, 2014.

Puckett, John L., ed. "University City Science Center." In *Encyclopedia of Greater Phila-delphia*. Camden, edited by Charlene Mires. NJ: Mid-Atlantic Regional Center for the Humanities, 2017. https://philadelphiaencyclopedia.org/essays/university-city-science -center/.

———. Unpublished notes from research in the University of Pennsylvania Archives, 2017.

———. *West Philadelphia Collaborative History*. https://collaborativehistory.gse.upenn .edu/.

Puckett, John L., and Mark F. Lloyd. *Becoming Penn: The Pragmatic American Univer-sity, 1950–2000*. Philadelphia: University of Pennsylvania Press, 2015.

Resnik, Henry S. *Turning on the System: War in the Philadelphia Public Schools*. New York: Pantheon Books, 1970.

Rodin, Judith. *The University and Urban Revival: Out of the Ivory Tower and into the Streets*. Philadelphia: University of Pennsylvania Press, 2007.

Royal, Camika. *Not Paved for Us: Black Educators and Public School Reform in Philadel-phia*. Cambridge, MA: Harvard Education Press, 2022.

Segal, Rebecca. *Got No Time to Fool Around: A Motivation Program for Education*. Phila-delphia: Westminster Press, 1972.

Simpson, Pearl S. "The Black Bottom." In *Black Bottom Picnic*, 35–50. Published by the author, 1998.

Smith, Neil. *The New Urban Frontier: Gentrification and the Revanchist City*. New York: Routledge, 1996.

———. "Toward a Theory of Gentrification: A Back to the City Movement by Capital, Not People." *Journal of the American Planning Association* 45, no. 4 (1979): 538–48.

Spencer, John T. *In the Crossfire: Marcus Foster and the Troubled History of American School Reform.* Philadelphia: University of Pennsylvania Press, 2012.

Taylor, Keeanga-Yamahtta. *Race for Profit: How Banks and the Real Estate Industry Undermined Black Homeownership.* Chapel Hill: University of North Carolina Press, 2019.

Thelin, John R. *A History of American Higher Education.* 2nd ed. Baltimore: Johns Hopkins University Press, 2011.

Warner, Sam Bass, Jr. *The Private City: Philadelphia in Three Periods of Its Growth.* 2nd ed. Philadelphia: University of Pennsylvania Press, 1987.

Weber, Lillian. *The English Infant School and Informal Education.* Englewood Cliffs, NJ: Prentice-Hall, 1971.

Wilder, Craig Steven. *Ebony and Ivy: Race, Slavery, and the Troubled History of America's Universities.* New York: Bloomsbury, 2014.

Wolf-Powers, Laura. *University City: History, Race, and Community in the Era of the Innovation District.* Philadelphia: University of Pennsylvania Press, 2022.

Yin, Karen. "Capitalizing for Equality." Conscious Style Guide, 2017. https://conscious styleguide.com/capitalizing-for-equality/.

Zemel, Andrea. "Fine Arts 349: Community, Collaborative, and Public Art." *Art Journal* 58, no. 1 (Spring 1999): 63–67.

Index

Edward M. Epstein is the Alan J. Lee Director at the Teachers Institute of Philadelphia. He is the coauthor of *Race, Gender, and Leadership in Nonprofit Organizations.*

Also in the series *Urban Life, Landscape, and Policy*:

William Issel, *For Both Cross and Flag: Catholic Action, Anti-Catholicism, and National Security Politics in World War II San Francisco*

Lisa Hoffman, *Patriotic Professionalism in Urban China: Fostering Talent*

John D. Fairfield, *The Public and Its Possibilities: Triumphs and Tragedies in the American City*

Andrew Hurley, *Beyond Preservation: Using Public History to Revitalize Inner Cities*

www.ingramcontent.com/pod-product-compliance
Lightning Source LLC
Chambersburg PA
CBHW050805270326
41926CB00025B/4543